Travels with a
Medieval Queen

Mary Taylor Simeti lives on a farm outside Palermo with her Sicilian husband and two children. She is the author of *On Persephone's Island*, an account of Sicily and its myths, *Sicilian Food: A History of the Island's Cuisine* and *Bitter Almonds: Recollections and Recipes from a Sicilian Girlhood*.

Travels with a Medieval Queen

The Journey of a Sicilian Princess

MARY TAYLOR SIMETI

PHOENIX

A PHOENIX PAPERBACK

First published in Great Britain
by Weidenfeld & Nicolson in 2002
This paperback edition published in 2003
by Phoenix,
a division of Orion Books Ltd,
Orion House, 5 Upper St Martin's Lane,
London WC2H 9EA

A CIP catalogue record for this book is
available from the British Library.

ISBN 1 84212 648 2

Printed and bound in Great Britain by
Clays Ltd, St Ives plc

For my sister
PAMELA TAYLOR MORTON
With love and gratitude on all fronts

CONTENTS

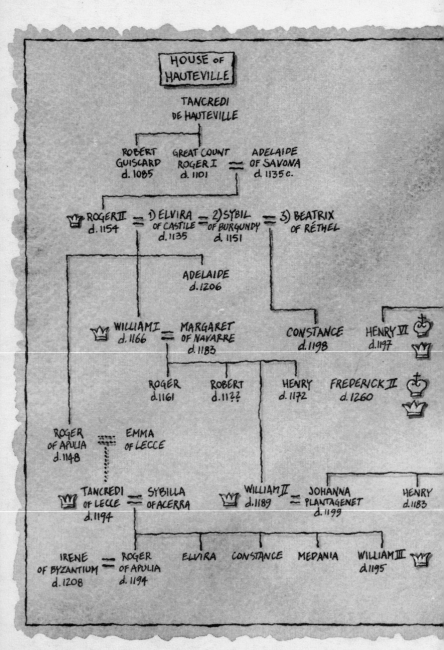

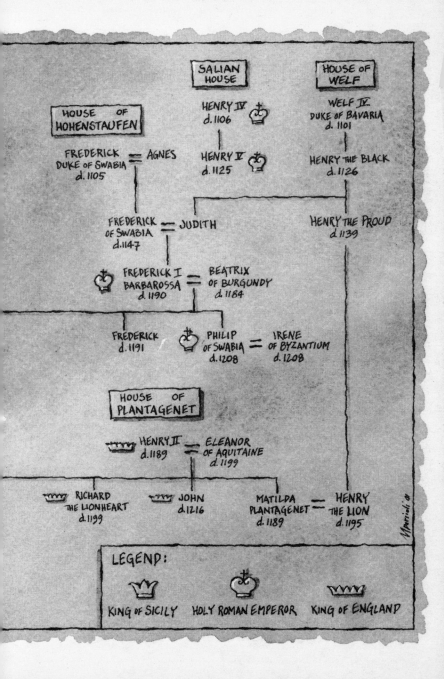

PROLOGUE

There are four tombs, imposing red porphyry caskets
borne by crouching lions, somber and elegant,
incongruous in the pastel neoclassic interior that
houses them. . . . But the Sicilians do not remember
their own: no flowers for Roger II, the most brilliant
of the Norman kings, or for his daughter Constance.
I am, as always, deeply moved by these tombs, and I
repeat to myself my old promise to bring some flowers someday for Constance; better still, someday I
shall write her story.

– On Persephone's Island

It has taken me seventeen years, but I have kept my word.
What follows is the story I promised to write, the story of
Constance of Hauteville, the twelfth-century Sicilian
princess who married a German king, was crowned Holy
Roman empress, and later returned to rule as queen in her
own kingdom.

The Kingdom of Sicily, which comprised most of southern
Italy as well as the island of Sicily itself, had been wrested
from Arab, Lombard, and Greek hands in the eleventh century by knights from Normandy, most of whom were
descended from the house of Hauteville and were cousins to
the William who conquered England. The Norman dynasty
in the South lasted little more than two centuries, but in that
brief period its capital, Palermo, became the wealthiest and
most cosmopolitan city of Europe, outdistanced only by
Constantinople.

It was this wealth that provided the dowry for Constance

Constance of Hauteville is buried in the Cathedral of Palermo:
no lions for ladies, but the red porphyry sarcophagus is
nonetheless very regal.

of Hauteville upon her marriage in 1186, the most magnificent dowry that Europe had ever seen. One hundred and fifty
mules were required to carry the burden of gold and silver,
of furs and rare silks woven in the royal silk workshops of
Palermo, a dowry worthy of the daughter of the greatest
of Sicily's Norman kings, Roger II, who had died at the end
of February in 1154, just a few weeks before Constance was
born.

First her half-brother, William I, succeeded to the throne,
and then his son, her nephew William II. Constance grew up

in Palermo amidst the gilded mosaics of churches and palaces, her youth blooming and fading among the flowers and fountains of Moorish cloisters and gazebos; as a potential heir to the throne, she was too valuable a pawn in international diplomacy to be ceded lightly. It was not until 1184, when the Holy Roman Emperor Frederick Barbarossa, in order to consolidate a newly signed peace treaty, asked for her hand to be given to his son, that William consented to his aunt's marriage. In August of 1185 Constance and her fabulous treasure were handed over to the imperial envoys at Rieti, some fifty miles northeast of Rome, whence she continued northward to Milan, where she was to marry the young king of Germany, Henry of Hohenstaufen. He was twenty-one at the time, she almost thirty-two.

The following years she spent on the road, first in central and northern Italy, and then in Germany, as the court progressed from city to castle to city. In 1191 Constance accompanied Henry to Italy, as far as Naples, where he made an unsuccessful attempt to seize the Sicilian throne. Three years later, in the spring of 1194, they crossed the Alps again, bent once more on conquering Sicily. For Constance, this proved to be the final journey home: it took her over a year to accomplish, and it wrought amazing changes in her life.

From the very beginning of her travels, Constance was caught between conflicting cultures, a pendulum suspended over the abyss that separated Norman Sicily from the Germany of the Hohenstaufens. As an American who has spent the greater part of her life in Sicily, I have always felt a strange affinity with Constance's expatriate ambivalences, and a gut sense of her motivations, intuitions that sometimes conflicted with the few scholarly interpretations I could find.

In writing her story, I have tried to remember the warning of the great medievalist Georges Duby: 'I must never forget the differences, the hundreds of years that separate me from my subject, the great stretch of time that hides almost all I am endeavoring to see behind a veil I cannot pierce.'[1]

But I am an incurable and incautious amateur, and so, while respecting the rules of historical research as far as I am capable, I have exploited the liberty that amateur status gives me. Hoping to come as close to Constance as I could, given the eight centuries that divide us and the scarcity of documents that speak of her, I decided to resuscitate my very limited and long-forgotten training in medieval history, and to make first a journey of the mind through libraries and bookstores, reading as much as I could about her era, and then a journey by car, retracing the route that brought her home to Sicily in 1194.

I would look at the landscapes she had passed through, stay in the cities where she had broken her journey, relive in my imagination the adventures that had befallen her. If I drew enough tangents on the empty page allotted to Constance in the history books, perhaps some hint of her outlines would emerge.

PART ONE

THE DUBBING AT
PENTECOST

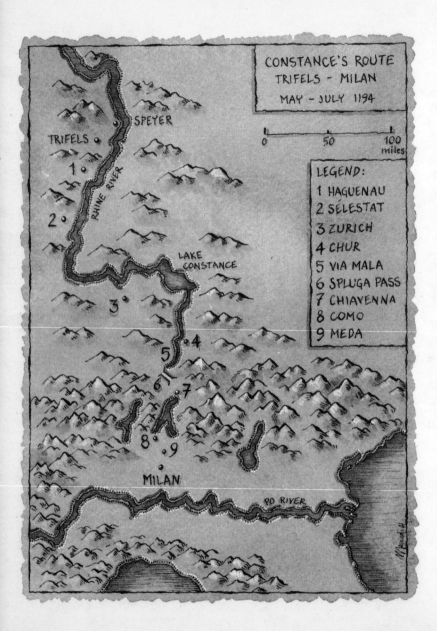

CHAPTER ONE : MAY

Arthur, good king of Brittany,
Whose knighthood teaches us
To be courteous, to be true knights,
Held court as a king should
On that holy day always
Known as the Pentecost.
    – *Yvain, The Knight of the Lion*
      Chrétien de Troyes, c. 1177[1]

The tower of Trifels Castle beckoned, dark red against the pale spring sky and the new green of the tree-covered mountainside below. Princes, dukes, barons, and bishops came riding from all parts of Germany, summoned by their suzerain, the thrice-crowned Henry VI, King of Germany, King of Italy, and Holy Roman Emperor, to attend high court on the feast of Pentecost, which in 1194 fell on the ninth of May.

Each came with a party of knights riding behind him, and a mule train laden with arms and armor, for once the court session had ended, they would move south, following their liege lord, Henry, and his wife, the Empress Constance, crossing over the Alps and down into the Lombard plain like the waters of the spring thaw. An army bent on conquest, their goal was southern Italy and the fabulously wealthy Norman Kingdom of Sicily, claimed by Henry through ancient imperial right, and by Constance as the only legitimate heir of the Norman dynasty. Whose claim was stronger depended on one's point of view.

Trifels beckoned to me as well. Although I had never seen it, not even in a photograph, I knew that it stood among the wooded hills of the Pfälzerwald, the Palace Forest that forms the northern border of the Palatine Rhineland, the ancestral possessions of the Hohenstaufen family, into which Constance had married. It was from here that she began her last journey south, and I sensed that in every way – culturally and emotionally as well as geographically – it represented the farthest point of her travels, her greatest distance from home. I would not be able to arrive at any understanding of Constance if I had not seen Trifels.

The knights arrive at Trifels armed for
the coming military campaign.

May

~

My own arrival in Germany in 1996 was easier, quicker, and considerably less dazzling than Constance's had been: I brought no mules, carried no treasure, made no perilous mountain crossings. My major challenges were to succeed in driving the car on and off the overnight ferry from Palermo to Naples, and thence find my way north to an apartment in Rome, that of Marcella Serangeli, the friend who was to accompany me.

Marcella was packed and waiting: a cup of coffee, and we were off. She had been unable to travel for several years and was delighted to explore a recently reacquired freedom by accompanying me on this trip. Marcella is a retired social worker, almost the first person I had met when I came to Sicily in 1962 to work in a community development project. We were co-workers and neighbors for two years, and then she left Sicily to work in Spain and then in Central America. Never a true expatriate, she knows nonetheless about living in a foreign country. Our children are contemporaries, and many vacations spent together had long since proved that we make good traveling companions.

We had agreed by phone that while the itinerary of our return journey southward, determined by that of Constance, would follow the secondary roads, on the northward portion we would take the superhighways, driving as fast as we could in order to get where we were headed as soon as possible. Travel as motion, not as experience.

It was May, the days were long, and we left Rome at noon. Except for the usual traffic jam crossing the pass over the Apennines between Florence and Bologna, and heavy traffic around Milan, there were no problems, and we arrived at Como in time for dinner. By eleven the next morning, we had zipped under the Alps and were in Zurich. It felt as if we had robbed ourselves of time and space.

We crossed the German border near Schaffhausen and,

going slowly now, drove west along the northern bank of the Rhine. The river itself is fairly wide in this part, but the fluvial plain is narrower: to the north a strip of rich fields tightly farmed with what appeared to be forage crops, and then a dark line of fir trees – the southernmost hem of the Black Forest. Across the river and to the south, the Swiss side of the plain rose rapidly into foothills, beyond which the snow-covered peaks of the Alps closed the horizon like a freshly painted picket fence.

The vision of the distant mountaintops glowing in the sunset was tamed by the well-fed placidity of the Rhine in the foreground, the prosperous fields, and the highway running straight. Had it been the twelfth century, however, we would have found ourselves surrounded by bogs and marshes, rotting bushes and fallen trees obstructing our progress, our path blocked each spring by the floodwaters of the great river obese with roaring masses of melted snows, the rafts at the fords drawn ashore for the season, the wooden bridges torn from their moorings.

We would have felt menaced by that ribbon of black trees to the north. The Black Forest hid bandits, beasts both real and mythical, and even wild men, long-haired and naked, who lived on roots and berries and ran amok. We would be thanking God that at least the mountains were behind us and that we had been brought this far in safety, and praying that we would arrive at some sure lodging before darkness fell.

After an hour or so, Marcella and I picked a turnoff at whim and headed up into the twilight of the Schwarzwald, where we sank gratefully into the first pine-paneled, feather-bedded *Gasthaus* we could find, happily forgetful of our first exercise in historical imagination.

～

My idea of the Black Forest had always been strictly out of Grimm – virgin, dark, and impenetrable, populated by Gauls who moved silently through the underbrush, as at ease as deer. Caesar claimed to have marched through it for months without seeing sunlight. So be it, but that wasn't the forest of today. It wasn't black, and it wasn't composed of Norway spruce. I hadn't realized that a forest of conifers cannot reproduce itself, since the saplings die for lack of the sunlight that their parent trees deny them. Without human maintenance, careful foresting, and clearance, the beech tree, the only tree that can reproduce itself in its own shade, will take over.

What we found as we drove northwest through gentle hills were stands of Norway spruce, dark indeed but with little or no underbrush, alternating with bright green meadows and threaded with carefully tended walking paths, quite crowded with young families, babies and backpacks bobbing on their shoulders, and older couples striding along with the help of stout wooden walking sticks.

The meadow grass grew paler as the mist crept over it, laying big banks of fog over the lower valleys. We had decided to take the Schwarzwald-Hochstrasse, the upper road that would carry us up through the highest and densest part, which supposedly offered the most spectacular views. Here, however, the forest became white, ceding its black to the rain clouds closing over us; the long needles of the spruces caught thick strands of mist as if they were combing wool. We followed the red taillights in front of us while great glowing eyes glared up out of the fog and slithered past us to the left.

It was a relief to come down out of the fog and to cross the valley of the Rhine. The late afternoon sky was overcast and prematurely dark when we arrived at Annweiler, the small village that lies in the valley below Trifels. The clouds hung low over the hills, releasing intermittent and desultory rain, but the village streets were full of people, and it required two hours of increasingly desperate research to find a room on the outskirts of town.

We were lucky to find a bed, for it was the Friday of the Pentecost weekend, something we had not taken into our calculations. Pentecost has lost status in Italy, but in Germany it is still a major holiday weekend, and for many contemporary Germans, it signifies the opening of the hiking season. The paths of the Pfälzerwald, which more or less begins at Annweiler, compete with those of the Black Forest across the river for vacationers from the southwestern German cities.

That night my sleep was agitated by dreams involving Constance and the castle that we would be seeing the next day. I woke early, and while Marcella slept on, I lay in bed musing about Constance in the irregular thought patterns that belong to dawn, and gazing at the walls around me. The owner of the bed-and-breakfast was a big, sunny bear of a man who spoke only Greek, and the decor of his establishment had immigrated to Germany with him: souvenir amphoras and wall hangings embroidered with pictures of the Parthenon, Mediterranean kitsch rather than German *Gemütlichkeit*. I felt at home here, as Constance would have: she had grown up in a polyglot society in which the Greek language and culture played a prominent role, and the sound of someone speaking Greek would surely have aroused her nostalgia.

～

The name Trifels derives most probably from Drei Pfälze – three castles. They stand on adjacent hills: Anebos, a mere stub of reddish-brown tower; Scharffenberg Castle farther off, of which only a much-restored tower is visible; and Trifels itself, the most important. They date from the eleventh or possibly the tenth century, but in the mid-twelfth century they were enlarged and strengthened by Constance's father-in-law, the Emperor Frederick Barbarossa, in order to enforce the northern borders of his family lands.

The road to Trifels took us up through a forest of beech and elms, magnificently tall trees with new leaves of soft green, interspersed with stands of darker pines. The effect in late May was of soft, gentle woods, where the light filtering through the

The imperial stronghold of Trifels, starting point for the journey.

green made the undergrowth luminous even when, as that morning, there was little sunlight. Occasionally the sun broke through the clouds, warming the stone to the color of cream of tomato soup, but a chill wind was blowing fairly steadily, and the tourists milling around the entrance all had wind jackets and heavy sweaters, with few short sleeves in sight. The majority of the visitors, and there were many, were Germans, perhaps attracted less by the sham beauty of the reconstructed castle than by the many stories of its treasures and its prisons, a symbol of the majesty and might of medieval Germany.

Today Trifels looks like every nineteenth-century engraver's idea of a medieval German castle. Towers of dark rose sandstone cluster on a mountaintop, their foundations hidden behind the upper branches of elms and pine trees on three sides and exposed on the fourth, where striated layers of the same rose-red stone descend in a sharp overhang. The towers are irregular: the original eleventh-century keep is flanked by a great tower and a chapel tower, unusual in that the apse of the chapel, located on the upper story, bulges out from the exterior wall, its semicylindrical weight resting on the heads of three cheerful lions. The lions are garlanded by gaping cracks, which explains why we were not allowed to enter the chapel but could only peer in from the doorway.

A great hall was added in the first half of the thirteenth century, then used as a quarry in later years. Extensive restoration after World War II, more enthusiastic than authentic, has given us the present hall, an impressive two-storied room with heavy arches on all four sides supporting the columns of the loggia above. The final touch was provided in 1960 by the construction of a squat square tower with a peaked roof, set off from the others and destined to be the custodian's residence. All that remains of the treasure are copies of the imperial insignia: a cross, a crown, an orb, and a scepter, none of which has anything to do with Sicily.

Scattered about the courtyard were billboards reconstructing the various stages of Trifels's construction, and a coin-operated loudspeaker told us its history. I read and listened diligently: first mentioned in 1081 as an imperial castle built by the emperors of the earlier Salian dynasty, it was then renovated in the middle of the twelfth century by the Hohenstaufen Frederick Barbarossa. Its dungeons were the prison of Richard the Lionheart when he was captured and held for ransom by Henry VI, the son of Barbarossa; and it served as treasure house for the fabulous spoils brought to Germany after Henry's conquest of the Norman Kingdom of Sicily. The spiel was well thought out and well executed. Yet it made not one mention of Constance.

They seem to care little about her in Germany. We searched the billboards in vain for her name, but the fabled Sicilian treasure had become the treasure of the Hohenstaufen, its presence there due only to the exploits of Henry VI. Yet Regine, my friend, neighbor, and translator, tells me that when she was a child growing up only a few miles from Trifels, it was the Treasure of the Kaiserin Konstanz that dominated her games and fantasies.

Only when we had climbed up to the tower roof did Constance begin to come alive in my own fantasy. The view from the top of the square tower could not have changed much in eight hundred years. To the north and west, wooded hills stretched as far as we could see, an undulating horizon craggy with ruined towers. Constance would have seen them newly built and been able to put a name and an owner to each. But I doubt she looked that way often; she would have been far more attracted by the view to the east, over the foothills to the valley where the Rhine, flowing down from the Alps, passed the great Holy Roman imperial cities: Speyer, Mainz, Worms, Cologne.

Better still was the view to the south, through the hills to the distant plain of Alsace, toward the palace at Haguenau, toward Sicily. This was the route by which Constance had first come to Germany, crossing from Italy to France, then coming up through Burgundy and Alsace. It was from the south that she had first seen Trifels, a lonely castle lit by a wintry sky and floating in a sea of leafless trees. Henry considered it the best-defended, most secure prison for hostages of rank. For Constance, daughter of the urban South, it must have looked like solitary confinement.

Imagine her standing there at the parapet, on the eve of their departure, looking south along the route they were to follow, a first leave-taking from her life in Germany. An older woman in the eyes of her contemporaries, she had recently turned forty. It is said that she was tall, blond, and good-looking, a description not improbable given her northern blood, but even in those days this was such a fairy-tale stereo-type for those of royal blood (since darkness was equated with impurity and sin) that it might be pure invention.

One German historian, Karl Hampe, describes Constance as 'a proud woman of independent spirit and passionate tem-perament,'[2] but gives no sources. He is handing us, perhaps, a bowdlerized version of a nasty comment made by the Francis-can monk, Fra Salimbene, who claimed 'she was a perverse woman who constantly caused trouble among her brothers' wives and the entire family.'[3] But the monk, who was writing almost a hundred years after her death, was a partisan of the papacy as opposed to the empire, and like all men of the medieval Church, he had a very low opinion of women in general. Here as elsewhere, Constance serves as a blank screen on which each can project the woman he or she prefers. Victim, for centuries to come, of gossip and legend and spite, she has often been the target for opinions and judgments directed more at other members of her family than at the Empress herself.

I myself have chosen to see a woman whose early pride and passion, if ever they existed, had been battered and quelled by eight years of exile in a marriage to a man whom only ambition could arouse. Except for her husband, she was alone in the world: no member of the family of her childhood had sur-vived. Cursed by her years, perhaps, or by her genes, she was barren, unable to fulfill the only legitimate purpose that the medieval world allotted to a laywoman, that of producing an heir. The future of thrones and dynasties depended on the issue of her fruitless womb.

At forty, the obsessive, raging ache of sterility, the yearning emptiness in her loins and in her arms, had dulled to resignation, and pride was a mask worn to hide failure and shame. If on the eve of their departure Henry was fired by the will to sit upon the Sicilian throne, Constance may often have entertained the idea of seeking refuge in a Palermo convent.

Departures were nothing new to Constance. Since the imperial office was an elective one, the empire had no capital city, and its court traveled continuously. Lacking any permanent bureaucratic structure or even any press through which to make his authority felt at a distance, the emperor had to rely on the persuasive powers of his own presence, journeying together with his empress and his court from one castle or episcopal palace to the next. Although by feudal law he had the right to demand hospitality from anyone in the realm, most often he stayed where he could feed his retainers from the produce of the imperial lands. Some princes had been exonerated from the duty of receiving the king, no mean privilege: the king's following might be composed of three hundred people or of four thousand, and his arrival had by law to be announced six weeks beforehand. A twelfth-century estimate of the court's daily consumption (probably exaggerated but nonetheless alarming) included one thousand pigs and sheep, ten barrels of wine and ten of beer, one thousand bushels of wheat, eight oxen, 'and other things besides.'[4]

Henry tended to confine his traveling to the southwestern part of Germany, within the lands that belonged outright to the Hohenstaufen family. The high courts of Christmas, Easter, and Pentecost were usually held in the imperial cities ruled by an 'ecclesiastical prince,' a bishop or archbishop of high noble birth who had been elected in accordance with the emperor's will and who administered for him the territory that had been granted in fief to the bishopric. The first cathedral city that Constance had visited in Germany was Speyer, where Henry had held court in March of 1188. They had spent the first two years of their marriage in Italy and had then come north along the western route, through the lands that Henry had inherited from his mother, Beatrix of Burgundy. At the beginning of March they had arrived at Toul, near Nancy; some days later they entered what is now Germany and proceeded to Speyer.

Speyer lies on the west bank of the Rhine, not far from Annweiler. Marcella and I drove there in the rain, across a plain of vineyards. Now a very pretty but modest town with lovely baroque houses, it was once one of the most important cities of the empire. At the height of its splendor in the sixteenth century, Speyer had sixty town gates topped by towers, as well as thirty-eight churches and chapels, plus an enormous Romanesque cathedral that had four spires so tall, they might well have inspired the city's name.

At a certain point we could see Speyer across fields and woods that blocked out all the modern part of the town, leaving us only a view of towers and spires. The road was empty of traffic; no crossroads required signs; and were it not for the asphalt, we might have been traveling with Constance, at a time when one had to rely on landmarks, river fords, passing merchants and pilgrims, and even far-off church steeples in order to find one's way. How grateful medieval travelers must have felt when the spires they were looking for came into sight.

In the past the Speyer cathedral was flanked by ever-spreading episcopal and imperial palaces and chanceries, where the court lodged when called to the imperial diet (the last took place in 1570), but all of this has disappeared. During the centuries the church has been burned, looted, demolished, bombed, deconsecrated, and reconsecrated, and its most recent restoration dates to the 1950s and 1960s. Much of the original crypt remains, but the upper parts have been reconstructed, supposedly according to the eleventh-century plans: the atrium is built in layers of beige and red stone, so that the façade is striped, while the rest of the cathedral is solid red stone.

The largest Romanesque church in all Europe and the first to have a vaulted ceiling, the cathedral has an interior impressive in its vastness. On that first visit Constance would have descended with her husband into the crypt, to pray at the tombs of his ancestors. Beatrix of Burgundy lies buried here, together with the five emperors of an earlier dynasty, that of the Salians. The imperial tombs are of the utmost simplicity – heavy slabs of unadorned stone resting on the floor, surprisingly stark compared with the elegance of royal burial in Sicily. In 1188 there was an empty space awaiting Beatrix's husband, Frederick Barbarossa, the first of the Hohenstaufen emperors. It remained empty for a century, until Rudolf of Hapsburg was buried there, for Frederick was destined to die far from Germany, on his way to the Holy Land, and despite the best efforts of the embalmers, his body never made it home.

Constance had never known her mother-in-law, who died in the year of her betrothal. Beatrix of Burgundy was by all accounts a highly cultivated and forceful woman who had done much to polish the rough intercourse of the German court, and her presence must have haunted Constance, who

The devoted imperial couple Frederick Barbarossa and Beatrix of Burgundy, as they were depicted on coins from the city of Frankfurt.

was unable to make a comparable impression in her husband's homeland. Wishing for someone to guide her in the role of a German queen, and missing her own mother, Beatrix of Réthel, who died at much the same time as the Burgundian Beatrix but in Palermo, Constance must have felt continually reproached by her mother-in-law's memory.

Beatrix of Burgundy had been brought up in Mâcon, at the cosmopolitan court of her father, Count William, the most powerful nobleman in the Kingdoms of Burgundy and Provence and the leader of the opposition to effective German rule over what was nominally part of the empire. Weaned on the literature of Provence and the poetry of courtly love, she was said to be herself a singer and a poet of some merit. She

A lady submits to her maidservant's attentions, just as I imagine
Constance submitting to Nahid. Double-sided combs cut from
bone or tortoiseshell, like the one on the lady's lap, are still in use
in Mediterranean countries today.

was still in her teens when the Holy Roman Emperor Barbarossa, some twenty years older than she, decided to quell the opposition by marrying the heir. A contemporary writer, Acerbus Morena, describes her as being 'of medium build with hair shining like gold and a very beautiful face, her teeth white and well formed. She had an upright bearing, a very small mouth, a modest gaze, bright eyes, and a chaste and gentle manner of speech.'[5] However stereotyped this description, too, may sound, this young slip of a girl had entranced and dominated the mighty Barbarossa, so enslaving him that he was considered a *vir uxoratus*, a man ruled by his wife. In what seems to have been a truly happy union, Beatrix had insisted on breaking with tradition and traveling by her husband's side in his perpetual movements, bearing him at least twelve children along the way. She was but forty when she died, much mourned by her husband.

If Beatrix was a ghostly presence, who were the living that populated Constance's years in Germany? I have no information. My German being just adequate to finding a bed-and-breakfast, I have been able to read only what has been translated for me, but I suspect that little is there to find: the titles of princes and clerics who served as witnesses for court documents, casualty lists from battlefields, with little attention paid to the women participating in court life. I do not even know if Constance followed her mother-in-law's example in traveling about with the emperor, but I will assume that she did.

Unable to bear the prospect of such loneliness for my protagonist, and hovering nearer to the edge of fiction than is perhaps licit, I have imagined some ties binding Constance to the people around her: a special susceptibility to the charm of her charismatic father-in-law, Frederick Barbarossa; a platonic, 'courtly' relationship with the poet Frederick von Hausen; and the company of a totally invented but not improbable childhood nurse, an Arab slave whom I have chosen to call Nahid. I have taken Nahid from the palace harem in Palermo when she was twelve, that she might serve Constance's mother upon her arrival from Flanders to marry Roger II, and I have appointed Nahid to be present at Constance's birth and to have watched over her ever since. Influenced perhaps by Shakespearean nurses, I imagine Nahid as devoted and imperious, taking more liberties than Constance might perhaps accept, were she not the Queen's only physical link with the world of her youth.

∼

However well surrounded by the friendship of the two Fredericks Constance might have been on her first visit to Speyer in 1188, as she prepared to leave Trifels in 1194 she was alone. We can allow her Nahid – she will need a female presence on this trip – but the others, the two Fredericks, were gone. She had taken her leave of them in Haguenau four years earlier, on the eve of their departure for the Holy Land.

∼

One more night in our bed-and-breakfast, and we were on our way. By the secular calendar we were late: Henry and Constance set out from Trifels on May 15th, but Marcella and I, stragglers in the imperial entourage, didn't get started until the thirtieth.

I know now that I have not given offense in being late: the liturgical calendar was much more important to Constance. Rulers of the Middle Ages were accustomed to holding high court on the great Christian feast days: Christmas, Easter, and Pentecost. The last, which falls on the seventh Sunday after Easter, is a feast day with many layers of significance: the Christian celebration of the descent of the Holy Spirit upon the Apostles mingles with pagan celebrations of spring. Medieval kings and emperors honored this feast by summoning their bishops and their knights to a last solemn high court before sending them off to a season of tournaments and battles.

It was on Pentecost that the ceremony of dubbing the new knights took place, that the Holy Spirit might descend upon them and guide them in their quests and their adventures, in their service to their lord and to their God. The dubbing at Pentecost was, according to Georges Duby, the first step in the education of the knight, the beginning of a 'long initiatory peregrination.' Then came adventure, which 'roved over a map whose two poles were the court and the forest,' while the third stage lay in the future, 'the place of dreams, inaccessible, always receding, a mirage.'⁶ All in all, the feast of Pentecost was the right moment for us to begin our journey.

We had no time that morning for a last visit to the castle, and as the road from Annweiler climbed up around the mountain, we took the fork that pointed south. We passed a large hawk sitting in a tree, and others wheeling in the sky; I took the hawk to be Constance's familiar and felt she was keeping an approving eye on us.

Our road climbed up into the Trifels mountains, then down through castle-studded hills to the French border. The hills got softer and softer, and the beech woods gave way to vineyards before we reached the plain. The border itself was deserted, the customs booth totally unattended. Nobody was in sight, nobody cared about our passing through, and yet we were crossing one of the most bloodied borders in Europe. A Europe united in the Peace of God had been the medieval dream, dear to both popes and emperors, who fought each other relentlessly in a struggle for supremacy. Had contemporary politicians and bureaucrats succeeded where the great figures of the past had failed?

Once in France the road descended slowly to a vast and rolling plain, a checkerboard of forage crops and grains – wheat, oats, and rye – mostly still a brilliant green, with here and there a field where the ears had already appeared and were

This hunting scene from an early fourteenth-century German manuscript
is later than our period, but it is so lovely that I am including it here, just as
I have used it in the logo of our farm.

turning yellow. They seemed somewhat stunted, perhaps by the short growing season: in Sicily the ears would already be tall and golden, just a few weeks from their harvest. On the horizon a thin band of darker green marked the beginning of the Holy Forest of Haguenau, where we intended to have our picnic.

Little remains of the Haguenau forest, once part of the vast woodlands that covered much of France and southern Germany, but we did not have to go far before the trees grew thick. The modern forest is mostly beech trees, and the new leaves were well along now in size but still of a tender green, mingling with oaks. It was an oak tree, very ancient and immense in diameter, that had rendered the forest sacred: oak trees were a principal object of worship in pre-Christian Germany, but on what pretext the Church converted this one to its own purposes, I do not know. The sacred oak was felled many centuries ago but its presence lingered: Marcella and I felt slightly uneasy and almost disrespectful sitting on a log in the middle of a clearing and eating our sandwiches, even though this opening in the trees was flooded with sunlight. Being modern women, we attributed our nervousness to the stares of the truckers driving by the small turnoff where we had sought our picnic spot, but there was more to it than that.

For medieval man, the forest had two faces: the carefully tended and nourishing forest that rendered wood for burning and building, game and fruit, mushrooms, honey, wild greens, berries, and tubers; and the other, the dense and hostile forest, full of mystery and fear, a dwelling place for bandits and dangerous beasts, for giant wild men, hairy and unpredictable, and for all manner of evil spirits.

The burgeoning economy and consequent growth in population during the twelfth century produced a great demand for more tillable land, and great spreads of forest land were cleared and tamed. At the same time a new type of forest appeared, the forest of Duby's 'initiatory peregrination,' the imaginary terrain of the new tradition of courtly poetry that was just

The damsel is definitely in distress, but the gentle, rather wistful expression on the wild man's face suggests an earlier version of King Kong.

arriving at the German courts. It was a forest with precise limits and characteristics, created ad hoc as a landscape in which the good Christian knight might gain honor and demonstrate his courage, slaying the dangerous giant or the evil knight, rescuing the captive lady, and fulfilling his quest.

～

Our forest came to an end at the foot of a hill on which once stood the imperial palace of Haguenau. The town itself has crept over the foundations – there are two lovely churches, but the only testimony of the palace itself are some reconstructions that are to be seen in the local historical society.

If any place in Germany came to represent home to Constance, it would have been Haguenau. The palace, at least in the form she knew it, had been built by her father-in-law, each room haunted by the force of his personality and by the poets and scholars who joined him there when he could take a rest from his travels, amidst furnishings and comforts that reflected the tastes acquired during the many years he spent in Italy.

Whatever pleasant memories the years in Germany had offered Constance were gathered here. In the falconry, the wicker cage would have been readied for Henry's eagle, the proudest and most powerful of birds, with which only an emperor or a king might hunt. Henry, a devoted hunter, would go nowhere without it, not even to war, and the eagle was already prepared for travel, hooded in embroidered crimson and tethered to his perch by golden jesses. But the pretty little merlin hawk that had ridden on Constance's wrist the last few times she went hunting would remain here: the journey in front of them would be arduous, and the strange lassitude that had been overtaking her in the past weeks told her that her body would not have the extra strength that hunting required. The royal falconry in Palermo, if they should get that far, would be waiting for her.

Frederick had assembled a large library at Haguenau, where Constance had spent peaceful hours studying the heavy tomes of philosophy and government, wondering at the miracles wrought by the saints, or browsing among the slight volumes of poetry. It was here that the troubadours came, journeying from France to sing their *lais* and recite their epics, exchanging rhymes and meters with the minnesingers, their German colleagues.

It was probably here that Constance bade farewell to her father-in-law. At Mainz, on Christmas of 1188, the Emperor had taken the cross, swearing to undertake a Crusade to rescue Jerusalem from the heathen, and the poet Frederick von Hausen, one of his most loyal followers, had joined him. Neither Frederick reached the Holy Land: lord and vassal died within a few weeks and a few hundred leagues of each other, in Asia Minor. I like to imagine that it was also here in Haguenau that Constance had parted from von Hausen, and had received from the poet a farewell gift, a book he had purchased for her in Burgundy, her own copy – small pages of parchment bound in leather and embossed in gold – of the romance of *Yvain, The Knight of the Lion*, which they had often read together.

A day of prayer and vigil had marked the Crusaders' departure, and then a banquet accompanied by music and song. Perhaps it was on this occasion that von Hausen sang to the court his last poem, a love lyric that followed all the rules, and yet – possibly – was no mere exercise, no simple taunt to lay before his rivals in the game of courtly composition.

> My heart and my body want to separate,
> that have ridden together all my life.
> The body wants to strike against the heathen,
> but the heart has chosen out a woman
> before all the world. It has weighed on me ever since,
> that one will not go in the steps of the other.
> My eyes have brought me to grief.
> May God alone break up that strife.

> I had hoped to be free of this great weight
> when I took the cross for the glory of God.
> It would be right if the heart were in it, too,
> but its own faith held it back.
> I would truly be a living man again
> if it would stop its ignorant desiring.
> I see now, to the heart it's all one
> how I shall fare at last.

And then, in a softer key, a final apostrophe:

> Heart, since I cannot turn you back
> from deserting me so sadly,
> I pray God reach down to send you
> where they will welcome you in.
> Alas, poor Heart, how will it go with you?
> How could you dare go boldly into this danger all alone?

Who will help you end your cares
with such loyalty as I have shown?[7]

It was at Haguenau, too, that the Sicilian expedition of
1194 began in earnest. We have no precise information about
the size of the army, to which each man, lay or cleric, who
owed his fief to the Emperor was obliged to contribute a given
number of armed and mounted knights, an army that swelled
in size as the Emperor moved south. The average size of the
imperial expeditions to Italy during the reign of the Hohenstaufen appears to have been between ten and fifteen thousand
knights, plus their followers. Perhaps the starting numbers
were much smaller in this case, since Henry could count on
the support of his vassals in northern Italy, no longer enemies
but allies. It should not have been difficult to recruit extra
hands: the wealth of Sicily was fabled, the expectations of
pillage and booty inflated.

This was not the medieval army that Hollywood sends
charging across the screen, plumes waving and steel plates
shining. At the end of the twelfth century styles of armor had
changed little from those embroidered on the Bayeux Tapes-
try. A tunic or hauberk of chain mail covered the soldier from
shoulder to knee; a hood of mail protected his neck; and a
conical metal helmet defended the top of his head from the
blows of enemy swords. The soldiers' shields were kite-
shaped, rounded at the top and pointed at the bottom, so they
could be stuck into the ground to form a defensive wall. The
use of heraldic devices had only recently been introduced, and
the coats of arms that were painted on their shields or embroidered on their tunics were still quite primitive.

Behind the knights, or perhaps well protected in their
midst, rode the ladies. How many and who they were remains
an unanswered question: given the Emperor's haste, the
number was probably limited. We must make do with the
Empress, riding sidesaddle; and Nahid riding by her side.
There were pack mules as well – no hundred and fifty this time,

This knight in armor, from a thirteenth-century Sicilian manuscript, has a strip of metal on his helmet that protects his nose. His tunic is made of metal platelets rather than chain mail.

for the bulk of Constance's dowry was locked up in the strongboxes of the Hohenstaufen, but a few beasts would have carried the cane baskets and leather chests packed with the Empress's personal belongings: enameled mirrors from Limoges, missals bound in gold, crosses studded with jewels, and the ivory caskets and combs and chess pieces from the workshops of Amalfi and Palermo that she had brought with her nine years before, together with the robes of Sicilian silk and the Flemish tunics and cloaks of 'scarlet' – the finest wool available, felted and dyed to a deep crimson – lined with the gray-white fur of vair and miniver, to protect her from the mountain air.

∼

Marcella and I went in their wake, as far as it was possible. At this point, in fact, we were faced with the problem of how to determine the route that the imperial party took, and how we might best follow it. I had come with a list of all the extant documents issued by the imperial chancellery that accompanied the Emperor, decrees and edicts with dates and place-names to indicate where and when the court sat, and who were the witnesses. From this we knew only that the next recorded stop was Chur, in the valley of the Rhine near the Austrian border, whence they would begin the climb over the high Alps. But after we reached Basel we ourselves would have to choose which way to go: along the valley of the Rhine, heading first east, then south, or along the string of lakes that cut diagonally across Switzerland. For the moment, however, the route posed no problems.

From Haguenau to Strasbourg, a big highway runs south and next to it a smaller route, which we took on principle. But we gained little; we were in a major industrial area, and the 'small' road was like America's Route 1. Warehouses and diners, gas stations and enormous trailer trucks roaring past brought us abruptly into the twentieth century, which we fled as fast as we could, turning inland, once we were past Strasbourg, to an area of small villages and flat fields divided one from the other by canals. Constance, too, would have had to travel inland, for this was the flood basin of the Rhine, and only in the nineteenth century were the waters brought under control by a network of canals. We spent the night here, at the spot where the river Ill and the Rhine-Rhone Canal converge.

∼

Our first stop the next day was Sélestat, to see the lovely Romanesque church of Saint-Foy (we had decided to stop for every Romanesque building we passed and nothing else), and to admire the Bibliothèque Humaniste, one of the great libraries of the French Renaissance. Many much earlier manuscripts were on display there as well, their margins crowded with comments in different hands, which made me reflect on my own complaint of not having enough time to read. It was not the sheer numbers of books piled up on my desk and on my bedstead table – greater riches than any medieval scholar could dream of – that bothered me, but the velocity and superficiality with which they would, if ever, be read. Constance had had access to the Haguenau library, but in her own possession she would have had at best ten or twelve books. So she would have read them and then reread them, culled and then culled again, commented and then, if she knew how to write, transcribed her comments in the margins. I have never had the discipline to read in this manner, except perhaps when it was imposed upon me in my college years, but as I looked at the neat yet (to me) illegible notations on the parchment pages, it seemed enviable.

The countryside between Sélestat and Basel was very tame and very pretty: fields divided by stands of trees, mostly oaks and robinias in full bloom. The pendulous bunches of their white flowers invaded the woods like an army of tiny clouds, and the open windows of the car swept up their perfume as we passed. We spotted a falcon as we drove, some turtledoves, and then on top of a tower an enormously big nest, with a stork standing in it, poised on one leg. I amused myself by speculating on what Constance might have thought on first sight of such a giant nest: the medieval imagination would have delighted in populating it with the oddest of beasts. But afterward I read that storks have now come back to nest in Sicily for the first time in three centuries, so presumably she already knew them. I was just beginning to get my bearings in Constance's world, awkwardly and with frequent error, and I still had much to learn before I could give free rein to my imagination.

By the time we reached Basel we had made up our minds to take the northern route to Chur, along the Rhine. It was an arbitrary decision, based on the fact that I had no information on the lake route, but later research has convinced me that at least the imperial party, if not the entire army, crossed Switzerland by boat via the lakes.

We saw the underside of Zurich, caught in an endless Friday-afternoon traffic jam in the tunnels that are supposed to let you pass beneath the city in haste, and then drove straight east through lush farms on gently rolling meadows and wooded hills, just south of the Rhine valley. It was a treat for the eyes only, since the meadows were being sprayed with liquid manure after the first mowing, and its smell was with us all through Switzerland. Marcella was indignant that the roadside inn where we settled for the night should charge us so much, given that the service included such a stink. Perhaps they were making us pay for period atmosphere: medieval nostrils were well accustomed to strong stimulation.

Whim took us first to see the famous library at Saint Gall, and then south, slighting the elbow of the Rhine and going farther into the hills to Appenzell, which according to my guidebook is one of the most unspoiled areas in Switzerland. Be that as it may, the town itself seemed entirely devoted to *Gasthäuser* and tearooms and souvenir stands; we lingered only long enough to take advantage of an excellent pastry shop. As we left, we drove by a bride in a white dress and an apron, who was standing at the roadside behind a wooden stall distributing what appeared to be fresh vegetables to her wedding guests. The groom flagged us down, then seeing that we were only passing tourists, he waved us on, leaving us wistful. We would have gladly asked a few questions and wished them well, even eaten a crudité or two in their honor.

The road continued through more wooded hills, past more toy farms and more sprayed manure, then dropped suddenly once more to the Rhine, which meanwhile had turned a corner and was now again running from south to north. We were across the river from Austria, not far north of where the lake route would have landed the imperial party. The mountains on either side drop abruptly from distant and snow-covered peaks to the river valley, which widens slightly, then closes again into a steep gorge guarded by a castle or a solitary tower, as the river crashes and falls over the huge dark boulders that litter the narrow chasms. The thought of inching one's way along the rock-strewn path on the back of a horse (we at least were driving on a modern albeit terrifying road) filled us with awe.

≈

The people of the Middle Ages thought of themselves as *homines viatores*, pilgrims and voyagers, their bodies trudging through life in penance that they might save their souls, even when they stayed put in their own villages. But they did travel, too, under great constraints and in the face of great dangers – and to a degree that should amaze contemporary tourists, for whom travel is so comfortable, so boringly easy, that they go on survival trips for their amusement.

Bishops, monks, and papal legates, students and scholars, pilgrims and Crusaders, merchants and soldiers, poets and jugglers and street musicians – all were in endless movement up and down the great routes of European commerce, many of which followed the old roads of the ancient Roman Empire. But in many places the Roman roads had fallen into ruin, and without the Roman hydraulic controls the valleys that they crossed had flooded once more. Rivers in flood, bridges washed out, mud in spring, torrential rains in the fall, mountain passes blocked by snow in the winter: this was the daily fare of the medieval traveler.

The seasons were the primary factor determining where and when one journeyed, especially if it was a question of crossing the ultimate barrier, the Alps. The passes were open from the end of May until the middle of September; to attempt them in winter meant great peril, as the Holy Roman Emperor Henry IV had learned to his discomfort. Excommunicated by Pope Gregory VII in February of 1076, he was ordered to do penance within a year or lose his throne, and so he set out the following January with his queen and his knights to cross the

30

pass of Mont Cenis. A contemporary, Lampert of Hersfeld, describes the journey for us.

> Arrived at the foot of the pass Henry 'hired for a price some of the natives, familiar with the neighborhood, and accustomed to the steep slopes of the Alps. These were to precede the party on the precipitous incline and through the masses of snow, to do what they could to make easier the passage of those behind. When under this escort, they reached, not without great difficulty, the top of the pass, there seemed to be little possibility of going any further. The mountain was precipitous and . . . owing to the icy cold, slippery, apparently forbidding any attempt to make a descent. Thereupon the men tried to the utmost of their ability to avoid the danger, now crawling on their hands and feet, now supporting themselves on the shoulders of those in front; now and again, as their feet slipped, falling and rolling. At last, after the greatest peril they reached level ground. The guides placed the queen and her ladies, who were in the rear of the party, upon ox-skins, and drew them down the slope. Some of the horses were lowered on various contrivances, others were dragged down with their feet tied. Some were killed in the process, many were maimed, only a few surviving the danger whole and sound.'[8]

Henry IV survived and made his penance by standing in sackcloth and sandals in the snow before the gates of Matilda of Canossa's castle, where the Pope awaited him – a humiliating experience, no doubt, but much less frightening.

In normal circumstances, however, the Holy Roman emperors preferred to cross the Alps via the central passes that depart from the Rhine valley where it divides Switzerland from Austria: the Spluga, the Septimer, and the Julier. Despite the danger of mud, they had to set out as soon as the passes opened in May, in order to accomplish their mission before new snows blocked their return route in the autumn and, if

Having successfully survived his Alpine crossing, Emperor Henry
IV supplicates Matilda to intercede with the pope on his behalf.

they were bound for the Italian South, in order to avoid the
onset of the August heat in the Palatine swamps between
Rome and Naples, where dysentery, typhus, and malaria had
decimated more than one German army.

Politics were another factor to be considered in choosing a
pass: the cities that guarded access to the passes and the hospices that could offer some succor to the traveler might or
might not be loyal to the emperor. And the road might lead
down into unfriendly territory. Often, if a large army was
involved, it had to be broken up and groups of soldiers sent
through different passes, for the problem of provisioning large
numbers of men in such difficult circumstances was acute.

Which of the central passes Henry chose for 1194 expedition is an open question. The St. Gotthard was not opened
until the next century, so the choice lay between the Spluga

and the Septimer, which lay a little farther to the east. It is said that the Hohenstaufen preferred to ford the Rhine at Chur and take the Septimer, thus avoiding the Via Mala, a gorge so narrow and impassable that travelers had to take a long detour up into the mountains before continuing south to the Spluga. Some historians claim, however, that this time the imperial party did take the Spluga, perhaps because the Septimer was still closed by snow. The Septimer can no longer be crossed by wheeled traffic, so our choice was made for us: the Spluga, Via Mala and all.

~

At Chur the great barrier of the Alps rose before us, and the valley split in two, one arm running east to Davos and St. Moritz, one west to the Ticino. We went west and spent the night in Tamins, whence we would start our ascent of the Spluga the next morning.

Our route from Tamins crossed the Rhine and went south to Thusis, then through a gorge so narrow that the rocky walls almost touched each other. Fir trees hung from boulders that tumbled down to a tortuous and dramatic riverbed white with boiling waters. This was the Via Mala, the evil way. Dynamite had carved out a road that saved us the detour, but the passage was daunting nonetheless. The snow on the peaks up above us was mostly hidden by clouds, the colors of the landscape were dark and threatening, and our relief at coming out the other side was not from empathy for Constance, but all our own.

At Splügen we left the highway and began a steep and very abrupt climb up hairpin turns, at first through woods and then, when the trees gave way, through a wider valley littered with big slabs of bare rock and pocked with sparse clumps of grass and miniature meadows of buttercups. A stream descended with great energy and splash, dividing itself into tiny rivulets. Occasionally there was a patch of violets, something pink that looked like saponaria, and deep blue gentians. I

·Rer aſcendit montſenis·

Emperor Henry VII crosses the Alps in 1310. There has been little
improvement since Constance's crossing: the Empress rides astride on the way
up, but everyone, regardless of rank, has to walk going down.

was driving around horrendous bends and at the same time trying to record the names of the flowers we were seeing; at a certain point Marcella firmly removed the tape recorder from my hand and echoed what I said into the mike, preferring that I give my full attention and both hands to the curves.

We finished the climb much sooner than we expected, for we had forgotten how high we already were when we started. There was nothing at the invisible Italian border but a small cabin belonging to the border police that offered coffee, dreary postcards, and a WC. Big humps of tired gray snow were melting onto the roadside. We were at the top of the world here – it was a shock to see that the snow looked so urban, so polluted – but banks of clouds blowing past deprived us of the view.

~

The idea of doing all this on horseback was staggering. The imperial party had been traveling hard and had covered the distance from Trifels to Chur in seven days. The climb up to the pass had to be done fast, leaving the highest hospice on the northern ascent, crossing, and then descending to the first hospice to the south, all in the space of a single day. If the travelers were caught in the dark in a sudden storm, not even the heaviest, richest Flemish wool and thickest squirrel linings would save them, and many of their followers had much less to protect them.

A drawing in a manuscript shows the Emperor Henry VII's ascent of the Alps in the fourteenth century; his queen is riding astride, for the precarious balance offered by the more usual sidesaddle was inadequate on the steep climb. Even so it must have been devastating: each step of the horse pulling himself up the mountainside would have translated into a spine-wrenching heave for the rider, each slip of the hoof and scramble to regain balance meant a desperate tensing of the rider's every muscle. There was no time to rest at the top, no more than a short stop to squat behind a boulder. Perhaps the soldiers at the head of the column had stopped to build a fire, perhaps there was a draught of hot broth ready for the Empress, to restore her before beginning the descent. For the descent was worse, too steep and slippery in many places to attempt on horseback. Often they had to inch their way down on foot.

~

'We have just passed the Spluga and have entered Italy. Now the descent begins, and it's going to be even more harrowing than the climb.'

Back in the car, Marcella had turned on the tape recorder. At first the descent looked much more gradual, an ugly lunar landscape of greenish slate punctuated here and there only by buttercups, their yellow muted by the mist that was moving through the pass. The road wound down with deceptive smoothness to Madesimo, and from there it dropped sharply in an amazing series of very narrow hairpin turns, which revealed glimpses of sheer cliffs and forests rising almost vertically across the valley, although between the mists and the need to keep my eyes on the road, I saw much less of them than I should have liked.

First we passed Madesimo, then Pianazzo, small villages clinging to the mountainside or taking advantage of a stretch of level ground, originally hospices for pilgrims crossing the pass. After Pianazzo the descent to Chiavenna was truly dramatic and most spectacular, with extremely steep, sharp curves running down through a forest of larches, the needles still very tender and very green. Henry had held court in Chur on the twenty-second of May, and then again on the twenty-sixth at Chiavenna: in three days they had accomplished more than fifty miles, including the agonizing descent on foot.

After Chiavenna the valley floor widens out into a little plain that follows the river Mera to the shore of Lake Como. High and snow-topped mountains rise steep on either side, and as we drove through, the clouds and mists still lingered about their peaks. But the temperature was very mild, and the vegetation by the roadsides began to look more familiar, more Mediterranean.

In the garden of the hotel in Loveno where we spent the night, there was a merlin, looking for worms. She flew all around the lawn with one in her beak until she was sure that the coast was clear, then made a quick dart into the bushes where her nest was hidden. We had seen merlins many times on our trip: perhaps Constance had one in a cage to keep her company, or remembered one from her childhood. Merlins are vulnerable birds – they build their nests low to the ground.

Two fish hawks were flying over the lake as we drove south from Loveno. The west coast of Lake Como is truly lovely: the villas have kept their space, and the landscape of the past remains. We passed several Romanesque churches, one in particular at Ossuccio that has a very peculiar bell tower with a bulge at the top that looks like a minaret. The flowers were incredibly lush: after all the tiny Alpine flowers we had seen, we were overwhelmed by the masses of roses and the budding hortensias five feet high.

But the road that we followed down the western shore of the lake is cut through rock, with lots of tunnels – a relatively modern construction. The last lap of Constance's Alpine journey, which took her to the city of Como at the lake's southernmost tip, was done by boat.

From Como the journey to Milan was brief, only about twenty-five miles of flat terrain easily traveled. The city awaited its lords, the gates of the Basilica of St. Ambrose were opened to receive them, and the high, arched galleries of the outer court were ablaze with hangings, so similar, with banners glowing bright against the warm rose of the bricks, to how it had looked on Constance and Henry's wedding day, eight years before. Within, the Archbishop prepared to celebrate a high mass to commemorate eight years of imperial matrimony and to invoke divine protection for their undertaking. It was to be a brief stop, time enough to receive homage before moving on.

But something happened in Milan, something that demanded attention, that altered everything. The Empress fainted perhaps, or was overcome by an exhaustion too deep and too pervasive to be written off to the effects of the Alpine crossing. It seemed that the two menstrual periods she had missed were not the onset of an early menopause nor yet the amenorrhea frequent in an age of inadequate diet poor in iron. It was most improbable, indeed quite unbelievable, but Constance in her forty-first year appeared to be pregnant.

CHAPTER TWO : JUNE

And so she began her quest,
And travelled through many countries, . . .
Which caused her such pain that she sickened
And grew ill. Yet that was lucky,
For it brought her to a friend's house,
Where she was dearly loved, and they saw
At once, looking at her face,
That her health was not very good.
And they made her stay. . . .
                        – *Yvain, The Knight of the Lion*
                        Chrétien de Troyes, c. 1177

Further travel was out of the question. Pregnant or not, the Empress had to rest and regain her strength before taking to the road again.

Henry could not wait upon his wife's health, however. The imperial army was moving southward, growing in numbers as each city it passed – Pavia, Lodi, Piacenza – sent the knights that it owed in service to its imperial overlord. Henry himself was due within the month at Genoa and Pisa to negotiate for the assistance of their fleets in his southern campaigns. The urgency was compelling, for the Sicilian throne was vacant.

Some sources claim that in 1185, just before Constance left Sicily to marry Henry, her nephew, King William II, had designated her as the heir to his throne and had summoned all the nobility of the Sicilian Kingdom to swear fealty to her. Historians disagree as to how much credit to give this story, but very few believe that in doing so William intended to unite the Kingdom of Sicily to the Holy Roman Empire. At that time he was only thirty-one, and his wife, Johanna Plantagenet of England, was not yet twenty: there was no reason then to suspect that William would die childless just four years later, or that the oath would prove anything more than a mere formality.

Yet on the eighteenth of November 1189, William had unexpectedly died, leaving open the question of succession. As the last living child of Roger II, Constance was the legitimate heir, but she was already thirty-five and thought to be sterile; moreover, if she were to return to Sicily, she would bring with her the much-feared Germans and their claim, as emperors of the West, to suzerainty over all of the southern kingdom.

Popular support went instead to the candidacy of Tancredi of Lecce, the illegitimate son of Roger, Duke of Apulia, the eldest son of Roger II, and of Emma, daughter of the Count of Lecce. Tancredi had been fathered by Constance's half-brother, yet he was some twenty years older than his aunt. Orphaned at an early age, he had been brought up at the court of Palermo, and although he had been involved in revolts against both William I and then Queen Margaret, once their son ascended the throne, Tancredi became an able administrator and a close and loyal advisor to the King, who had appointed him great constable and master justiciar of Apulia.

In January of 1190 Tancredi was crowned King of Sicily. Henry was outraged by this usurpation of his wife's throne, but he could not leave Germany just then: Henry the Lion, the Welf prince of Bavaria, had rebelled, and then news came that Henry VI's father, the Emperor Frederick Barbarossa, who had embarked on the Third Crusade the year before, had fallen from his horse and drowned while crossing the river Salef in Asia Minor. The need to secure his own election to the imperial throne vacated by his father's death prevented Henry from launching an expedition against Tancredi until the beginning of 1191.

That first expedition began in glory on Easter Day of 1191 in Rome, when Henry and Constance received the imperial crowns from the hands of Pope Celestine III. It ended in disaster the following August. The imperial army, engaged in a fruitless siege of Naples, was defeated once again by the heat and dysentery of the southern summer and forced to flee northward before the autumn snows closed the Alpine passes to Germany. The flower of German knighthood lay dead on the Campanian plains and the Empress, betrayed by the people of Salerno who had offered her hospitality, was a prisoner in the hands of Tancredi. As we shall see later, Constance eventually made a lucky escape, returning to Germany unharmed but greatly humiliated.

The Emperor had greater hopes for this, the 1194 expedition. In February he had finally collected the ransom that was owed him for the release of Richard the Lionheart, the English king whom he had held captive for more than a year. It was a vast sum, enough to pay the Pisan and Genoese fleets and reward the loyalty of the southern nobility. And then in March the couriers had arrived at court, floundering through the snow-blocked passes to bring the news, first of the death of Tancredi's elder son and appointed heir, named for his grandfather, Roger of Apulia, and then, a few weeks later, of the death of Tancredi himself.

Before dying, Tancredi had designated as heir to the Sicilian throne his younger son, who was crowned shortly afterward as William III. But William was only four years old, and for all her reluctant courage, the young Queen Regent, Sybilla of Acerra, had yet to win the confidence of a people who still remembered the troubled times of Queen Margaret's regency. The road to the throne in fact lay open, but Henry VI would have to take it at the greatest speed, before the humors of the Sicilians coalesced in favor of the boy-king and his widowed mother. Henry could not linger by Constance's bedside.

Pregnant queens did not take to their beds as a matter of course, even in the Middle Ages. Beatrix of Burgundy bore most of her many children en route and without noticeably delaying the imperial progress; Eleanor of Aquitaine was equally mobile during her ten pregnancies. There must have been something particularly worrying about Constance's condition, if Henry was willing to forgo the propaganda value of arriving in Sicily with his wife, the legitimate heir to the throne, at his side.

We can only hypothesize the sources of such concern: extreme exhaustion after the forced march over the Alps, signs indicating a possible miscarriage, or even a feverish delirium, refuge for a mind reluctant to grasp this radical change in destiny. A first pregnancy at the age of forty might not have struck Constance as a cause for unmitigated joy; in the twelfth century the odds were against her, and the chances slim that she and her child would survive.

Whatever the reasons, Henry decided to leave Constance behind. The chronicle of the city of Milan tells us that at the end of May in the year 1194, the Empress was at Meda.

∼

Meda was a surprise, and in fact our friends in Milan, once we got there, were amazed that we should have found a reason to look for it. None of them had ever been there, nor had they ever heard of the Convent of San Vittore, which had given shelter to Constance in June of 1194.

The town of Meda lies some nine miles north of Milan, just off the old road from Como in the middle of the Brianza plain, one of dozens of old towns and villages that have now been knit together into a depressing continuum of characterless suburban sprawl, furniture factories, and other small industries. I had not been able to learn beforehand if anything still remained of the convent, and as we drove round and round the outskirts of the town, it seemed less and less likely that we would find it. But we did find the town hall, and armed with the booklets and the directions which we were given there, we finally located a road that curved up the flank of a low hill. At the end of the road a flight of marble steps led up to a wide piazza ringed by buildings. In front of us stood the baroque façade of a large church; to our right was an imposing palace, austerely Renaissance in style, flanked by another, slightly smaller baroque church. The history of Meda is centered in these three buildings, or at least in their earlier and more modest versions.

The earliest building was the Church of San Vittore. Named after a Milanese martyr of the first half of the third century, it was first described in documents of the eighth century as a small rural chapel standing atop a wooded hill and shaded by two enormous laurel trees. Around the year 780 a convent of nuns adhering to the Benedictine rule was founded at its side. It was here that Constance stayed in the summer of 1194.

The community survived until 1798, when it was closed under the rule of Napoleon's Cisalpine Republic and the convent building became a private residence. The town booklet does not say when the convent assumed its present aspect, but its drawings show a cloister with Renaissance arches, and it describes the rebuilding of the church tower of Santa Maria, just across the way, in the early 1800s, in defiance of a twelfth-century ban, no longer in force, on any tower tall enough to allow impious eyes to spy upon the nuns.

A sign on the gate indicated that it was possible to visit the palace by appointment, but we had no time to return to Meda another day; nor, we thought, would we have been particularly enlightened by a visit to the palace interior, where only the foundations of the medieval convent were to be seen. What it looked like in Constance's day was left to our imagination.

The bigger of the baroque churches, now known as the Sanctuary of the Holy Cross but formerly dedicated to Saints Mary and Sebastian and referred to as Santa Maria, was founded later, at the beginning of the eleventh century, through the donations of pious landowners. During the decades that followed, both institutions – convent and church – expanded their territorial possessions: the Holy Roman

Emperor Henry II granted the Abbess seigneurial rights over Meda and its surrounding territories, while Santa Maria became the parish church for the inhabitants of Meda, the village that had grown up around the convent.

In the early years of the twelfth century, the convent bought the church and all its possessions, and the Abbess declared her right to nominate the parish priest – a claim strongly contested by the people of Meda, who were infected by the communal spirit of independence widespread throughout Lombardy at that time. Years of legal battles ensued, until Henry VI put an end to the quarrel, confirming his predecessor's edict and all the rights that the convent had acquired, including the abbess's right to nominate the priest.

Small wonder then that Henry should choose to leave his pregnant wife in the care of the Abbess of San Vittore, Letizia by name, a powerful woman who had excellent reasons for being grateful and loyal to the imperial cause. The Milanese had less incentive to loyalty: the imperial army had razed their city in 1162. Barbarossa and the Lombard League had signed a peace treaty at the Swiss city of Constance in 1183, and the Commune of Milan, convinced that it was a good omen that the bride bore the same name as the city where the treaty had been signed, had insisted that the wedding of Henry and Constance take place at St. Ambrose (the only church that Barbarossa had left standing). Nonetheless, Henry could have had little doubt as to where the real sympathies of the Milanese lay.

The Abbess Letizia, on the other hand, knew that her power depended on her fealty to the Emperor, and that the presence of his wife would greatly enhance the prestige of the convent. Constance would be an honored guest, never a hostage, and Henry could continue southward with an easy mind.

~

We cannot be sure that Constance, in the depths of her exhaustion, was aware of where she was, or that she had any memory of her husband's leave-taking – unaccustomedly solicitous, perhaps, now that she was carrying his heir – or of being brought to Meda. More likely hers was a slow return to consciousness, eased and comforted by the familiar attentions of Nahid.

Imagine her, more and more wakeful as the days went by and her strength began to return, as she lay propped up on cushions, listening to the sounds of convent life moving outside her chamber door. What would she have heard?

Bells most often penetrated her silence – the deep bell that rang from Santa Maria's stunted church tower to announce the hour to the people of the small town clinging to the hillside in the shadow of the convent, and the clear silver bell that hung within the cloister, ringing both night and day to call the nuns to prayer. The brassier call of the bell mounted outside the convent's great wooden gate sounded frequently in the daylight hours as visitors tugged at the cord: townspeople pleading their innocence of some offense against the imperial laws, pilgrims looking for a roof and bread, peasants come in from the convent lands to pay their tithes of eggs, cheeses, a brace of squawking geese or a recalcitrant and bawling spring lamb to be slaughtered and roasted in the great convent kitchen; merchants seeking to purchase the convent's surplus, the fading rattle of their wheeled carts carrying off sacks of barley and oats, bundles of fleece, bellowing calves destined for the markets of Milan.

The noise dwindled in the evening as the late sun slanted into the cloister, low enough to reach under the stone arches and find her door, partially opened to the resinous perfumes of early lavender, of thyme and rosemary and sage growing in the cloister garden. Then the Empress could hear the low hum of bees on the lavender, the ringing of the bell for vespers, and a rush of hurried footsteps as the nuns gathered in the chapel.

These same sounds echoed in cloisters throughout Christendom, and clocked a routine reassuring in its sameness from

Hildesheim to Milan, from Fontevrault to Palermo, a routine well known to Constance, recalling her to some part of her former life.

∽

From the day of her birth in 1154 until the moment she became betrothed to Henry VI, Constance is hidden behind a veil of silence. Contemporary Palermo chronicles make no mention of her presence; the *Liber ad honorem Augusti*, Pietro of Eboli's poem in praise of Henry VI, tells something of Constance's story, but only as an appendix to that of the Emperor. In the Bern Stadtsbibliothek manuscript the illustrations leap from a picture of her at her mother's breast to one of her wedding. Those who wrote of Constance in the following century were so swayed by partisan interests as to be quite unreliable.

Among the various rumors put into circulation was one claiming she had been a nun, and had been forced to break her holy vows in order to marry the German king. It is in this guise that she was immortalized by Dante:

> This other splendour that is here enrolled,
>> Who on my right displays herself to thee
>> In all the radiance that our sphere can hold,
>
> Saith that as I even so was she –
>> A sister also, from whose head they tore
>> The sheltering holy wimple, as with me.
>
> But though they flung her to the world once more,
>> Against her will, in decency's despite,
>> Ne'er did her heart put off the veil it wore.
>
> Constance the Great her name, and this her light;
>> By Swabia's second gale engendering,
>> She bare the third – the last imperial might.[1]

Most historians today feel that there is no question of Constance ever having become a nun: she was far more valuable to the Sicilian Kingdom as the potential consort of some crowned head than as a bride of Christ. It does seem likely, however, that at the time of her betrothal in 1184, she was residing in the Convent of San Salvatore in Palermo.

∾

It seems reasonable to assume that Constance's mother, Beatrix of Réthel, remained in the royal palace after the death

The Bern codex of Pietro of Eboli's poem in honor of Henry VI gives us a unique, almost comic-strip vision of Constance's life. The first illustration shows Roger marrying Beatrix of Réthel, who then mourns her dead husband as she nurses his posthumous daughter Constance. Below, Constance is betrothed to Henry with a rather large engagement ring and travels north to wed.

of her husband, Roger II, and the coronation of her stepson as King William I of Sicily. Most likely she lived with her baby daughter in partial seclusion, never quite comfortable with the strange customs and exotic habits of these Southerners to whom she had been sent to bear a royal heir, yet secure in the respect that her stepson had shown to her as queen mother.

In the absence of evidence to the contrary, I have chosen to create an early life for Constance in the palace. She would have been entitled to all the prerogatives of a female member of the royal family, such as they were, and nothing in her actions as an adult intimates a woman brought up from infancy within the walls of a convent. We have a letter, often attributed to a certain Hugo Falcandus, thought to be the mysterious author of an earlier *History of the Tyrants of Sicily*: the letter is a political pamphlet urging the Sicilians to cease their internecine feuding and unite against the German invader. The author attributes to Constance the same ingratitude that he notes in the whole of Sicilian society:

> You are an island whose condition is wretched, and fate damned. You have nurtured and educated your children to the end that when they grow up to the hoped-for strength, they first tested that strength on you, and then – fattened on the abundance of your breasts – trample upon and tear your womb! . . . Constance too, brought up from her first cradle for many years in the riches of your delights, educated and moulded by your instruction and manners, later left to enrich foreigners with your wealth, and now returns with huge forces to repay you with a disgraceful recompense, so as to violently tear apart the apparel of her most beautiful nurse and stain with foreign filth the elegance with which you exceed all other realms.[2]

The author's enthusiasm for a political cause obviously outweighs his historical objectivity at this point, and rhetoric plays a

The city of Palermo is divided into different neighborhoods, each with its own costume and religion. In the upper left-hand corner, beyond the city walls, are the rare birds and plants in the gardens of the Genoard, and to the right lies the palace with the Palatine Chapel. At the bottom is the port, closed by a chain and guarded by a fortress, the Castrum Maris.

49

large part, but if the author was indeed Hugo, he had been present in the palace and knew the facts of Constance's upbringing.

~

And how could I not give Constance the palace in Palermo to grow up in, deny her such beautiful, magical surroundings for her childhood? Much changed by the centuries, only pieces of the original Norman palace remain, difficult to gather into a coherent whole, yet sufficient to give us at least a fragmented idea of its magnificence. With the help of Hugo Falcandus, we can attempt a reconstruction:

> This city, then, lies in a plain: on one side she is subjected to the frequent lashings of the sea, the beating of whose waves is, however, checked by the former palace (called the Sea Castle) and by walls armed with a large number of towers. The New Palace sits on the opposite part of the other side, built with amazing effort and astonishing skill out of squared stones; the outer side has walls which wind far and wide, while the inner side is remarkable for its great splendor of gems and gold. On one side it has the Pisan Tower, assigned to the protection of the treasury, on the other the Greek Tower overlooks that part of the city which is called Kemonia. That part of the palace called Joharia glorifies the middle section; it is particularly beautiful, sparkling with the glory of many kinds of adornment, and the king used to spend his time there intimately when he wanted to enjoy peace and quiet.[3]

Walled off from the main body of the city, this royal precinct was known as the Galca and corresponds approximately to what is today the palm-filled Piazza Bonanno and its surrounding buildings. It contained palaces, churches, chapels, and even the remains of a Roman amphitheater, as well as gardens, fountains, and the cages of the royal menagerie.

This gold pendant, which originally contained a
relic of Saint Thomas à Becket, was a gift of Reginald, Bishop
of Bath, to Queen Margaret of Sicily, probably on the occasion
of her son William II's marriage to Johanna Plantagenet.

Over the rest of the site there are spread various mansions
placed all around for the married ladies, the girls of the
harem, and the eunuchs who are assigned to serve the king
and queen.[4]

Here Beatrice would have had her apartments, living in what
was most probably a luxurious but uneasy coexistence with the
new queen, William's Spanish wife, Margaret of Navarre, whose
insensitivity to those around her would become manifest in the
coming years. Ambitious for herself and for her sons, Margaret
would have had little time for the young widow and no interest
at all in Constance, her husband's half-sister, a mere baby and a
female to boot, too far removed from the succession to be a
threat to her own offspring.

It was different for the royal children. I like to think that the
close friendship between Constance and the future King
William II – a friendship documented once he assumed the
crown – had its roots in these early years, when Constance ran

through the halls and the gardens of the palace, struggling to keep up with the little boys who, older than she, were yet her nephews: Roger the eldest, the beautiful favorite of the king; Robert, destined to die early and unsung; and William, born just a year before Constance, golden-haired, gentle, and loving.

> There are some smaller palaces there, shining with great beauty, where the king either discusses the state of the realm in private with his *familiares*, or invites the powerful when he is going to talk about the great public affairs of the realm. Nor is it appropriate to pass over in silence the high-quality workshops which belong to the palace, where the threads of silkworms are spun most finely into separate threads of different colours before being knitted together to make multiple strands. Here you can see how single-stranded, double-stranded and triple-stranded thread is finished with less skill and expense; and there six-stranded thread is pressed together using richer material; here the red thread meets your eyes with the gleam of fire; and there the color of green thread gives pleasure to the eyes of onlookers with its pleasant aspect; over there damask cloth, marked by patterns of different kinds, requires greater application from the craftsmen and richness of raw material, and is consequently finished at greater cost. You may see many other adornments of different colours and types there, among them gold threaded into the silk, and a variety of different-shaped [patterns] . . . made by sparkling gems [and] pearls.[5]

These were the *tiraz*, the palace workshops where the descendants of the weavers carried off from Byzantium by Roger II's admiral, George of Antioch, continued to labor, weaving brilliant silks and samites and embroidering them with gold.

I like to imagine that Constance came here to watch these marvels taking place. Once the boys began their initiation into the military arts, where she could no longer follow, her nurse

Nahid sought to distract her from the hurt of exclusion by taking her to explore the hidden treasures of the palace, to the workshops of the *tiraz*, where the scarlet and emerald and azure shuttles flew back and forth between the glistening threads of the warp like the exotic birds that fluttered about the aviaries in the royal gardens, and the tongues of the weavers gossiped and chattered in Greek and Arabic and Norman French, as the heavy combs thumped rhythmically against the woof.

Perhaps they visited the Arab quarters as well, and the harem that the Norman kings had captured from their Saracen predecessors and maintained for their own pleasure. This was Nahid's birthplace, but she, not beautiful enough to merit the king's favors, had been taken away as a girl to serve the new queen Beatrix upon her arrival from Flanders. To Constance, a blond-haired, blue-eyed child of northern genes, the dark beauty of the Arab slavewomen would have been as familiar as it had been exotic to her mother; for her, the hennaed decorations of hand and foot were a delightful game rather than a heathen practice, and veils and scented oils and Saracen ornaments represented only the comforting figure of her nurse.

Would Nahid have accompanied her to the Palatine Chapel as well? Many of the Muslims in service at the palace had converted to Christianity, often a ruse for survival rather than an act of faith, for they were known to call out to Allah in moments of stress. Either way, the Saracen girl would have taken pleasure in showing the child the chapel ceiling, a triumph of her own culture.

Further on, for those who enter the palace from the side that overlooks the city, the Royal Chapel first meets the eye, paved with a floor of costly craftsmanship and with walls whose lower level is decorated with plates of precious marble, and the higher one with mosaic stones, some gold and others of different colours, with representations of the story of the Old and New Testaments. The [ceiling] . . . is adorned by an outstanding elegance of carvings, and an amazing variety of [paintings], . . . with the splendour of gold shining all around.[6]

Passing centuries and poor light make it difficult to make out the kings and their houris, their musicians and their cupbearers who dwell in the niches of what is considered the finest extant example of a painted wood ceiling in the Arab tradition, but the gleam of gold in the mosaics of the Palatine Chapel is as bright as ever.

Roger II built the chapel in the 1130s as his private place of prayer, and he called upon all of the craftsmen who were his subjects – Arabs, Greeks, and Latins – to work together to create a masterpiece in what has come to be called the Arab-Norman style. The wooden ceiling and the geometric inlays are Arabic; the floor plan and the mosaics are Byzantine; and the inlays in red porphyry and green marble that cover the floor and ornament the royal throne, raised on a dais facing the altar on the back wall, are of Latin influence, yet all merge into a perfect whole.

One can be thankful that the Christian knights who sacked the palace in 1161 spared this sacred space. It did not fare so well in 1943, however, when Allied troops occupied the palace and it became the seat of the Allied Military Command in Sicily. A local historian claims that the heads of two saints and two angels disappeared from one of the arches; understandably, given the circumstances, but nevertheless unfortunately, no fuss was made, and the 1946 restoration replaced the holes with perfect copies. Given the sad record of American collecting, the story is credible: it would be interesting to know where the original heads have ended up.[7]

Some of the earlier restorations were very poorly done, but they are unable to destroy the perfection with which this small, dark, yet glittering space depicts the sacred mystery and might of divinely appointed kingship, the sacrality of the power with which Roger II considered himself to be invested.

Aside from the chapel and the dungeons that tunnel from the palace into the very foundations of the city walls, relatively little of the original palace remains. In later centuries most of the southern construction was altered beyond recognition by order of Spanish and Bourbon viceroys who wished to live on a scale grander than what the small proportions of the medieval Norman rooms allowed. The Pisan Tower and a part of the Joharia are beautifully preserved, and two of the rooms are open to the public. It is here that we can find the principal testimony to the royal intentions: here is the Garden of Eden, here paradise on earth. The theme held great interest for the budding humanists of the twelfth century, who most often sought to re-create it in an ecclesiastical context, a garden protected from temptation and sin by the high walls of a cloister. But in Palermo the Norman kings, through their just rule, claimed to reestablish an earthly paradise, an Eden reflected in the exotic beasts and lush foliage that decorated the walls of the palace.

The first room, known as the Sala dei Venti (Room of the Winds), is a square hall of beautiful chiseled stones forming a high vaulted ceiling. Although very handsome, it is appreciated less for its own merits than for the fact that it is the antechamber to the Sala di Ruggiero, attributed to Roger II but more probably built by his son William I. This second room is the perfect lay counterpart to the sacred decorations of the chapel. Above the marble-lined walls and in the arched niches runs a mosaic frieze of palm trees where lions and peacocks gather and centaurs hunt with drawn bows. It too has suffered over the years, and an awkward marble fake chimney of nineteenth-century origin fills up a niche that must have been a second window before the Renaissance façade of the Spanish addition encroached upon it. I particularly like the description that the English historian John Julius Norwich gives us:

What really matters in this enchanting room, this gorgeous bestiary in blue and green and gold, is the way it speaks to us . . . of the happier and more carefree side of Norman Sicilian life; reminding us how, despite all the intrigues and conspiracies and rebellions . . . the sun still shone through the forest and men still looked on the world around them, and laughed, and were grateful.[8]

Next to the Room of Roger stands the Pisan Tower, a truly amazing construction, now unfortunately closed to the public since its rooms have been allotted to the president of the Sicilian Regional Assembly as his private offices. On the ground floor is the Zecca, where the kingdom's gold coinage was minted and stored; it now contains the Assembly's library and may eventually be opened to public use. The offices overhead

The Pisan Tower was the stronghold of the Norman royal palace.
It was at the shuttered and balconied center window that William I
and Roger stood in 1161 to address the crowd.

occupy the main room of the tower: the inner sanctuary, built like a tower within a tower. Its massive stone walls rise three stories to a vaulted ceiling; when the palace was restored, a wooden ceiling that divided the space into two rooms was removed, but possibly some such vertical division did exist in the original structure as well. About a third of the way up are two rows of mosaics, each about ten inches high—all that is left of a double frieze that must once have covered walls decorated much like those in Roger's room. One can see only a parade of hooves, the hooves of horses ridden by hunters, perhaps, or by the Norman knights that conquered Palermo. Beautiful as the raw stone is, it is painful to have such a miserly hint of the former glory of this room.

From the eastern wall a large window looks down to the square far below and out over the whole city of Palermo. Small arched windows pierce the thick stone of the other walls, narrowing into slots just wide enough for an arrow to pass through. These smaller windows open onto a corridor, so narrow that one soldier alone, armed with shield and sword, could man it. Embraced by the corridor, the inner room is accessible only through a heavy double door. How safe William must have felt there, in a vault that a mere handful of knights could defend, but how illusory that safety.

~

It was in this room, in fact, that the luminous years of Constance's childhood came to an abrupt and violent end. In March of 1161, just as she was reaching the age of seven, the age at which medieval children were considered to leave infancy behind them, the nobility revolted against William I, and the palace was taken by storm and sacked.

When William's grandfather, the Great Count Roger de Hauteville, had conquered Palermo from the Arabs in 1072, he had found an efficient court bureaucracy, which he adapted to his own purposes and then bequeathed to his son, Roger II, whose chief counselors, both civil and military, were mainly Greeks and Arabs, occasionally even eunuchs and slaves. With the gradual latinization of the Norman Kingdom in the second half of the twelfth century, an increasingly aggressive and ambitious (and fiercely taxed) nobility grew more and more resentful of the fact that so much power should lie in such common hands, while the knights themselves were generally excluded from court decision making.

The revolt of 1161 was plotted by the barons and led by a young knight named Matthew Bonello. They intended to murder the Chancellor Maio of Bari, the son of a mere merchant who was William I's closest advisor, and to dethrone William and put his young son Roger in his place. On the morning of March 9 the traitors stormed the palace dungeons, releasing among others the King's nephew, Tancredi of Lecce, the illegitimate son of William's long-dead brother, Roger of Apulia.

Unlike most of the Hauteville men, Tancredi, who was nearing thirty, was very short in stature and of an extremely

Justice is administered in several different languages and law codes at the court of Palermo, keeping the Greek, Latin, and Saracen notaries so busy that their scribes even work at night by candlelight.

ugly countenance – a contemporary writer likened him to a monkey. He had a poor record in terms of loyalty, having spent five years in prison for his part in the 1156 revolt of the barons of Apulia against the newly crowned William.

Was Constance old enough to have heard and understood the palace gossip? Was the misbegotten and unsightly traitor locked in the dungeons already a menacing shape in her seven-year-old's imagination? Or was she oblivious to any possible danger to her world, totally unprepared for the noises of the revolt, the roaring mob outside the palace windows, the shouts and running footsteps in the corridors, the crashing and banging as the royal treasury was looted, the silken hangings torn from the walls, the chests of gold and silver coins carried off, together with the gem-encrusted vestments of the king, the golden plates and goblets, the chiseled ivory caskets, even the wondrous silver planisphere made for her father by an Arab astronomer. High above this metallic cacophony, she could hear screaming in the Muslim quarters, the sound of the women of the harem being raped and of the eunuchs being slaughtered.

In the tower King William was a prisoner, and Queen Margaret and her sons were under arrest in her apartments, where – most probably – Beatrix and Constance waited with them. Armed knights came to take young Roger away, not, as the women had feared, to harm him but to crown him and to lead him on horseback through the city before the cheering crowds.

The revolt eventually failed, defeated by its own excesses of violence and sacrilege. The bishops and the other high clerics, repelled and frightened, called on the people of Palermo to rout the barons from the palace and restore the rightful king to power. But the damage had been done; nor was it finished.

In control once more of his stronghold in the Pisan Tower, the King stood at its window, preparing to address the crowd of Palermitani who were gathering below. The young Roger stood by his father's side, the King's hands lay on the shoul-

William I on his deathbed, attended by an astrologer, then mourned by his
queen and courtiers before the altar of the *cappella regia*, the Palatine Chapel.

ders of his firstborn, most-loved son and heir.

Suddenly there was a muffled scream and a soft thud as the
nine-year-old child slumped to the ground. By some unbear-
able fluke, a stray arrow loosed by an unknown hand had
penetrated the window and pierced Roger's eye. The King,
huge, heavy, and fierce-looking under his full black beard, a
man whom Constance rarely saw but had always known as the
ruler of her universe, crumpled to the marble floor, next to
Roger's still body, and there he sat, sobbing like a small child.

～

Nothing would be the same again. Unable to recover from the
loss of his favorite son, the King retired more and more to the
private joys of his harem and the beautiful pleasure palaces he
was constructing. His health declined, and five years later, in
1166, he died.

An illustration in Pietro of Eboli's *Liber ad honorem Augusti* shows him on his deathbed, surrounded by his queen and his courtiers, and by an Arab astrologer who looks to the stars to see if the end is at hand. If history has called him William Malus (the Bad), his subjects mourned him sincerely: the codex shows the people of Palermo – Christians, Arabs, and Jews – each in his proper costume and in his own neighborhood – as they bewail his death. According to Hugo Falcandus,

> all the citizens, dressed in black garments, kept the same clothes on for three days. Throughout these three days women and noble matrons – especially the Muslim ones, whose grief for the King was not feigned – symbolically went around in sackcloth with their hair loose day and night, in groups, with a crowd of slave-girls preceding them, and filled the entire city with their wailing and their rhythmic chanting in time to the beating of drums.[9]

The King's presence had intruded upon palace life but lightly in his last years; it was not so much the loss of her half-brother that twelve-year-old Constance mourned as the loss of stability and companionship. The boy William, just one year older than she and more of a brother to her than his father had ever been, was now king. Together with her mother, Constance took her place in the entourage that accompanied him across the Galca along the Covered Way, the underground route that led from the palace to the cathedral. She watched the Archbishop Romualdo place the crown of Sicily on William's golden curls, and she saw the Palermitani go wild with excitement when their beautiful young boy-king appeared to them, first in the Loggia of the Incoronation, then riding through the city on horseback. She stood there watching as William entered into a new game, one in which there was no role for Constance to play.

William may have been king, but Margaret was regent, and Constance's mother, Beatrix, had nowhere to turn for protection.

It seems likely, therefore, that it was at this point that Beatrix decided to seek the protection of God in the Convent of San Salvatore, perhaps taking her young daughter with her so that Constance might continue her education at the hands of the nuns, safe from palace intrigues. This convent, the oldest in the city, is not far from the royal palace: ten minutes' walk through the gardens of the Galca, under a gate that no longer stands, and down Palermo's main street, the present-day Corso Vittorio Emanuele, known now as then as the Cassaro. Ten minutes, more if the stalls and markets of the Arab merchants were open, with all the temptations of their multicolored merchandise.

Today the convent is a school; the side that faces on the Cassaro is covered with modern stucco, but from the Via Protonotaro (named for one of the Norman court officials) one can see on the upper story a remnant of the original façade, a row of arched windows surrounded by typical Norman zig-zagged brickwork, and glimpse a schoolgirl peering down much as the young princess might have done, had she been living here. Something remains of an inner court, once a cloister with a garden more tropical, with jasmine twining among the roses, but not unlike the garden at Meda. If convents did not signify happiness for Constance, at least they must have offered a synonym for refuge and safety.

Although I do not believe that Constance remained at length within the convent, a reasonable, if purely hypothetical, explanation for her presence there at the time of her betrothal might be looked for in the date of her mother's death, somewhere between 1183 and 1185. Although we know nothing about Beatrix's life from the time she gave birth until her burial in the Galca church of St. Mary Magdalene, it is quite probable that she, like so many dowager queens of her era, spent most of her remaining years in the convent, and that Constance had returned there in those last months in order to attend her mother's deathbed.

The same problems that had been at the root of the 1161 revolt re-emerged during the regency. In the hope of maintaining an independent position, Margaret called her French cousin, Stephen of Perche, to her side. She named him chancellor and archbishop of Palermo and probably took him as her lover as well. His rapid rise to power, and the arrogance and insensitivity that Stephen and his band of French followers demonstrated toward the Sicilians – barons, ecclesiastics, and commoners alike – endeared him to none. After another period of unrest and revolt, in 1168 Margaret was forced to expel Stephen and his fellow Frenchmen from the kingdom, and from then until 1171, when her son William came of age, she remains in the background. We hear nothing more about her until her death in 1183 except that she founded the Benedictine abbey of Maniace, built at the foot of Mount Etna, which later became the seat of the Duchy of Bronte, awarded in gratitude to Admiral Nelson by the Bourbon king Ferdinand IV of Naples during the Napoleonic Wars and inhabited by Nelson's descendants until just a few years ago.

Whether or not Constance spent the years of Margaret's regency in the convent, her presence was not forgotten: in fact, one of the causes for the popular alarm and hostility toward Stephen of Perche was his scheme to marry Constance to one of his brothers, considered by some as an indication that he himself had ambitions for the crown.

In any case, Constance probably returned to court after William II's coming of age, if for no other reason than to complete her education. Unlike the royal families of northern Europe, who sent their sons out to be educated in other courts at an early age, the Normans of Sicily seem to have had the habit of keeping their children at home. Or at least the boys: what happened to the girls, or even if there were any girls, is something we don't know.

In this conspiracy of silence, Constance proves an exception because of whom she married. The reasoning of John Carmi Parsons, in *Medieval Queenship*, concerning the royal daughters of northern Europe probably applies to her case as well:

> It hardly stands to reason that royal or noble parents would ignore the daughters who were to serve as matrimonial ambassadors. For one thing, the idea that royal daughters were raised in isolation from their families implies that for them, the imperatives of that group were greatly attenuated; if they were meant to represent a father's interests as informants or go-betweens, it is more likely that parents would cultivate relationships with them and train them for their future roles. . . . These daughters are prepared from childhood for their roles as peace-weavers; since their early marriages are seen as deplorable events that consign them to the authority of tyrannical mothers-in-law or to hostile environments where they lack the support of relatives, they are indulged with every luxury while under their parents' roof.[10]

Constance had the bad luck to have no father and a mother who surely had very little voice in court matters, but William I no doubt considered himself *in loco parentis* with regard to his little half-sister, and all the evidence indicates that William II held Constance in great esteem.

Just who were the other women of the court is almost impossible to know: very few names have survived from an era chronicled exclusively in a masculine hand. We know that Constance had a much older illegitimate half-sister, Adelaide, who returned to the court of Palermo as a widow in 1156 after the death of her husband Ugo, Count of Molise. Her name comes down to us mainly because she became the beloved of Matthew Bonello, the ringleader of the 1161 revolt. As such, she would have fallen from the King's grace, and probably it was soon after Bonello's imprisonment and death that she returned to Molise, where she died in 1206, leaving her worldly goods to the cathedral at Boiano. She would not have been an important presence after Constance's childhood years.

One chronicle reports that an illegitimate daughter of Roger II was married to Margaret's brother Henry of Navarre, but it is not clear whether this was Adelaide or another woman. I can find no report of Roger's having any legitimate daughters other than Constance, although it is perfectly possible that they existed but did not live long enough to acquire the reflected fame of an influential husband.

Life at court under William I did not allow much space for women in any case. It had not been expected that he would become king, and he had not been trained to rule. An excellent soldier when roused, William had preferred to leave the everyday business of government in the hands of his *familiares*, the advisors and bureaucrats (chief among them the above-mentioned Maio di Bari) whom he had inherited from his father. When forced to meet with his *familiares* or do business with the barons of the realm, he would do so in the Sala Verde. This was a two-storied structure with arched colonnades on the ground floor, and apartments on the second, so rich in vines and flowering plants that it was called the 'Green Room.' It appears to have been built, possibly on ancient Roman foundations, in the middle of the verdant gardens, full of fountains, palms, and fruit trees, that lay within the walls of the Galca, the fortified citadel that protected the palace.

But William I preferred to spend his time at the Zisa, the summer pavilion that he was building in the great park outside the city walls known as the Genoard. But it was not the ladies of the court, however, who kept him company there.

If Margaret's regency was a nightmare of foreign intruders, offended locals, and restless barons, the tenor of court life must have changed drastically in 1171, when William II came of age. He was a very different man from his father, and was greeted with enthusiasm, according to Lord Norwich, by the Sicilian people:

Christ anoints William II, as portrayed in a mosaic in the
Cathedral of Monreale. The pendants hanging from either side
of his crown are typically Byzantine, similar to those on the
crown pictured in the color insert.

Not that they knew much about him. His beauty, to be sure, was famous; he had preserved it intact through his adolescence, and the boy who had seemed like an angel on the day of his coronation now at eighteen reminded people of a young god. The rest was largely rumour. He was said to be a studious lad, who read and spoke all the languages of his kingdom, including Arabic; mild-mannered and gentle, given neither to those brooding silences nor to those sudden outbursts of rage that had rendered his father so formidable; deeply religious, yet tolerant of faiths other than his own.[11]

They saw in the young King hope for a new era of peace and tranquillity and an end to the continual unrest that had followed upon the death of his grandfather. The first matter that lay before him was the choice of a bride, a matter which was turning out to be extremely complicated.

Wealth, power, and beauty made William II a most desirable husband, and the offers poured in. The first, in 1167, had come from Manuel Comnenus, proposing his daughter Maria, who at that time was heir to the Byzantine Empire. Queen Margaret, still regent at that time, left the Greek proposal dangling and appeared to be much more interested in an offer that arrived the following year from the King of England, the Plantagenet Henry II, offering the youngest of his three daughters, Johanna. Educated in Poitiers at the court of her mother, Eleanor of Aquitaine, Johanna spoke the same Norman French that was spoken in Palermo. The idea of tightening the blood ties between the kingdoms of England and Sicily was very appealing, especially as the Plantagenets ruled a good part of western France as well as England itself. But in 1170, before this offer could become formalized, the saintly Thomas à Becket was murdered in Canterbury Cathedral, and the blame fell upon Henry's shoulders. The marriage negotiations were broken off.

The following spring a new offer arrived from Byzantium,

and this time Margaret accepted it. William and his royal party (there is no evidence of Constance's participation) journeyed to Taranto to receive the imperial princess, but the promised bride never arrived. The young King was left standing humiliated at the wharf, and relations between the Norman Kingdom and the Eastern Empire never recovered.

The following year, an invitation to marry one of the daughters of Frederick Barbarossa arrived. To the papacy, however, the possibility of a unification between Sicily to the south and the Holy Roman Empire to the north was extremely threatening: the Papal States would be caught in a vise. To avoid such a union, Pope Alexander III immediately set out to revive the negotiations with the English throne. Henry II had done penitence for his share in the responsibility for Becket's death and had been absolved, so his daughter was once more acceptable, as a contemporary chronicler, Benedict of Peterborough, tells us:

> In the same year (1176) the Bishop-Elect of Troia, the Bishop-Elect of Capaccio, and Count Florian of Camerota, ambassadors of William, King of Sicily, and with them Rothrud, Archbishop of Rouen, a relative of said king of Sicily, came to England. And when they came to the Lord King in London, they petitioned him to give his daughter Johanna in marriage to their lord, William, King of Sicily. He summoned the archbishops and the bishops and the barons and the wise men of his realm to London and consulted them as to how he should answer the ambassadors of such a great king. And on their advice he accepted, and sent the ambassadors to Winchester, to see if this daughter was pleasing to them.[12]

Johanna was indeed pleasing to them, the negotiations were completed, and Henry II ordered a fancy trousseau for the young bride. The Pipe Rolls of the Exchequer for the twenty-second year of the reign of Henry II speak – one can almost hear the outrage – of a 'robe costing the enormous sum of £114 4s 5d.' Other amounts are recorded for the purchase of furs and scarlet silks, and for lengths of linen cloth and the dyed canvas hangings for the cabin of the royal yacht that was to carry Johanna and the Sicilian ambassadors across the Channel with an escort of seven ships.

Henry II placed Johanna and the ambassadors in the care of her brothers: the young Henry brought her overland as far as Poitiers, and then Richard, soon to be known as the Lionheart, accompanied the party across Aquitaine and Toulouse to Saint-Gilles at the delta of the river Rhône. There William's English advisor, Richard Palmer, was waiting, together with the Archbishop of Capua and a fleet of twenty-five ships.

Johanna was formally delivered into Sicilian hands, and the party embarked on the ninth of November, but the weather was terrible, and it took them until Christmas to reach Naples. Johanna had been so seasick that the Sicilians feared for her health, so the rest of the journey was made by land, ending at the gates of Palermo on February 2nd, 1177. In the words of another chronicler, Roger of Hoveden:

> When she had arrived in Palermo, in Sicily, together with Gilles, bishop of Evreux, and the other envoys of our lord the king, the whole city welcomed them, and lamps, so many and so large, were lighted up, that the city almost seemed to be on fire, and the rays of the stars could in no way bear comparison with the brilliance of such a light: for it was by night that they entered the city of Palermo. The said daughter of the king of England was then escorted, mounted on one of the king's horses, and resplendent with regal garments, to a certain palace, that there she might in becoming state await the day of her marriage and coronation.[13]

William had denied his mother any further say in the affairs of state once he took them into his own hands, and it was highly unlikely that he would have encouraged a close relationship between Margaret and the new queen. Who would make a more suitable companion than Constance, now twenty-three years of age, equal in rank, entirely loyal to her nephew, and still young enough to become Johanna's confidante?

It is on record that Johanna, after her husband's death, was a staunch supporter of Constance's legitimate right to the succession, as opposed to that of Tancredi, so I do not think that I risk too much in assuming that a firm and lasting friendship grew up between the two women. Life in the palace took on a different quality in the presence of the daughter of Eleanor of Aquitaine and those who visited her. Poetry, romance and courtly love, a whole new cultural life in which women were both inspiration and actors was being introduced to Sicily from the north, and Constance would have been there both as witness and as participant.

∾

Let us imagine Constance in Meda as June of 1194 came to a close. Her strength had come back to her; she could distinguish between the devastating weakness of her first weeks there and the gentle lassitude that now pervaded her body as she walked about the cloister, or sat in the chair that the Abbess had ordered set in the garden. The lavender and the thyme were in full bloom, each plant quivering under the assault of fat bumblebees, smaller and more agile honeybees, swallowtails, and cabbage moths, a miniature marketplace in perpetual motion scaled down to the level of her energy.

Occasionally she lifted her eyes from the bees to the sky, to watch a hawk circling above and feel a pang of regret for the merlin hawk that she had left behind in Haguenau. But it was very brief, this regret, for now the measure of her life fit comfortably within these cloister walls. She was not yet

Although this is in fact a scene from the story of David and Bathsheba,
I like to imagine that it is Constance supervising the bath of the newly arrived
Johanna, while the young bridegroom William kibitzes from a distance.

ready to face open horizons again. It was the past that preoccupied, as if she felt the need to reconstruct each step that had
brought her to this moment, to this columned square of sunlit
flowers.

How many convents had seen her as their guest, how many
palaces had welcomed her. A life of constant motion, constant
traveling, even as a child: from palace to convent to palace.
Imagine her as she thinks back to the palace in the Galca and
the apartments destined for William's bride-to-be, the new
damask wall hangings – a pattern of peacocks and rabbits
chosen by Constance herself – mounted, the copper bathtub
and the brass braziers bright with their recent polishing.

The hot coals in the braziers, sweetened with dried orange
peel, had taken the chill off the night air, and the emptied tub
still smelled of perfumed oils. The damp and rumpled linen
towels and the cast-off robes of wool and sable had been

removed and all was in order. Johanna, who had managed to stay awake through the ritual of the bath only because its novelty piqued her curiosity, was already fast asleep under the scarlet coverlet, her long fair hair spread out around her.

Imagine Constance sitting in Meda and smiling to herself as she remembered slipping into bed next to Johanna and feeling the small body next to her move closer in her sleep, seeking the comfort of human warmth. When William asked his aunt to be chaperone and companion to his eleven-year-old bride until she was old enough to enter her marriage bed, Constance had accepted gladly. She had been happy to have a new role for herself at court, and felt an instinctive sympathy for one so young, so far from home, so precocious in experiencing that exile which Constance knew might soon be her own lot. She had not imagined how dear to her Johanna was to become in the future, how deep a friendship could grow from the maternal feelings of the early years, and with what great affection and sympathy she would watch the child grow to girl and then to young woman, participating in Johanna's delight and pleasures, receiving her confidences, and sharing her growing anguish at her inability to produce an heir.

How acutely she missed Johanna now; how greatly she desired to confide to her dearest friend the joys and the terrors of her own late and long-awaited pregnancy.

CHAPTER THREE : JULY

The knights gathered there
Where the ladies called them,
And the young ladies, too, and the girls.
Some gossiped, told and retold
Stories, some spoke of love,
The anguish and the sadness of Love
And its glories, as Love's disciples
And followers knew them, then
When Love flourished, and was rich.
    – *Yvain, The Knight of the Lion*
        Chrétien de Troyes, c. 1177

No chronicler thought it important to record the Empress's progress southward from Meda in the late summer and fall of 1194. We know with certainty only that she was in Meda by the end of May, and that before Christmas Day she had arrived in Jesi, a town in the Marches, in central Italy, not far from Ancona. Taking into consideration that this was a very belated first pregnancy, and therefore fraught with uncertainty and anxiety, as well as enormous political significance, Constance's journey was surely not planned lightly.

We shall assume that Constance chose to remain in cool and peaceful Meda until she was safely beyond the first four, most precarious months of gestation, and until the worst of the muggy heat of summer in the Po valley had passed. When she resumed her travels, she would have done so with slow caution, following the easiest and safest routes and making frequent and lengthy stopovers, timing her progress to bring her near the border of the Sicilian Kingdom, and to a town loyal to the Emperor, well before the nine months were up. It would be unthinkably dangerous for the Empress to be overtaken by labor pains as she traveled, and to give birth by the roadside.

Let us give her another month of peace, then: July in Meda, more time to rest and to remember, before she has to turn her face to the future. Let us assume too that with the return of her energy, her curiosity revives as well; that her need to flee from intolerable present weakness into the past has been placated, tempered by a need for company, a need to be entertained.

~

Midsummer was a busy season for the Abbess of Meda. The earth is most generous in its bounty then, and she would have had to devote much time to her agents, reckoning the tithes due to the sisters, seeing that their share of the harvest arrived at the convent gate, and arranging for it to be properly stored or advantageously sold. Nonetheless she would have been attentive to the Empress, paying her almost daily visits not only in the interest of her own duty and of the abbey's advantage, but also for the pleasure of the company of an educated woman, one who was at least acquainted with the management of an imperial household and could sympathize with her own burdens.

Picture the two ladies sitting together and chatting, perhaps on a bench in the cloister garden. The shape and cut of their clothes differ little: a linen chemise, a long gown with sleeves tight at the wrists, an overtunic with wider sleeves, and a veil to cover their heads and shoulders and to hide their hair, arch-symbol of seduction to the medieval eye.

Whether monastic or lay, female attire had changed little since late antiquity. In the north of Europe, men had abandoned the long garments of Rome in favor of the short tunic and loose trousers of the Germanic tribal tradition, but even in the thirteenth century, when the pace of changing fashion was

74

to accelerate greatly, the dictates of modesty allowed little leeway for radical innovation in feminine apparel.

The Abbess, being a nun of the Benedictine order, wore a habit of black wool, which was black in name only: by our lights, it would be a faded shade of blue. According to the French historian Michel Pastoreau, in the early Middle Ages color was perceived according to a ternary system, completely different from our modern and 'scientific' perception of the color spectrum. The basic color was white, with all its symbolic charge of purity: black was the opposite of white, darkness rather than a specific hue. The other opposite of white was red, which ranged from yellow through scarlet to purple and meant anything colored, as the Spanish words *tinto* and *colorado*, both meaning 'red,' still testify. The gamut widened with the development of improved dyes and mordants, and during the course of the twelfth century, an increasingly organized and hierarchical society required a greater range of coats of arms and of clothing to reflect its differing levels of status. But the rich black that would be produced in the fifteenth century was neither available nor of interest to the people of Constance's era, who aspired to the reddish tones obtained through inexpensive madder dyes; to the rich scarlet of costly kermes and cochineal; and increasingly, to blue. During the twelfth century the washed-out blue of woad was flanked by the deep and intense blue produced from indigo, imported from the southern Mediterranean, which gained steadily in popularity, rising in the thirteenth century to a position of prominence that lasted into the twentieth.[1]

To the nuns passing under the cloister arches at Meda, the Empress sitting next to the drably gowned Abbess must have seemed like some rare butterfly escaped from the Garden of Eden. She was still wearing what she had brought with her from Palermo – clothing was very expensive in the Middle Ages and was worn until it was threadbare: silks that had been dyed and woven in the *tiraz*, brilliant colors that were audaciously combined according to a Near Eastern sensibility the likes of which had never been seen in northern Europe, where silk was reserved for ecclesiastical vestments. But in Palermo even the Christian women, in the words of a visiting Spanish Muslim, 'dressed in silken robes embroidered in gold, and wrapped themselves in splendid mantles and colored veils, and walked in golden slippers . . . adorned with all the ornaments of Muslim women, with jewels, with paints, and with perfumes.'[2] Even dressed at her simplest, Constance must have evoked wonder and awe.

~

What would an empress and an abbess talk about? Prayer and good works, naturally, for the Abbess would have felt a responsibility for the soul of her guest as well as for her physical recovery. No doubt they told each other tales of saints and miracles, the Empress introducing the Abbess to the martyrs she had learned of during her German stay, and to the stories of Sicilian saints of her childhood, of Lucy and Agatha and perhaps of Rosalia, the Norman noblewoman who is said to have lived as a hermit in a cave on the mountain above Palermo and to have died just about the time when Constance was born.

The Abbess would surely have given Constance an account of the martyrs whose tombs lay beside the altar in the convent chapel, a very old story that began in the third century, when Maximinus was emperor in Rome. The holy martyr Victor, imprisoned in Milan by imperial order, managed to escape and fled to the woods, where he was murdered and his body left to rot. The wild beasts of the forest did not feed on the holy remains but guarded them faithfully until a chapel was built in the woods at Meda to house them.

Five hundred years passed, and the laurel saplings that had been planted at the sides of the chapel grew tall and strong. One day Aimo and Vermondo, two young knights hunting nearby, were attacked by enormous boars and took refuge in the laurel trees, where they sat until the boars tired of waiting for them and wandered away.

Aimo and Vermondo vowed to found a monastery in honor of Saint Victor, on the very spot where his laurel trees had saved them. Renouncing earthly glory and riches, they offered themselves to a life of prayer and charity and mortification. The monastery attracted many young people, among them a group of Benedictine nuns, and when Aimo and Vermondo died, they were buried in the chapel at Meda.

The tombs in the chapel were not those where Aimo and Vermondo were first buried, but more beautiful ones into which their bodies were later translated. When the old tombs were opened, a most wonderful perfume issued forth, which spread everywhere and brought many new people to dedicate their lives to venerating the saints.[3]

～

On days when the cloister's business was pressing and the Abbess had no time to tell stories but only to inquire after the Empress's health, she might have urged upon her guest a book of sermons, a breviary, or a collection of Mary miracles to read and contemplate.

Meda was renowned as a center of economic and political power, but not as a seat of learning: its library, if it existed at all, would have contained very few books, and even those were most probably limited to religious matters. It is unlikely that Constance would have found in the nunnery the kind of entertainment to which she had become accustomed at court.

Living as she did in the second half of the twelfth century, Constance had high standards in entertainment. Her appeal in fact lies not only in the events of her own life but also in their timing, for she was both witness to and protagonist in what could be considered the most exciting period in medieval history. The economic depression and intellectual pessimism that had accompanied the approach of the year 1000 had

Holy Roman Emperor Frederick Barbarossa with two of his sons:
on the left King Henry of Germany (the future Emperor Henry VI); on the
right Frederick, Duke of Swabia, who died in 1191, leaving his ducal title to
his brother Philip, who was originally destined for the clergy.

given way in the following years to a new optimism, a remarkable growth in the population and economy of western Europe, and a consequent expansion of cities and commerce. Life and society became much more complex, institutions multiplied, and new classes emerged.

To the individual, this complexity meant a multiplicity of new roles and new groups with which to identify, and choosing among them required a greater awareness of the inner self than medieval man had known before. Thoughts now dwelled on more intimate, more human levels, both in the forms of religious devotion – a concentration on the bodily suffering of the crucified Christ, and the maternal joy and suffering of the Virgin Mary – and in the new literary forms that emerged in the courts of the nobility and that served to define the behavior appropriate to the members of those courts.

It is in fact in the last half of the twelfth century that knighthood becomes institutionalized, a process encouraged both by secular rulers, be they kings or emperors, and by the Church. For the former, dubbing a knight meant channeling the unruly and brutal energies of the landless younger sons of the nobility into service, and to the Holy Roman Emperor in particular, it meant giving vent to the ambitions of the *ministeriales*, the men of lower social status who had become the backbone of the imperial administration. For the Church, the code of chivalric behavior reinforced the new sacrality of marriage and banned rape and concubinage, which had been common components of the Germanic warrior tradition.

Many historians consider that the exact moment in history in which knighthood became an institution can be identified with the knighting of Henry of Hohenstaufen and his younger brother Frederick in 1184, the same year in which Henry became betrothed to Constance. For the occasion, Barbarossa summoned a great assembly – so extravagant and impressive that it is recorded by almost every contemporary chronicle – to convene at the city of Mainz on the day of Pentecost.

On the eastern bank of the Rhine at Erbfordie, an entire

city, complete with imperial palace, church, and houses for guests, had been constructed all of wood. Invitations had been sent out to all the leaders of the empire, both lay and ecclesiastical, as well as to those of the imperial cities of northern Italy, who arrived with full regalia and entourage. Together with the nobility came, for the first time to the German court, the troubadours of France and the young German minnesingers – Guiot of Provins, Doetes of Troyes, and Henry von Veldeke – who brought with them the new school of poetry, the school of courtly love.

> On Sunday, 20 May, Frederick and Beatrix and their son Henry wore their crowns [Henry had already been crowned King of Germany] in a festive procession and, in the evening of that same day, at a banquet, dukes and margraves, all members of the new class of princes, acted as cup-bearers, marshalls and chamberlains. On the next day, after early morning mass, Frederick's two sons received their swords and took the oath of knighthood. For the main political object of the celebration was to prepare the ground for their succession. Henry from now on became a real co-regent and Frederick was made, officially, duke of Swabia. There were rich presents to reward wandering knights and singers. Then there was another banquet and finally a great tournament in which Frederick himself took part; and on the following day, more banquets and tournaments. The gaiety of that Tuesday, however, was marred by a sudden storm which destroyed the wooden church and several other buildings, killing fifteen people.[4]

The popular mind seems to have made much of this unfortunate conclusion, which was no doubt laced with terrible omens. The chronicles dwell upon it at length – more so, almost, than on the events of the festival itself. In the words of one chronicler,

Then the royal house at Erbfordie where they were gathered collapsed, and a great multitude of counts and free men and men of all different ranks fell with it, and sank miserably into the sewer which lay beneath. Some of these were with difficulty rescued from the Gera river that flowed through the latrines. Others, discovered in the sewage, were almost beyond recognition.[5]

One cannot help wondering, given the ubiquity of meticulous detail in this and other chronicles, whether the humble monks who transcribed them were shocked by such an ill-omened ending to the event, or simply taking sly pleasure in the thought of all those aristocrats flailing about amidst the excrement.

Among the survivors of the Mainz debacle was Frederick von Hausen, one of the first of the lyric poets writing in the German vernacular to adopt the style of the French troubadours and to devote himself to the pursuit and celebration of courtly love. In these lyrics the poet-lover declares his unrequited and unconsummated love for a woman – older and of more elevated rank – who was most often the wife of his lord.

The unattainability of the lady and the suffering of the lover are ethical necessities in the fiction of courtly love. Courtly love, *fin' amors*, is the love of courtliness, of the refinement that distinguishes a class. . . . This love-relation enables the courtly man to declare his commitment to the ideals of his class, and to exemplify the behavior in which those ideals are realized: steadfastness, optimism, devoted service, formality, personal grace, self-esteem, self-sacrifice.[6]

The French poets rendered this unlikely and slightly ridiculous ideal of love to their courtly audiences with considerable irony – a perspective that generally appears to have been lost upon their German followers. Early poets such as von Hausen composed narcissistic contemplations of their own sufferings, whereas their successors tended to refute the courtly ideals and dwell upon love as a mutual relationship. But in many cases, the love relationship is indeed a fiction, an excuse for a demonstration of poetic skill. This is not necessarily true, however, in the case of von Hausen:

> The account of his death at Philomelium in 1190 makes it clear that he was a well-known and respected nobleman, far more famous as a soldier than as a poet. It is a reasonable assumption that he was an amateur in both senses of the word, a man who wrote poetry because he liked it, with no thought of establishing a professional reputation or of pleasing a patron. Such a poet would be likely to show two characteristics: he would work within the form and framework of imagery already established by the professional poets in the Romance languages but would express his personal feelings more directly.[7]

Von Hausen's career as a faithful and esteemed servant in the imperial court can be sketchily traced through the documents he witnessed (as his father had done before him). He followed

Young men in the throes of courtly love woo their ladies with music and poetry on this enameled casket from Limoges.

Frederick Barbarossa to Italy in the 1175 expedition against the Lombard League and then again in 1185–88, the years of Constance's marriage and travels in northern Italy. He is recorded as being present in Germany at Henry's knighting in 1184 and was also in Germany in 1188, when he followed his emperor's example and took the cross. He died on May 6th, 1190, during the battle of Philomelium, near the center of present-day Turkey, by falling from the saddle while chasing a Turk.

This is the man whom I have chosen to be the great, perhaps the only, love of Constance. This relationship is pure invention on my part – not impossible, maybe not improbable, but totally undocumented. Moved by a quite unscholarly wish to offer her some compensation for what I see to have been great unhappiness, I have elected Frederick von Hausen as the pious and courteous Christian knight who initiated Constance into courtly love.

It is quite probable that von Hausen was waiting for her in Rieti in 1185, one among the knights and clerics whom Barbarossa had sent to receive his future daughter-in-law from the hands of her Norman retinue and escort her to the north. We can imagine the diffident curiosity with which she greeted them. Her expectations had not been high: the Germans did not enjoy a good reputation at the Norman court, where they were thought to be crass and uncultivated at best and more generally to be brutally violent. It was well known, moreover, that Frederick Barbarossa's imperial appetite extended to all of the Sicilian Kingdom, which he had considered to be a rightful part of the empire of the West well before he acquired Constance as a daughter-in-law. Constance, for her part, could boast not only impeccable lineage but wealth and cultivated refinement as well; she had held her head high as she rode into Rieti, followed by a train of one hundred and fifty mules laden with her trousseau of precious jewels and silks and silver, and with her dowry of forty thousand pounds of gold, a treasure that had left all of Europe agape.

The court at Palermo, where Constance had lived until

then, was very cosmopolitan, but the visitors from northern Europe were mostly Frenchmen and, especially after Johanna's arrival, Englishmen. They had brought with them the first lyrics, the epics and romances that were being produced in the north, and in Johanna's company Constance had first discovered 'courtesy,' the ideal of courtly love, service, and loyalty. Johanna had imbibed these ideas with her mother's milk: Eleanor of Aquitaine was one of the great patronesses of troubadours and poets, and Johanna's childhood had been lulled by constant music and song. Constance had doubtless listened to her stories, half incredulous, half wistful, for she herself was not yet too old to dream of *fin' amors*. But she would not have expected to find these ideals embodied in a German.

Her nephew William II had sailed with her as far as Salerno, and from there she had traveled by land to Rieti, where with great ceremony she and her treasure were handed over to the care of Barbarossa's emissaries. Picture her as she resumed her travels, this time in the company of the imperial party, and imagine the intense and ill-concealed curiosity with which she was examining her new escorts, searching for clues as to the nature of the foreigner awaiting in the north who was destined to become her husband.

It pleases me to think that her friendship with von Hausen began here, that more and more often she found him riding by her side during the long journey and was pleasantly surprised by the grave courtesy and well-turned phrases in heavily accented French with which he addressed her. I imagine him winning her with his considerate comments and explanations, for the countryside they were passing through was all new to her, and the stories and poems that he recited helped to while away the long hours in the saddle.

Perhaps it was von Hausen who first gave her lessons in German, naming the parts of their bodies and those of the horses, the saddles and bridles, the clothes they were wearing, the animals and the scenes that they passed as they rode.

Perhaps he taught her simple rhymes and jingles to aid her in mastering the strange and craggy syllables, and laughed with her at her attempts to pronounce such unfamiliar sounds. I like to think that it was one such rhyme, an ancient travel blessing that she had learned from him during the first weeks of their journey, that was the last thing she had said to him as he rode forth from Haguenau, headed toward Jerusalem:

> I look after you as you go,
> With my five fingers I send fifty-five angels after you.
> May God send you home in health,
> The Gate of victory stands open before you
> And the gate of happiness, too.
> May the gate of water be closed to you,
> And the gate of death by sword.[8]

And so it had been, for he had passed none of these gates, yet his destiny was not to be avoided.

We know from the documents that during the first years of her marriage, as Constance followed her husband and her father-in-law around northern Italy, von Hausen was present at the imperial court more often than not. He was a companion, a teacher, an ever dearer friend. As a foreigner from what the Germans considered an excessively extravagant culture, who had yet to master the Swabian dialect, Constance would have been slow to assume the running of the imperial household, and Henry, absorbed in questions of terrestrial power and spiritual salvation, may have had little time for her. I have asked von Hausen to mitigate her loneliness.

It might have been through his eyes that she learned to look at her father-in-law and so fell under the spell of his enormous charm. Frederick Barbarossa had kept all warmth for himself, bequeathing little upon his son Henry. Despite the terrible rages that reminded Constance of her long-dead half-brother William, in the evening hours, when the aging Emperor was relaxed and in search of entertainment, his pleasure in the

Leave-taking in the fourteenth century. The fancy tournament helmet, decorated with peacock feathers, is very different from the somber Crusader's helmet that Constance might have handed to Frederick von Hausen.

parade of jugglers, acrobats, minstrels, and storytellers that passed through the court was heartfelt and contagious.

Only then (or so I choose to believe), when the Emperor called on von Hausen for a song, did the poet allow his true feelings for her to show through the formalities of the love lyric. His piety, his deep desire to participate in the salvation of the Holy Land, and above all his utmost devotion to the man into whose service he was born and to whom he had pledged loyalty unto death, would not allow a word, a gesture beyond what his art could accommodate.

And perhaps, if indeed she did love him, it was in the end this that Constance loved the most. She had seen enough of treachery and betrayal in her former life; von Hausen could become for her the incarnation of the virtues of the Christian knight. And still now, at Meda, as she thought of him, it was thus that she chose to remember him, offering his songs to the Emperor and to the young King and Queen:

> My heart has been wounded
> and ill for a long time now
> (as it should be, for it is foolish),
> ever since it knew a lady –
> if he who is Emperor of all realms
> should give her just one kiss
> on her crimson mouth,
> even he would feel the better for it.
>
> Since I have entrusted my heart
> to one of the loveliest,
> I should be rewarded
> by the very person whom I mean.
> Though I have never let her know,
> I am nonetheless the man
> who could bring her greater happiness
> than anyone else in the world.

Who could console me but
the same beautiful lady
who brings greater woe to my heart
than any can imagine?
I suffer such grief perforce,
for my heart has aimed too high.
If love should treat me so unkindly,
let no man ever trust it.[9]

I first chose Chrétien de Troyes's *Yvain, The Knight of the Lion* to be von Hausen's parting gift to Constance simply because I had happened upon Burton Raffel's delightful translation, devoid of archaisms and needless flourishes, which makes it both readable and quotable.[10] The story is based on the Arthurian tales that had become extremely popular in the twelfth century. Yvain, knight at the court of King Arthur, departs to challenge the knight of the fountain who has defeated his cousin Gawain, but he does so in a most unchivalric manner – in secret, and without taking leave of the king. He is successful, kills the wicked knight, and with the help of a servant girl wins the love and the hand of the widow, Laudine, and becomes the lord of his victim's castle.

Gawain arrives and tempts him back to the court and to knightly adventures. Laudine consents reluctantly to Yvain's departure, making him promise to return within a year. Distracted by his success in the tourneys and by the camaraderie of court life, Yvain forgets his promise, the year passes, and not until the servant girl, Lunette, brings back the ring he gave Laudine and says that her mistress wants never to see him again, does he realize what he has done.

The thought that he has lost his lady and his fortune through his thoughtless and unchivalrous behavior drives him mad. He flees to the forest, where he runs naked like a wild man, forgetful of who he is and what he has lost. Succored first by a hermit and then by a lady who cures him and asks his service, he gradually comes to internalize the ideals and virtues of the courteous knight. A lion that he rescues from a serpent becomes his follower, an example of fidelity that is a lesson to him. Keeping his true identity hidden, he presents himself only as the Knight of the Lion, and more and more his adventures are selfless and disinterested, rescuing helpless damsels out of charity rather than for glory. In the end he wins back the love of Laudine and is at peace, and they live happily ever after.

I could not have made a better choice, as I was to discover in the course of my reading. Chrétien de Troyes is probably the greatest author of twelfth-century romances. Troyes was the seat of the County of Champagne, and much of Chrétien's work was produced for the court of the Countess Marie. Marie de Champagne came from a long line of poetry lovers: her great-grandfather was William IX, Duke of Aquitaine and the

Working in tandem, Yvain and his lion manage to slay a giant.

first known troubadour poet, and her mother, Eleanor, was a famous patroness both at the French court while she was married to Marie's father, King Louis VII of France, and in the early years of her marriage to Henry II. Marie was thus our Johanna's half-sister, and Johanna had spent part of her childhood with Marie.

Chrétien himself is now thought to have been a cleric rather than a member of the court aristocracy; hence the didactic undertones of his works. One of the first of the French poets to use the material of Arthurian romance, in *Yvain*, which was probably written about 1177, he manipulates the conventions of romance and questions its artificial values: 'The serious part of his poem consists in the rehabilitation of Yvain as a human being by separating him from the Arthurian world and allowing him, as the Knight of the Lion, to demonstrate natural principles of human kindness and charity to his fellow-men, not the artificial behavior of the romance hero.'[11]

My summary does not in the least do justice to Chrétien's lovely story, beautifully told. The poet portrays personalities with considerable complexity and makes liberal use of irony and humor – the lion is fierce in his defense of his master, but otherwise as lovable as the Cowardly Lion of Oz. In the scholarly debate over the degree to which the people of the twelfth century had developed a sense of their own identity and individuality, *Yvain* is held to be a major piece of evidence. I am not competent to take part in that debate, and it is too early in our story to even consider its terms as they might apply to Constance. But I feel I chose well in giving her the Knight of the Lion as a fictional companion in her travels.

The great adventure of chivalric romance is the adventure of becoming what (and who) you think you can be, of transforming the *awareness* of an inner self into an *actuality* which impresses upon the external world the fact of personal, self-chosen destiny, and therefore of an inner-determined identity.[12]

The Abbess Letizia was a woman accustomed to wielding economic and political power, worldly in the sense of being able to manage the secular affairs of her abbey. But she was also no doubt provincial in her personal experience: she would rarely have ventured farther afield from the San Vittore lands than an occasional trip to Milan. Constance, on the other hand, although she had little power of her own, had met popes and kings, princes and poets, and her firsthand knowledge of the greater world must have intrigued the nun. One can imagine Letizia listening openmouthed as Constance described the palaces of her youth, the mosaics of the churches in which she had prayed, the wild beasts of the royal menagerie, and the strange plants in the palace gardens. As their familiarity increased, Letizia's curiosity would have outweighed her discretion: I can hear her begging the Empress for her account of the most talked-about event in Western Christendom: how her husband Henry had held for ransom the King of England, Richard the Lionheart, an affair that had come to a happy conclusion just six months earlier.

Richard had been taken captive at the end of 1192, as he was returning to England from the Crusade, his dream of rescuing Jerusalem betrayed, his kingdom in the West beset by enemies both without and within. He had been late in leaving the Holy Land, sailing in October, when the season of safe navigation was coming to an end, and enemies awaited him at every Mediterranean port. So he had chosen a route no one might have expected: overland from Venice through Vienna to the lands of Henry the Lion, Duke of Saxony and Bavaria, who had been the husband of his late sister, Matilda, and who was hostile to the Emperor. Richard had counted on Henry the Lion to escort him across Germany, going north of the Hohenstaufen territories to the mouth of the Rhine, from where he could sail to England. But Duke Leopold of Austria had been alerted to a suspicious party of merchants traveling

Although he is wearing the clothes of a commoner, Richard is
discovered and taken captive by Austrian soldiers.

through his lands, and near Vienna, the King in disguise and
his small party were taken.

Some said the King himself was at fault: disguised as a
servant, he gave himself away by wearing his magnificent royal
ring. Others claimed that his servant boy, going off to buy
some food for the party, tucked the gold-embroidered gloves
of the King into his belt and thus unwittingly betrayed his
master.

Constance had first seen Richard when he was brought to
the high court at Ratisbon, after Duke Leopold had delivered
him to her husband in exchange for a share of the future
ransom, guaranteed by two hundred young hostages. Henry
had at first been extremely hostile to his captive, in part
because of Richard's friendly relations with his enemy, Henry
the Lion. Moreover, on his way to the Holy Land, Richard had
stopped off in Sicily to obtain the release of his widowed sister,
Johanna, who after William II's death had been practically a
captive in Tancredi's hands – and there Richard had signed a
treaty with Tancredi, whom Henry considered a usurper to the

Sicilian throne. Richard was furthermore accused of having betrayed the Holy Land by making a truce with Saladin, the leader of the infidels, and of having arranged the murder of one of the Emperor's cousins.

When the young English king stood up to defend himself against these accusations at Ratisbon, he spoke to the imperial court not as a prisoner captured like a common thief, but as if he were seated on his own throne. His bearing was so regal, his words so well chosen and so courteous, that he won the hearts of all those who were present. Even Henry was moved, and embraced him and exchanged the kiss of peace. The chroniclers tell us that there was not one among the members of the court who was not deeply affected by the sight or could refrain from weeping.

The ransom was fixed at 100,000 marks of silver, plus fifty galleys and two hundred knights to serve for a year in the Sicilian campaign, an enormous sum that had astonished the whole of Europe. It took time for the English Kingdom to raise the money, and in the meantime Richard's brother John was conspiring against him with the King of France, Philip Augustus, who offered Henry an even greater price for his prisoner. The months of captivity were not easy for the English king, for Henry changed his humor and sent him to Trifels for safekeeping; the chronicles speak of Richard's courage and good spirits in the face of hardship, and how he passed the time drinking, joking, and playing dice with the soldiers guarding him.

Then Henry relented once more and had Richard brought to Haguenau, where he was treated as a guest rather than a prisoner. The Emperor and the King vied both in brilliance and in verse, for Richard had been brought up at his mother's court in Poitiers and loved poetry and, like Henry, was himself a poet. A song that he is said to have written for his half-sister, Marie of Champagne, laments his long captivity and the indifference of his countrymen.

No prisoner is happy with his fate
And he complains that life is misery.
But to console himself, he can write songs.
My friends are many, but their gifts are few:
Shame on them, if for want of ransom paid,
   I spend two winters here.

For all my men and barons know this well,
English, Poitevin, Norman and Gascon,
That I would never leave the poorest man
Lying a prisoner for want of gold.
Although I do not hold this against them,
   I am still in prison.

Now I begin to see quite clearly that
Dead men and prisoners can have no friends.
Since I am here for want of coins and gold
I am unhappy, and they will regret
Their idleness, when I am dead and gone,
   In leaving me so long.[13]

Perhaps Constance remembered enough to sing these first three verses to the Abbess; surely she must have felt, if ever she heard them, a stab of sympathy for the English king in his unwelcome exile.

It was the great Eleanor herself who brought the ransom to Germany, and Constance had been present at the final meeting in Mainz in February of 1194. Eleanor had become an old woman, and her hair had grayed with seventy-two years of bearing children, traveling, and fighting to assure the succession of her sons to the English Kingdom and to the rule of her own beloved lands in the south of France. But the traces of her famous beauty were still visible, and she had lost neither her regal bearing nor her command of the situation. When the Emperor unexpectedly requested that Richard do homage to him for his kingdom, it was Eleanor who whispered in the ear of the reluctant King and persuaded him to place his cap in Henry's hands in sign of vassalage. And when Henry decreed Richard's liberation, Eleanor broke down and wept on the bosom of her adored son.

∾

One can imagine that Eleanor of Aquitaine became a favorite topic of conversation between Constance and Letizia – even of gossip, if one can so call exchanges between an empress and an abbess. Eleanor was perhaps the most famous woman of her century and certainly the most talked about. By all accounts a ravishingly beautiful and irresistibly charming woman, heiress to the Duchy of Aquitaine with its brilliant and refined court and poetic tradition, she had been married to the young King of France, Louis VII, at the age of thirteen, and she managed to scandalize Christendom for most of the rest of her life. When she and her husband arrived in the Holy Land during the Second Crusade, they first went to Antioch as guests of Eleanor's uncle, Raymond of Antioch, whose familiar southern charm induced his niece to ever greater familiarity. It was only by carrying her off bodily that Louis was able to enjoy his wife's company in Jerusalem. Although Eleanor was never formally charged, the aura of adultery has clung to her until the present, and the adulterous queen became a stock figure in medieval romance literature.

Eleanor had two daughters by Louis but could not produce a male heir, and eventually by mutual if, on the side of the besotted Louis, reluctant consent, the marriage was proclaimed null. The excuse was consanguinity, a transgression of the canon law that forbids marriage between even distant cousins, which throughout the Middle Ages was ignored or deplored according to political convenience. Dull and boring Louis was quickly replaced at Eleanor's side by the young and dashing Duke of Normandy, Henry Plantagenet, whose maternal grandfather had been Henry I of England. Gossip even claimed that Eleanor had bedded the father, Geoffrey, before marrying the son. Henry was nineteen, ten years younger than Eleanor, and she bore him three daughters and five sons. She was forty-two when Johanna was born and forty-five when she gave birth to her last child, John.

In her later years the sexual scandal gave way to the political, when she championed her sons Henry and Richard against their father and encouraged their rebellions. Their eldest son, William, died in childhood; young Henry was early designated as his father's successor to the throne of England. Richard, who had been named by his father as heir to the Duchy of Aquitaine, grew up at the Poitiers court, his mother's favorite, and it was he who survived both his father and his elder brothers and became Richard I, King of England, Duke of Normandy and Aquitaine, to name just a few of his titles. This was the son to whom Eleanor had given her strongest support and for whose ransom she had struggled ceaselessly.

Constance had had a previous meeting with Eleanor, in 1191, in Lodi, just south of Milan. She and Henry were traveling south to Rome for their coronation, and Henry was bent on the first, disastrous southern expedition to dislodge Tancredi from the Sicilian throne. Eleanor was also on her way to Sicily, where Richard was encamped at Messina together with the French king, Philip Augustus, where he was negotiating with Tancredi for the release of his sister Johanna and the restitution of her dowry, before embarking for the Holy Land. Eleanor was bringing with her a bride for Richard, Berengaria of Navarre. (Richard's inclinations lay in a different direction, however; the marriage was possibly never consummated, and he died without heirs.) The Lodi meeting is recorded as taking place between Eleanor and Henry: what they discussed is not revealed to us, but the news of such an encounter must have been most alarming to Tancredi, who was at that moment seeking Richard's support for his own permanence on the Sicilian throne.

As usual, nothing is said of Constance's presence, but she

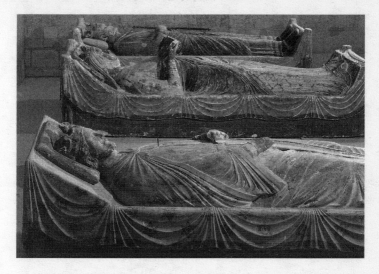

Not even death has separated Eleanor from her beloved son Richard:
their tombs lie side by side in the Abbey of Fontevrault.

was traveling with her husband and had every reason to wish
to meet the English queen. The Sicilians had been instrumen-
tal in saving Eleanor from a shipwreck on her return from the
Holy Land in 1149, and she and Louis had had what was
reported to have been a very congenial stay with Roger II in
his palace at Potenza, in Calabria, as they made their way up
the Italian peninsula and back to France. How eager Constance must have been to press Eleanor for her memories of
the father whom Constance herself had never known, and how
even more probable that she would have entrusted Eleanor
with gifts and letters for her dear friend Johanna, who would
be waiting for her mother at Messina.

The meeting between Eleanor and Constance at Mainz in
February of 1194 was of quite different tenor: the Queen and
the Empress were on different sides of the controversy over
Richard's ransom, and it is impossible to know if the two
women had any personal exchanges. Yet of all the spectators at
the imperial court who wept to see the English queen sobbing in

her son's embrace, Constance had perhaps the most reasons to be moved. Eleanor was much older, of course, and according to what she herself is supposed to have written in a letter to the pope, she was 'worn to a skeleton, a mere thing of skin and bones, the sap consumed in her veins, tears all but dried in the fountains of her eyes.' Yet there was much in Eleanor's life with which Constance could have sympathized: a woman of the South received not without suspicion into a northern court; the shame of not producing a male heir for the French throne; the marriage (albeit of her own choice) to a man ten years younger than she; and now, in Meda, as Constance began to feel the first stirrings of her own child in her womb, the fierceness of Eleanor's maternal love. It was a moment Constance would not have easily forgotten.

~

Constance's second month at Meda came to a close with the feast of Saint Anne, the mother of the Virgin Mary. This feast normally would not have been observed with particular solemnity by this community of virgins, but in 1194 the prayers of the nuns were needed to invoke the intercession of Saint Anne for the Empress, for Anne was the patroness of late and difficult childbirth. I like to think that Letizia prepared the office of vespers especially to this end, choosing a particular hymn, perhaps one of the songs of the German visionary Hildegard, Abbess of Bingen, and that she searched at length through her small collection of books for a fitting lesson.

> Hail, o greenest branch,
> sprung forth in the airy breezes
> of the prayers of the saints.
>
> So the time has come
> that your sprays have flourished:
> hail, hail to you, . . .

98

For the beautiful flower sprang from you
which gave all parched perfumes their aroma. . . .

Whence the skies bestowed dew upon the pasture,
and all the Earth was made joyful
because her womb
brought forth corn,
and because the birds of the firmament
built their nests in her.[14]

Imagine the Empress, restored to health and relatively tranquil now, as she kneels in the convent chapel and commends herself and her child to the protection of Saint Anne. Imagine her face as she listens to the sisters singing, the wonder, the joy, and even the pride with which she hears their words.

How did Constance explain to herself the fact that she, like Anne, had conceived so late in life? Had there been something unusual in the act of conception itself? Four months earlier, at the end of March, the news of Tancredi's death had reached Nuremberg, where the Eastertide court was sitting. The Lenten ban on sexual intercourse between man and wife had been lifted, and the Sicilian throne was now vacant, Henry's for the taking. How had he taken its heiress – with lust aroused by ambition, forgetful of the holy water and the gesture of crossing himself and the asking of God's pardon, thrusting harder and deeper than in the passionless, dutiful lovemaking of the past?

Was Constance herself different, more receptive in the deepest recesses of her psyche to his seed, now that she could hope to bestow her own Sicilian throne upon its issue?

Or was it simply a miracle, a belated answer to the candles lit, the altar cloths embroidered, the masses sung, and the reiterated prayers? Whatever the reason and whatever the cause, Constance could feel slight flutterings in her womb as she knelt in the chapel at Meda, the first tangible evidence of a pregnancy so long desired, so long despaired of. The time had come when she must look ahead.

This twelfth-century mosaic represents the Virgin's birth, although Saint Anne, reclining on her childbed, does not look particularly advanced in years.

The lesson that followed the hymn was not the one indicated by the calendar but was taken from the writings of Saint Jerome. The Abbess spoke of Anne and Joachim, who lived together in holy matrimony, following the word of the Lord and observing his feast days; who divided what little riches they had between the temple and the poor and needy, keeping only a third part for themselves; who despite their prayers and sacrifices remained barren for twenty years. She told of how Joachim, going to Jerusalem for the feast of the Dedication, was chased from the temple, the priest saying that it was unseemly that one cursed by the Lord with barrenness should offer prayers before His altar. And she told how Joachim fled from Jerusalem, too ashamed to return to his family, and dwelt among the shepherds, and how an angel appeared to him, saying:

I, the Lord's angel, am sent to thee, to announce to thee that thy prayers are granted, and thine almsworks have ascended in the sight of the Lord. I have seen thy shame, and heard the reproach of barrenness wrongfully cast upon thee. For God indeed punishes not nature, but sin; and therefore, when He closes a womb, it is only that He may later open it more wondrously, and that all may know what is born thereof is not the fruit of lust, but of the divine munificence. Did not Sara, the first mother of your race, bear the shame of barrenness until her ninetieth year, and yet bear Isaac, to whom was promised the blessing of all nations? Did not Rachel also long remain barren, and yet beget Joseph, who was the ruler of all Egypt? Who was stronger than Samson or holier than Samuel? Yet both of these were the sons of barren mothers! Therefore believe my words and these examples: those conceived after a long delay, and begotten of sterile mothers, are wont to be the more admirable![15]

PART TWO

THE FOREST

CONSTANCE'S ROUTE
MILAN – BAGNARA CALABRA
AUGUST 1194 – APRIL 1195

0   50   100
miles

MILAN

PO RIVER

RAVENNA

ANCONA

ADRIATIC SEA

SICILIAN KINGDOM

ROME

BORDER

1194

NAPLES

SALERNO

TYRRHENIAN SEA

MESSINA

PALERMO

CATANIA

BAGNARA CALABRA

IONIAN SEA

LEGEND:
1 PIACENZA
2 CASTELL'ARQUATO
3 CHIARAVALLE DELLA COLOMBA
4 FIDENZA
5 PARMA
6 MODENA
7 BOLOGNA
8 JESI
9 SAN VITTORE DELLE CHIUSE
10 FOLIGNO
11 TREVI
12 SPOLETO
13 RIETI
14 SAN CLEMENTE A CASAURIA
15 TERMOLI
16 S. LEONARDO DI SIPONTO
17 TRANI
18 BARI
19 GIOIA DEL COLLE
20 S. GIOVANNI IN FIORE

CHAPTER FOUR : AUGUST

I was very well lodged, that night,
And as soon as one could see
The morning light, my horse
Was ready, exactly as I'd asked
The night before.
– *Yvain, The Knight of the Lion*
Chrétien de Troyes, c. 1177

It was almost time for Constance to take to the road again, and there were many preparations to be made, and decisions to be taken. Marcella and I too were confronted with choices, but they would be arbitrary, decided on the basis of whim or curiosity, for the next lap of Constance's journey is entirely undocumented. It is commonly assumed, however, that she took the easiest route leading from Milan to the town of Jesi in the Marches, where she was to give birth. This route would have brought her along the southern edge of the Po valley to Bologna, then across to the seaside town of Rimini and south along the Adriatic coast almost as far as Ancona. Jesi lies twelve miles inland, just to the north of Ancona.

The journey covers roughly three hundred miles. If we assume that the Empress and her escort traveled very slowly, at an average of ten miles a day; that for every day of travel there followed at least one day of rest; and that the party often had to detour in search of safe lodging, it would have taken them a little over two months to arrive in Jesi.

Contemporary medical knowledge, based mainly on the writings of Hippocrates and Galen, considered that the ties that bound the fetus to the uterus of the mother were strongest in the fifth and sixth months of pregnancy. Thus with the arrival of August, Constance was theoretically able to travel in relative safety.

The months from August through October were considered, moreover, to be the best time for travel in northern Italy: the worst of the heat was over, and the rivers and streams were at their lowest, their flood basins dried and hardened by the summer sun. If the Empress started out in mid-August, she could have hoped for good weather to accompany her until the end of October, by which time she would have arrived in Jesi, where she could spend the last two months of her pregnancy in safety and repose.

How would she travel? Constance was an accomplished horsewoman, having traveled up and down the Italian peninsula on horseback, not to mention her four Alpine crossings and her frequent tours of Germany. But the roads that lay before her now were not necessarily smooth, and the lurching gait of a horse picking its way over rough paths would hardly have been considered advisable for a delicate pregnancy. A cart was out of the question: even the much-traveled Via Emilia would be uneven and full of potholes, the old Roman paving stones wrenched apart by frost, flood, and centuries of neglect, and the wooden-wheeled carts of the period were without springs and without mercy. It is most probable that Constance rode in some sort of sedan chair or litter, a luxury conveyance that at that time was just arriving in Europe from Byzantium together with the returning Crusaders. Very possibly Constance's father, with his passion for whatever Byzantium had to offer that might exalt his majesty, had used a litter for ceremonial purposes, and in Germany litters had made their appearance by the middle of the twelfth century: the Archbishop of Trevirs arrived at the synod of Rheims in a leather litter lined with the finest linen, astounding the assembly with such luxury.

So let us assume that, except for the most difficult passages, Constance rode in a litter slung between two mules, one that did justice to her exalted rank, lined in scarlet wool and embroidered in gold, with some sort of roof to protect her from the rain and hangings to hide her from view when she wished. Let us also keep in mind that all this splendor would soon be dimmed by the dust kicked up by the mules' hooves, splotched by raindrops, and marred by mud.

When I was fourteen years old, I toured the castles of the Loire with my parents and was surprised to find that so many of them had belonged to the same man. Why did he need so many? I asked. Because the castles got too smelly, answered my father, and they had to open the windows, burn the straw from the floors, and move on to the next. I now realize that this was a rather simplified explanation from a historical standpoint, but it was very effective. I have never since forgotten that one must look at the past through a glass darkly: Constance's journey may have been a glittering royal progress, but it was also long, tiring, dirty, and often dangerous.

Nahid, or whoever it was that served as maid to the Empress, would have ridden next to the litter, but who else was in the party? An armed escort for certain, with a sufficient number of knights that two could ride ahead, harbingers to announce the imminent arrival of the Empress at her next resting place. We have no way of knowing who these knights were, or if they were under the orders of a high dignitary summoned from Germany to escort the Emperor's wife, or some Italian commander honored by the Emperor's trust. Each host would have accompanied the Empress to the border of his territory, where she would find her next host waiting to receive her.

Neither do we know if Constance had ladies-in-waiting attending her, or who they might have been. Had she made close friends among the ladies of the German court? Did the Abbess Letizia send a pair of her nuns to watch over Constance with their prayers?

However numerous Constance's escort may have been, it surely was not meant to go unobserved. The passage of the

Queen of Italy and Germany, wife to the Holy Roman Emperor and gravid with his heir, on her way to claim the Kingdom of Sicily, was too good an occasion for propaganda. But the space around the figure of the traveling Constance can be populated only by our imaginations, and for our purposes that is enough: it is her interior dialogue that matters to us, not what she said to her traveling companions.

A last problem: how would she have decided on the date of her departure? The Church calendar would have been important, of course, and perhaps the need to wait for whatever armed reinforcements might be arriving from Germany. But would she not look to the stars on the eve of resuming such a momentous journey, pregnant with far greater significance than it had seemed at the outset, and would she not ask their blessings?

> The sun, which moved regularly in a circle, controlled the more ordered events of nature, such as night and day and the four seasons. The planets, on the other hand, less certain in their motion, governed the more variable events in the world, the happenings that make life so uncertain. It was to the assessment of the factors governing these events, in a zone between the sure and the unsure, that astrology set itself. . . .
>
> In making predictions, astrology dealt with the following: *nativities*, the determination of a person's temperament from the positions of the constellations at the time of his birth; *revolutions*, the predictions of general events, weather, crops, and political changes; and *elections*, the art of selecting the right moment to do anything from planting a bean to deposing a king. The belief in all this sort of thing was so ardent, and the possible combinations of the movements of the stars and the actions of men so immense, that generations of astrologers were kept busy figuring out all these possibilities. Every prince hoped to have an astrologer at his court.[1]

This astrolabe from the early twelfth century might well have
been used by the Arabic astrologer who attended William II's
deathbed. Both astronomy and astrology were pursued with
great enthusiasm at the Norman court.

The early Latin Church had banned astrology, which had
been so much a part of Greek science, but its study lived on in
the Byzantine world and in the writings of Arab scholars. In
the twelfth century many of these Greek and Arabic texts were
being translated into Latin, by Arab and Jewish scholars in
Spanish Toledo and, to a lesser extent, in Palermo itself. Roger
II had been passionately interested in both astronomy and
astrology – witness the great silver planisphere he had commissioned, which disappeared during the sack of the royal palace
in 1161 – and Constance would certainly have grown up
believing deeply in the power of the stars.

Let us have her send to Milan for the advice of an
astrologer, then consult with the Abbess as to the most seemly
course of action. Let us have her settle upon the twelfth of

August as the date for her departure from Meda, then dispatch a courier to Henry, who at the head of the imperial army was nearing Naples, to inform him of her decision. She planned to cover the twenty-some miles that separated Meda from Milan in two days, rest for a day, and then celebrate the Assumption of the Blessed Virgin in the Basilica of St. Ambrose before continuing on her journey.

It must have been difficult for her to depart from Meda, to abandon the safety and the kindness of the convent for the uncertainties and dangers of the road, and to take leave of a friend who had given her succor and strength in a moment of great need. Perhaps the Abbess accompanied the Empress as far as Milan, out of affection as well as feudal duty, and went with her to hear mass at the basilica.

It pleases me to think that after the service Constance asked that she and the Abbess be accompanied to the little chapel of San Vittore in Cielo d'Oro (Saint Victor in a Sky of Gold) and that there, under the golden mosaics of the cupola, they prayed to the patron saint of the convent of Meda for his continued blessing and for protection of those who had dedicated their lives to his service; that they gave thanks for the recovery of Constance; and that there, privately and with many tears and loving embraces, Constance and Letizia parted.

～

While Constance spent two months recuperating in Meda, Marcella and I spent two days relaxing in Milan. Or we relaxed as well as was possible: the heat and noise of the big metropolis were brutal after the restful landscapes of rural Switzerland and the cool Alpine air. We shopped, met friends, and paid a long and pleasant visit to Sant'Ambrogio.

I don't understand why no one (as far as I know) has ever filmed a movie in the atrium of the Basilica of St. Ambrose. It cries out for a medieval coronation or wedding scene, better still a royal wedding like that of Constance and Henry VI,

The atrium of St. Ambrose, large enough to accommodate
a quite spectacular wedding procession.

which took place here in 1186. Even under the hazy Milanese sky, the rosy-red bricks are warm and welcoming, and the double-tiered galleries that flank the courtyard on both sides seem designed for silken hangings and banners embroidered with the coats of arms of knights gathered in assembly.

The courtyard is large enough to accommodate at least a hundred mounted knights in armor, with plumes trembling from their helmets and brightly painted shields. The heralds could stand in the upper gallery of the façade, their brass trumpets glinting in the sunlight over swags of roses hanging from the arch sills. And of course the royal bride would ride into the courtyard, accompanied by damsels in elaborate headdresses, a veil covering her face, her golden circlet entwined with flowers, and a ring of roses lying around the neck of her milk-white charger.

Very pre-Raphaelite and not at all authentic – medieval brides actually wore red. The vision was delicious nonetheless, and as I stood in the courtyard, transported by its beauty, I forbade myself to look for the historical flaws in my creation. Even leaving aside the more brazen Hollywood touches, this was indeed a great place for a wedding.

The actual marriage of Constance and Henry, certainly different in detail but surely no less spectacular, had been

celebrated in January [1186] with a festive wedding in Milan. A large number of magnates were invited. They came from Lombardy, from Burgundy and from Sicily. In the park which lay between the Porta Romana and the Porta Tosa a large wooden assembly hall had been erected. The church of St. Ambrose, the oldest and principal church of the city which had luckily survived the destruction of 1162, was splendidly decorated. The grille which usually protected the golden altar had been opened, and there, on 27 January, the marriage was solemnized. The wedding was followed by a festival crown wearing, at which the archbishop of Vienne placed the crown on Frederick's head, the patriarch of Aquileia placed the crown on Henry's head, and Archbishop Conrad of Mainz placed the crown on the head of the new queen. Thus the clergy of Italy, Burgundy and Germany were united in this act. The festivities ended with a sumptuous banquet in the wooden hall.[2]

Despite so many centuries of sack and destruction and bombing (St. Ambrose was very badly damaged in World War II), the golden altar before which Constance was married still stands there today, and the gleaming tesserae of St. Victor's golden sky still cling to their cupola as they first did fifteen hundred years ago.

~

Undoubtedly the stars had been consulted in fixing the date of the wedding, yet the same stars appear to have been somewhat sybilline as to what was to follow:

> In that year that king [Henry] celebrated his nuptials with great glory in Milan, ... an astronomer of Toledo, Johannes by name, sent letters to all parts of the world, warning that in the month of September of the following year all the planets would converge in one house, and a wind would blow which would destroy all crops and buildings, and there would be famine and death and many other calamities, and the end of the world and the coming of the Antichrist would follow, and in this all the astronomers and the other philosophers were agreed, whether Christian or Gentile or Jew. Wherefore a very great fear invaded many, and some even built themselves houses underground, and in many churches there were fasts and litanies and processions.[3]

It was not an auspicious year to begin a marriage, but in the medieval world omens and marvelous happenings could be

The marriage of Constance and Henry VI, as illustrated in a
fourteenth-century manuscript of Boccaccio's *De mulieribus
claris (Of Famous Women)*. The costumes are those of a later
era; here, too, Constance's fame seems to be the reflected
glory of marriage to a famous man.

seen wherever one looked; the difficult part was not to discover them but to interpret them correctly. Johannes was
proved wrong, and even presumptuous, and we can hope that
at least for that first year, the marriage went relatively
smoothly.

But in order that the wisdom of this world be proven fool-
ishness before God, at the appointed time there was great
serenity and tranquility, and nothing of that which had been
predicted took place.[4]

Nor has the wisdom of the world improved much: the exact same and rare alignment of planets took place on the fifth of May in the year 2000, and the same apocalyptic warnings of doom and destruction traveled across the globe via e-mail and Internet, this time predicting that the stock market would collapse.

~

We were on our way again. This time our general route was clear – all we had to do was follow the Roman roads: the Via Emilia as far as the Adriatic Sea, and then down the coast on the Via Flaminia until it turned inland toward Rome. We could only guess at Constance's stopping places. Nor did we have time to stop every ten miles to look for some trace of shelter, since we had only two weeks left to complete the journey that Constance had employed – albeit with many long halts – over a year to cover.

The best we could do, we thought, would be to read our guidebooks carefully each night, mark whatever architecture from the twelfth century lay along the next day's lap, and visit each of those sites, always hoping that unbeknownst to us at least a few of our choices might coincide with those of our Empress.

Neither Marcella nor I had ever done more than pass this way on the autostrada, but the towns that lay along the Via Emilia were not new to Constance. Imperial armies had been descending from Germany and tromping through and over these cities since the tenth century, when Otto I, King of the Eastern Franks, conquered the Lombard Kingdom of Italy, thus reestablishing the domains of Charlemagne as the Holy Roman Empire. In 962 the Pope gave Otto the imperial crown, and in the following centuries the *regnum Italicum* remained theoretically under German rule, but until the second half of the twelfth century, German sovereignty was largely honorific.

German emperors-to-be traditionally made an expedition into Italy early in their reign, to receive the 'iron crown of the Lombards' at Monza or Milan, and to march south to Rome to be crowned emperor there. It was the duty of the Lombard towns to provide aid and sustenance to the German king on this *iter Italicum*, but it was also understood that the purpose of the visit was largely ceremonial: the king would show himself, receive homage, take his crowns and go.[5]

All this changed drastically in 1152 with the election of Frederick Barbarossa, the Hohenstaufen duke of Swabia, as king of

The portrait of Frederick Barbarossa on this gilded bronze reliquary attempts to stress the connection between his empire and that of ancient Rome.

the Germans. Three years later he was crowned emperor in Rome, and in 1158 he called a great meeting at Roncaglia, just outside of Milan, where he attempted to reclaim for the empire the *regalia*, the royal rights of fiscal, juridical, and administrative authority over the towns of the *regnum Italicum*. But during the decades of imperial absence that preceded Barbarossa, the Lombard towns had gained a great measure of independence and self-government, which they had no intention of relinquishing. Barbarossa's sack of Milan in 1162, which had spared only the Basilica of St. Ambrose, was a consequence of the Milanese rebellion over the decrees of the Diet of Roncaglia, as well as an attempt to repress the city's own imperialism with regard to its neighboring rivals.

Many explanations have been given for the change in German policy toward Italy during the reign of Frederick Barbarossa. The first of these is Frederick's desire to realize in concrete terms a replica of the Roman Empire of classical times, one strong enough to rival the Byzantine Empire to the east and deriving its authority directly from God through election by the German princes (and not through coronation by the pope – hence his continual struggles with the papacy). Another motive lay in the fact that both northern Italy and Sicily (which he also claimed as part of the empire) were potentially unparalleled sources of revenue, with which he could strengthen the position of the Hohenstaufen dynasty within the empire. Since the imperial crown was not hereditary but elective, one's ability to secure the succession for one's own heirs depended in great part on the amount of land, revenues, and therefore prestige and power one could command within the borders of one's family holdings.

The twelfth century was a period of intense interest in political and juridical theory. The old Roman law and in particular the legal codes of Justinian were being rediscovered, carefully studied, and interpreted, as each party – imperial, papal, royal, or communal – searched for texts that would reinforce its own claims to rights and sovereignty. Whether Barbarossa, as an

117

heir to the old German warrior tradition, was really able to assimilate the ideas of empire, or was merely using them as a pretext for enriching his family and ensuring the succession of his lineage, is much debated; so is the question of whether his struggle with the Italian communes was due to his inability to understand the significance of this new drive toward independence or simply to his unwillingness to tolerate it. After his defeat at Legnano in 1176 at the hands of the Milanese army, Barbarossa signed the Treaty of Venice of 1177, thereby coming to a truce with the Lombard League, and making peace with both the pope and with the Sicilian king; but scholars even disagree on whether this treaty was a defeat or in fact a clever victory for him.

For our purposes, it is not necessary to pick and choose from among these various theories. Suffice it to say that the truce Barbarossa made with the towns of the Lombard League became a definitive peace with the Treaty of Constance in 1183, and that the resumption of good relations between the empire and Sicily led to the announcement, at Augsburg in the fall of 1184, of Henry's betrothal to Constance. By November of 1185, when Constance arrived with her German escort in Piacenza, where she was to await her marriage, all hostilities were over, and Milan claimed the honor of hosting the wedding.

~

Northern Italy was still familiar and friendly territory to Constance in 1194, when she started south once more, although one wonders just how much nine years of fairly constant traveling had done to bridge for her the great differences between the city of her childhood and those of the north. Recent and microscopic examinations by the new school of medieval historiographers belie the old generalizations about medieval unity, and reveal that even neighboring towns (much less the geographical regions that we now call nations) differed significantly from one another in their traditions and institutions. Translating the implications of this variety from the institutional level to that of mentality is still difficult. We had to be content with the consideration that both of us – Marcella of Umbrian-Roman background and I with my thirty-five years in Sicily – felt these northern cities to be quite foreign.

Our itinerary soon revealed unexpected limitations. What had seemed like such a long time when we were planning this trip now appeared unhappily brief. It was the fifth of June by the time we left Milan, and we had promised to arrive at the house of Marcella's parents in Stroncone, a small village in Umbria that lies almost as far south as Rome, on the ninth. And since, unlike Constance, we were not traveling under armed escort, we decided that in the cities we would not leave the car unattended when our suitcases and the portable computer on loan from my daughter were in the trunk.

Adhering to this rule wasn't a problem in Germany, where the towns were all furnished with ample and excellent garages, but the farther south we got, the scarcer the garages became, and the more difficult it was to find one in a warren of small streets. The difficulty of parking proved critical at Lodi, our first stop south of Milan.

The periphery of Milan had seemed an endless string of uninteresting buildings in an undistinguished countryside, further flattened by a thin haze, even though it was a sunny day with a good breeze. Whether this haze was modern pollution or a timeless meteorological condition (the Po valley is famous for thick and treacherous fogs in the wintertime) was hard to tell, but it would accompany us all the way across the peninsula to the Adriatic.

Lodi was where Constance had first met Eleanor of Aquitaine, and she and Henry had sat court there many times in the early years of their marriage. Not much remained for us to see, for Lodi had been destroyed by the Milanese in 1158 and rebuilt by order of Barbarossa. (The Lodigiani returned the favor by participating in the 1162 sack of Milan.) The city was still rebuilding its cathedral when Constance was in residence.

Marcella and I would nonetheless have liked to take a look, but fate was against us: when we arrived, some sort of fair was in progress, and all the streets that led toward the center and to some hope of a garage were closed except to pedestrian traffic. After half an hour of circling in vain, we gave up and headed on to Piacenza, a strategic city in the Middle Ages because it offered, across a bridge of boats tied one to the other, the most reliable crossing of the Po River.

We arrived at Piacenza at noon, just as the great church doors were swinging closed. This was to be a leitmotiv of our journey: Marcella is one of those people who is very, very slow in getting going in the morning, and I had known her long enough to realize that I could not do anything but accept this if we were to travel together in harmony. On the other hand, when at the end of a day of driving and sight-seeing five o'clock arrived and my energy level plummeted dramatically, Marcella took over the wheel and tackled the problem of finding us someplace to sleep with great cheerfulness. It worked out beautifully, even if we saw fewer church interiors than we might have. Fortunately it is the exteriors that remain most faithful to the twelfth century.

So in Piacenza we saw the outside of the austere brick basilica dedicated to Saint Anthony where the final details of the Treaty of Constance were hammered out, and we admired the façade of the Duomo, which would still have been under construction at the time of Constance's visits to Piacenza. If the carving of the portal had already been completed, then Constance's eye might have lingered on the scenes from the Nativity; Marcella and I had more fun with the caryatid who was waving her hands in the air and dancing with bended knee in some medieval forerunner of the Charleston.

The church doors were indeed closed to us in Piacenza. Constance was very elusive: we could connect her to nothing more solid than a series of carvings on a portal, one not much different from nor more meaningful than the many Romanesque portals that we would be seeing in the days to follow, and I had yet to see the significance in that sameness.

Although I tried my best, I was unable to to enter into the mind of Constance as she passed Piacenza traveling south in 1194, much less on her first visit in 1185. Of this earlier stay we know only that she arrived, a bride-to-be, at the beginning of November, but we do not know who greeted her, nor how long she remained. Was it here that she met her father-in-law and first saw her future husband? How was she entertained, and by whom, during the nearly three months that separated her from her wedding day? Where was she lodged? Questions that had not impeded my imagination elsewhere posed obstacles that here I could not overcome. The cathedral itself was too hemmed in by buildings from a later date; nor did the busy market in the square before it suggest a medieval fair in the same way as those we had seen hugging the apses of the German cathedrals.

I was disappointed and discouraged by this first morning on the road in Italy. As we left St. Ambrose, Constance seemed to have slipped from my grasp, and I wondered if I would find her again, or if all my elaborate travel plans would in the end leave me with empty hands, the veils of the past too thick to pierce, the book for which I had already signed a contract too thin to write. Marcella, sensing my mood, took over the car and drove us out of Piacenza and back onto the Via Emilia.

≈

The waters from the Alps run downstream in many rivulets into Italy and gather on the valley floor that the Italians call the *pianura padana*, the plain of the Po. There the Po River carries them eastward to the Adriatic Sea. In Roman times this plain was crisscrossed by canals and dams that kept the river waters under control, allowing not only cultivation of the fertile flood basin but safe travel on roads such as the Via

Emilia, which runs straight and smooth across the valley floor, with the river itself to the north and the foothills of the Apennines to the south.

With the collapse of the Roman Empire, all flood maintenance ceased, and the plain returned to forest and swamp. When the Lombards invaded in the sixth century, they found a nature almost as untamed as that which they had left behind them in the north. Hunting and shepherding were more congenial to them than agriculture, so it was not until the eleventh and twelfth centuries that increased demographic pressure led to widespread deforestation and land clearance.

> [T]he soil, liberated from trees and shrubs, no longer held the rainwater, the rivers swelled and flooded ever greater tracts of the plain, a story particularly true of the Po valley. From the beginning of the thirteenth century the chroniclers mark the passage of time by recurrent and disastrous floods, and describe the formation of big lakes, ever vaster and ever nearer the cities.[6]

Even when the river was quiet and its waters flowed within the boundaries of its natural bed, travel in the *pianura padana* was not always easy, for the bridges and the beautifully paved roads of the Romans had suffered the same devastation as their canals and dams. New paths had to be traced along higher lands, skirting the foothills, beyond the reach of the floodwaters. Just where the Via Emilia had been viable in the year 1194 and where instead Constance's party had had to deviate, as we had done in the Rhine valley, was a question that had no clear answer, leaving us free to be guided by our curiosity.

~

From Piacenza, we followed the Via Emilia – not the neatly paved Roman road, but the modern, tarred, and well-trafficked Route 9 that follows the old roadbed in a straight line drawn with a ruler across Emilia and Romagna to Rimini – a few miles to Fiorenzuola d'Arda, a town that, seen from the outskirts, did not live up to the beauty of its name. At the beginning of the tenth century, the nobility of northern Italy made war here on the Emperor Berengar I; the slaughter was so complete as to decimate the aristocracy of both camps, thus giving the Italian cities leeway to develop their rights and independence.

Here we made our first detour off the Via Emilia, driving south along the Arda River to visit the medieval village of Castell'Arquato, which sits on a promontory at the spot where the valley of the Arda, flowing down through the foothills of the Apennines, dissolves into the plain of the Po.

Once again we found ourselves on a movie set. A cobbled road winds up between old stone houses to the piazza at the top, flanked to the north by the Palace of the Podestà, a crenellated thirteenth-century building whose stern exterior is mitigated by a graceful staircase and a loggia added in the *Quattrocento*. To the south rises an impressive and many-turreted fortress known as the Rocca Visconti, built in the fourteenth century; a terrace overlooks the Po valley to the east; and to the west stand the rounded brick apses of the Collegiata, an enchanting Romanesque church founded in the eighth century by a local lord of Lombard origin and reconstructed in 1120 in its present form.

Both within and without, the Collegiata is a simple and sturdy structure. A massive and undecorated baptismal font about six feet in diameter, carved out of a solid block of stone, occupies a side apse, and thick brick columns hold up the small cloister. Above the portal there is a carving of the Madonna and Child; she leans with tender affection toward the under-sized man sitting on her knee, in an outpouring of emotion that we had not seen in northern Madonnas. The altar is composed, or rather recomposed, of carved panels, which are thought to have come originally from a choir railing: an

The apse of the Collegiata and the Palace of the
Podestà at Castell'Arquata.

Annunciation on one side, the meeting of Mary and Elizabeth on the other, with the prophet Isaiah in the middle, magnificent carvings that, like the Madonna on the portal, give a sense of archaic forms struggling to contain the new emotional piety of a burgeoning renaissance.

On the panels of the pulpit are carved the four Evangelists, whose symbols have been easy for me to identify ever since I memorized the jingle invented by my sister Emily while we were traveling in Europe with our parents in 1955: 'Be ye Jeagle [John the Eagle] or you may Mark the Lion Loxed [Luke the Ox] in the Mangel [Matthew the Angel].' My other sister says that for her this jingle just complicates things, but after almost half a century I am still dependent on this mnemonic device and, with Emily's permission, offer it to those readers whose minds quirk as ours do.

The piazza of Castell'Arquato represents, of course, a jumble of centuries. The only building that was already there at the end of the twelfth century was the church of the Collegiata, although some archaic fortress no doubt stood where the Rocca Visconti now rears its crenellated towers: the position was so strategic, and the view from its walls, up the Arda valley and down onto the plain, so commanding, as to offer a visual explanation of what fortresses were all about. A booklet on sale at the souvenir shop related a long tradition of fierce and independent civic pride: not good humus for imperial partisans.

We were forced to conclude that Constance would never have stayed here, and yet as a medieval microcosm, it was perfect: small houses reached up the hillside for the protection of the cross and the sword and, for a brief period at least, of their own *podestà*. After the big cities, Castell'Arquato brought us back to the measure of medieval man, to a scale in which Constance would have felt at home, and we were grateful.

No sooner were we back on the Via Emilia than we turned off again, this time to the north, in search of Chiaravalle della Colomba. Here it was the name that called us, a clue to the presence, or at least the remains, of a Cistercian monastery.

The Cistercian order, probably the most influential of the reforming monastic orders of the twelfth century, took its name from its mother abbey at Cîteaux (in Latin, Cistercium), founded in 1098 in reaction to the wealth and luxury that by then prevailed in the Benedictine monasteries ruled by Cluny. The rule spread rapidly throughout western Europe, its daughter houses being built in deserted tracts of land that the brothers were expected to reclaim through hard physical labor, performed with extreme austerity and spirituality. The abbeys themselves were built according to the precepts of the mother house: a church of unadorned severity was flanked by a large square cloister, around which the dwellings of the monks were built.

Chiaravalle della Colomba stands tall in the middle of a small and scattered farming community. The small houses – mostly quite modern but built on the form of the traditional *casa colonica*, with an arched portico shading the ground-floor stables and an outdoor staircase leading to the living quarters on the floor above – were surrounded by flat and verdant fields. Tractors and haying machines stood parked at the edge of the roads, and great bales of rolled-up hay waited to be carted to the barns.

The Cistercian abbey was established here in 1135, and construction went on well into the thirteenth century. Of this once large and impressive establishment, only the church and the cloister remain, built of red brick with simple marble decorations. The church, which was started first, is less ornate than the thirteenth-century cloister, built when the original severity of the rule was growing lax.

It is a lovely cloister, large and sunny with lush lawns, well-trimmed shrubs, and a bush of pale pink roses flowering discreetly in each corner. The warm red of the brick sets off the double row of delicate marble columns: the pale gray stone is veined with pink, as if the bricks above had bled their color in the rain. At the corners the columns meet in a group of four, tied together with stone loops as in a knot, and the vaults of the portico brace themselves against the walls on marble corbels carved with saints and animals.

To the Cistercians, the enclosed gardens of their cloisters suggested the possibility of returning, through the rigors of the monastic life, to the Garden of Eden, just as the Norman kings in decorating their palaces invoked their ability to rule an earthly paradise. Both cloister and palace reflected the growing optimism of the twelfth century and its increased expectations for a better life here on earth.

Inside the church itself, the decoration is much sparer, simple alternating stripes of gray marble and red brick that form the arches supporting the barrel-vaulted ceiling of the long, high nave. Our attention was riveted, however, by the decoration going on below. In shorts or jeans, bent double or crawling about on all fours, the ladies of the parish were preparing the *infiorata*, the carpet of flowers over which the procession honoring the feast of Corpus Domini would pass the next day.

When my mother-in-law was still alive, she would send us out to the farm to gather flowers on the morning of Corpus Domini. When, at the end of the day, the procession came down the street, she and the other pious women of Alcamo would stand on their balconies and toss the flower petals down before the feet of the archpriest, who walked in the shade of a silken canopy, holding high the crystal and golden monstrance that carried the host.

Corpus Domini (also known as Corpus Christi) celebrates the bodily presence of Christ in the host, the thin round wafer that represents the bread broken at the Last Supper. It is not a very ancient feast – the earliest recorded celebration was at Liège in 1220 – but flowers had such decorative and symbolic value, both in the classical world and in the Middle Ages, that to find them in a procession would hardly have been surprising to Constance.

I'm not at all sure that at Chiaravalle della Colomba the procession would have walked right over this *infiorata*, for it was an unusual example. Reproductions of large paintings, mostly portraits of saintly monks, had been laid out in a long line down the nave, each one about four feet from the next. They were being framed and linked together by a thick carpet of evergreen branches – bluish spruce, silvery cypress and cedar, dark green fir. No flowers were in sight, but ambitious swags and curlicues were chalked out on the marble floor on each side of the portrait frames, which perhaps were to be given a touch of color with flowers picked freshly on the morning of the procession. Or perhaps not: the somber palette of evergreens might have been a lingering expression of the severe Cistercian heritage.

A priest wandered in and out, his long skirts rustling with authority as he kept an eye on things and gave an occasional order, but this was obviously a familiar service to the women, a sphere of creative participation handed down from mother to daughter, and they didn't really seem to pay much attention to the priest, even if the subdued formality of their creation might not have been of their own choosing.

The success of the Cistercian order owed much to the enormous influence of Saint Bernard, a Burgundian nobleman who entered Cîteaux at the beginning of the twelfth century and shortly afterward became abbot of one of its first daughter houses, the Abbey of Clairvaux (Chiaravalla in Italian), a name lent to many later Cistercian foundations. An orator of great intelligence and charisma, thronged by huge crowds of devoted followers wherever he went, Bernard was one of the foremost exponents of the new intimate and emotional piety that was so characteristic of that century, and in particular of the growing cult of the Madonna. In his time, however, no one other than the monks themselves was allowed to enter the abbey churches, and although Bernard himself was extremely devoted to the Virgin, he took a very dim view of the rest of her sex. I suspect he would have been truly horrified to see those weak and wicked daughters of Eve crawling about in his church with their bottoms in the air!

As we left the church in the slanting sun of late afternoon, a hawk planed in slow and lazy circles above us, seemingly uninterested in what was moving far below. We were back in tune, it seemed, with Constance.

CHAPTER FIVE : SEPTEMBER

> trusting
> In his prowess, sure of his strength,
> Believing he must be a hero
> If he shares his journey with a lion
> Who goes along beside him
> As sweetly as any lamb.
>   – *Yvain, The Knight of the Lion*
>   Chrétien de Troyes, c. 1177

Our next stop was to have been Borgo San Donnino, once a town of some importance, to judge by the number of times it appears on the different imperial itineraries. When I was working out Constance's route south, I spent a lot of time trying to locate Borgo San Donnino on the map. It wasn't there, at least not under that name. In 1927 Mussolini had attempted to reawaken the descendants of the ancient Romans to their imperial calling by abolishing the medieval names of many towns and rebaptizing them with their classical precedents. Thus Girgenti returned to being Agrigento, Monte San Giuliano, in memory of Eryx, became Erice, and Borgo San Donnino became Fidenza, the Italianate echo of a very remote Fidentia.

Once I figured this out, it was easy to learn more: the small and somewhat modern town of Fidenza had once been a bustling center of medieval commerce, an obligatory stopping place for those who wished to worship at the tomb of Saint Donnino, a much-revered Christian martyr who had been decapitated on the banks of the Stirone, the stream that runs through the town, at the end of the third century. It had also offered hospitality to all those who passed on business and on pilgrimage, located as it was at the point where the Via Francigena split off south from the Via Emilia.

Neither Marcella nor I had ever heard of the Via Francigena: it is a medieval term once reserved for scholars and recently rediscovered by the tourist industry. The local information offices were well stocked with maps showing the pilgrim route that led from Canterbury across the Channel to Calais, then to Rheims, Besançon, and Lausanne, crossing the Alps via the Grand St. Bernard Pass, then down into Italy by way of Ivrea and Pavia. From Fidenza the road twisted up over the Cisa Pass and down the southern flank of the Apennines to Lucca, Siena, Viterbo, and finally Rome. The maps plotted the climb through the Cisa with photographs of medieval villages, rustic Romanesque churches, and enchanting archaic stone carvings – a tempting sidetrack that we had to save for a future visit.

When Constance passed this way in 1194, it was one of the busiest stretches of the Via Emilia, and despite the arrogance of her mounted escort, her party would have made slow progress. Imagine her dozing in her litter in the heat of midday, lulled by the slow and swaying gait of the mules, or waking as the air grew cooler and even the laziest dawdlers left the shade of the trees growing along the roadside. Then she might have opened the curtains wide enough to enjoy the tumble and flow of people around her, a motley throng of people crowding the road, reminding her of the streets of Palermo in her youth.

Merchants leading a train of pack mules, farmers returning from market, slow-paced oxen drawing wooden-wheeled carts that bumped noisily on the broken paving stones, humble monks walking barefoot, ascetic Cistercian abbots riding donkeys on their way north to the annual chapter general at Cîteaux, silk-clad bishops on horseback heading south with letters for the pope, young clerics and wandering scholars traveling by foot to study law at Bologna, jugglers and troubadours and troupes of actors pushing east with the hope of earning a few pennies at the inns of Borgo San Donnino – all fighting their way through a throng of pilgrims. The pilgrims flooded the route, some traveling alone, others in groups, each with his cowl and staff. Those with a scallop shell sewn to their hats were returning from the great shrine of St. James in Compostela; others were starting out for Rome or even for Jerusalem.

After Borgo the crowd would thin out. Those going on to the Holy Land would keep the Empress company along the Via Emilia and then down the Adriatic coast to Bari or Brindisi, where they would embark for the East. The others would turn south at Borgo, crossing the Apennines at the Cisa Pass, following the Via Francigena.

A swarm of beggars pushed their way through the crowds or crouched at the roadside, animating an already hectic scene with a chorus of plaintive cries and thrusted palms. The halt, the blind, and the homeless knew how to choose with expert eye or ear the rich merchant or cleric, or the pilgrim who

Pilgrims and travelers make their way across the façade of the cathedral at Borgo San Donnino, now known as Fidenza.

might have a few coins in his pocket, and how to ignore those who had to beg their supper themselves that night. Occasionally, on the farthest edges of the roadside, veiled figures stood a pace back from their alms bowls, sounding the wooden rattles that announced the invisible and inviolable barrier of leprosy that divided them from the rest of the world.

The knights escorting Constance's party would have been brutal in using their horses and the threat of their swords to keep the beggars at a distance from the imperial litter. Constance was accustomed to the sight of so much misery, and it would not have occurred to her to question the way God had ordered the world, but at each stop she would bid her knights scatter a handful of copper coins to the crowd, the charity of a good Christian, the largesse required of a great empress.

∼

Fidenza was full of discoveries for us, the most magificent being without a doubt its cathedral. Under construction from the first decade of the twelfth century, it acquired its definitive aspect as one of the greatest examples of Padanian Romanesque architecture when a new project for its completion was drawn up by Benedetto Antelami.

Only in very recent years, in particular since the restoration of his masterpiece, the Baptistery of Parma, has the figure of this genius emerged from the mists and gained widespread and well-merited notoriety. Antelami's surname indicates that he was born near Genoa, in the valley of the Intelvi, where he was part of a corporation of master builders known as the *magistri Antelami*, and it is believed that he was trained as a sculptor in Provence and worked on the Cathedral of Saint-Trophime in Arles.

In 1179 Antelami was in Borgo San Donnino and was commissioned to draw up plans for the completion of the cathedral, adding to its spare, elegant, but unfinished interior a cross-vaulted ceiling over the nave – a daring departure at that time – plus a new apse, a crypt, the central portal of the façade, and the two towers flanking it.

And what a wonderful job he did! There is no discontinuity between the old and the new. If the inside of the cathedral gives a feeling of great height, from the outside it looks almost stubby: the square towers are lower than the peak of the roof, with only small bell spires to raise them up. The façade remains unfinished, the lack of height reinforced by a horizontal line dividing the lower half in stone from an upper part in plain and weathered brick, which still awaits its marble facing. The inside reveals the architectural genius of Antelami, but it was the carvings on the exterior that captured my imagination.

I have tried very, very hard to read what Constance might have seen in these carvings as she looked at them. First, she would have seen the story: they tell the faithful about the life and martyrdom of Saint Donnino. Donnino was a *cubicularius*, the bedroom attendant of Maximianus Herculius, the co-ruler of the Emperor Diocletian in the late third century, who had his court in Milan. When it was discovered that Donnino had converted to Christianity, he was condemned to death, but he attempted to escape.

On the lintel over the main door runs a frieze, no more than a foot high. To the left, Saint Donnino, carrying a cross, gallops through the gates of Milan with mounted soldiers in hot pursuit as the townspeople peer down from the gate towers. Just right of center, a man with a crown – the Emperor Maximianus, no doubt, although with his chain mail and his flowing beard, he could easily be mistaken for Frederick Barbarossa – is brandishing his sword in the air. The decapitated body of Donnino sways uncertainly upright like – I can't resist – the proverbial chicken, and his severed and haloed head rests on an elaborately decorated chopping block. To the far right, the saint walks across a river gingerly carrying his head in his hands, while above these last figures, a pair of angels are flying his soul to heaven. At least I presume it is his soul, as represented by still another head, but this time clean-shaven,

Above the cathedral doorway, San Donnino flees for his life
but encounters martyrdom.

reflecting the Platonic ideal of the martyr rather than his flesh
and blood and bearded corporal reality.

Other friezes set into the cathedral walls show the apotheo-
sis and miracles of the saint, a parade of mounted knights or
lines of hooded, staff-bearing pilgrims. In one isolated rectan-
gle a foot soldier runs to keep up with a king charging ahead in
a wooden cart drawn by a pair of horses. The two horses are
rendered in an odd perspective that makes it look as if one
horse is riding piggyback upon the other. Still another plaque
depicts the three Magi, but there is nothing exotic about
them, and they might as well be three European kings off to
the Crusades. In all, the carvings are a veritable textbook of
medieval travel, a collection of figures with which to people
the roads that we have been traveling. (But, as far as I could
make out, no women.)

Something about the rows of soldiers, knights, and pilgrims, stylized and repetitive yet quick with gesture and
movement, reminded me of the flickering march of soldiers in
old newsreels, seen now on television and remembered from
the movie theaters of my early childhood. The marble grays of
black-and-white photography, the aggressive forward thrust
of the step, the familiarity of the figures removed into time by

Three kings gallop across the cathedral on their way to
the manger – or to the Crusades.

their rigidity: this was perhaps as close as I could get in my own
experience to what Constance saw.

Only in later reading did I discover that she saw something
altogether different. Like most Romanesque sculpture, Antelami's carvings were once painted in bright colors, an idea I
find as difficult to digest as I first found the thought of gaudily
painted Greek temples.

In the Middle Ages . . . the church was the place of color
par excellence. Almost all of it was colored: walls, pavements,
windows, ceilings, sculptural decorations; and these fixed
colors, animated by the sunlight, were accompanied and
echoed by the colors of the temporary decorations, of the
liturgical vestments and the ritual objects. In a society that
venerates color, that finds it warming and reassuring, the
church is the true temple of this color, even if some, like the
Cistercian monks of the twelfth century, abandon it or are
scandalized by it.[1]

One's sense of the past is so subjective. Quite apart from
questions of color, my own personal and irrational sense is that
the twelfth century lasted a long, long time, whereas the sixteenth and seventeenth centuries, about which I know very

The main portal of Antelami's cathedral, guarded by our first lions.

little, passed in a flash. Constance must have thought about history in almost biblical terms, of lineages and kings who begat kings who begat her father Roger who begat herself. She lived in a time when intellectual life went on in the shadow of great names from the past, and when scholars spent much time striving to reconcile present and direct experience with the texts they revered. But it was also a century in which a famous scholar said that the modern scholar was a dwarf standing on the shoulders of a giant – he could see farther.

In any case I must remember that Constance did not look at the carvings of Antelami from a historical standpoint, but from a Christian one. They tell the story of a servant, possibly even a slave, who had achieved man's highest aspiration – sainthood – and who now had the power to intercede, should he choose, for her own salvation. Above everything else, she would have been eager to pray at his tomb.

We have no way of knowing exactly which parts of the cathedral at Fidenza had been completed by 1194, although we know that in 1196 Antelami was already at work in Parma. The new crypt was not consecrated until 1207, the year in which the remains of Saint Donnino were translated into the Roman sarcophagus in which they still repose, and Antelami's statue of the Madonna was placed to its right. I like to hope, however, that the statue was already finished and on view somewhere when Constance passed through.

It is a Virgin and Child: the mother, seated on a throne, looks straight ahead. The Child, quite adult in his proportions, sits sideways on her knee, turning his badly damaged head away from us, his left hand raised in blessing, his near hand holding an orb. It is a full statue, not a relief, that stands alone and has no context to distract from the gravity of the larger figure, the weight of her responsibility as the mother of Christ. There is a certain hieratic rigidity in how she sits, and she does not give way to emotion as the Madonna in the Collegiata of Castell'Arquato does. Yet she is not a passive presence, but one that is aware, that accepts.

As we left the cathedral, I not only photographed the lions that crouch at the base of the columns on either side of the main door but patted them as well. I couldn't help myself, they are such wonderful beasts, large, not too weathered despite centuries of caresses, and full of roar. Their heads are turned to face each other; according to the pamphlet we obtained from a very obliging tourist office that was full of hopes for what the rediscovery of the Via Francigena might bring to Fidenza, the lions are in antithesis: 'one stares at the rising sun, ready to pounce, and symbolizes the resurrected Christ; the other, crouching down to watch the sunset, is a symbol of death.' That is a neat trick, unless the Cathedral of Fidenza is the only church in Christendom to be oriented along a north-south axis.

These were not the first lions that we had seen on our trip, and certainly I had seen others supporting columns all over southern Italy, some accepting their burden with a winning smile, others writhing in pain from the weight of it. But these were the first to penetrate my consciousness. Constance had traveled from city to city, welcomed at each church by a pair of lions guarding the entrance. The similarity of these Romanesque façades would put my descriptive powers to the test, but to her the lion at the door was a traveling companion, a welcome element of familiarity in a strange environment, protective of her sense of identity, just as an ad for Coca-Cola or Adidas might mitigate today the acute sense of solitude of a tourist in a foreign city.

~

The ideas that I had about travel and pilgrimage when I began the research for this book were much altered and expanded when I discovered a book by Eric J. Leed entitled *The Mind of the Traveler*. I must confess I owe Mr. Leed royalties – each time I returned from the States, my suitcase held a few more chapters Xeroxed from the New York Public Library copy – and a great deal more. He caused me to think about the difference between the classical journey, be it the *Odyssey* or that of Gilgamesh, the medieval journey, and the modern voyage of exploration, differences that have proved very helpful to me in my search for the elusive concept of self that the people of the twelfth century either did or did not possess.

He also distinguishes between the three separate moments of travel – departure, passage, and arrival – and between different kinds of journeys and genderings. The distinctions he draws and the points he makes furnished me with a theoretical structure into which I was able to fit my own intuition about Constance: that in the course of her travels, she underwent a process of transformation, triggered by the physiological journey of a female body from conception to childbirth, that was all the more radical because it took place within the context of a geographical journey from place to place.

In speaking of departure, Leed claims that 'the essence of departure does not change. Always, everywhere, it separates the individual from a defining social and cultural matrix,'[2] a separation in which 'the social being of the traveler becomes ambiguous and malleable.'[3] Still more pertinent are his reflections on passage:

> Passage is qualitatively different from both departure and arrival: it is an experience of motion across boundaries and through space, while departure and arrival are experiences of detachment from and attachment to places. . . . Certain invariant and persisting features of character and mind arise within the flux and change of passage. And the condition of motion produces a structure of experience with its own logic and order, distinct from the logic and order of place, locale, territoriality. . . . [P]assage is not simply the experience of an 'interstitial' zone.[4]

How might Constance have experienced passage? It must have seemed that her world was becoming ever smaller, the farther she traveled. The two months she spent cloistered in

Meda had given her time to redefine herself, nurtured by a company of females, inspired by the Abbess's own confidence and self-esteem; time to accustom herself to the idea of this late and unexpected maternity. Now within the confines of the litter, alone with the cramped and plaintive kicking of the child in her womb, she would have been traveling to an inner rhythm, immobilized in time and space.

Imagine the Empress as the mules carrying her litter picked their way along the edge of the Po valley. Stretches of uncleared land and swampy bracken alternated with small cleared plots divided one from another by a row of trees. A claustrophobic landscape, its flatness blocked out the horizon and robbed the world of contour and variety, yet Constance would have observed it with detached interest, unable to shed the habits of a lifetime of travel with rulers, calculating the bounty of the fields, judging the quality of the crops and the welfare of the farmers, and assessing the possibility of finding food for her escort and fodder for their horses.

Her years of travel had taught her to recognize the crops and the methods of farming that differed in their seasons and their aspect from those of her homeland. Each plot was a microcosm of activity: goats and sheep grazing on the unplowed stubble and weeds of harvested wheat and barley fields; vines heavy with grapes, strung out along a trellis of elms, where oxen yoked to carts and sledges waited patiently as the pickers filled the wooden tubs with grapes; straw-hatted peasants dressed in undyed hemp stooped to set out a row of winter cabbages.

Even the uncultivated land was alive then: a herd of lean and dark-bristled pigs rooted in the underbrush while their swine-herd beat at the oak trees with a stick to make the acorns fall; women bent double gathered into their upturned skirts wind-fall apples or dead twigs for the hearth; foresters and poachers set rabbit traps. At the outskirts of a wood, a sooty-faced collier surveyed his slow-burning pyramids of charcoal. A swirl of invisible motion circled above a row of beehives the pale yellow of plaited straw. A child tended geese at the edge of the marshes where fishermen stretched nets woven from leather strips, and cutters harvested reeds and willows with which to thatch their roofs and weave their baskets. A Book of Hours unfolded, page after page, along the wayside.

Each scene was different yet seemed the same, repeating itself again and again in the monotonous tilt and sway of the litter as Constance watched passively from behind the curtains. Perhaps her attention was caught by a party of mounted hunters breaking from a stand of poplars, hawks lodged on their gauntlets. Would she have felt a moment of wistfulness for a former self, younger and lither, heedless of the consequences of a fall, or did that self belong to a too distant time, an ill-remembered context?

At day's end a town or a monastery appeared in the twilit distance, similar to the one that had grown smaller behind her in the morning sun. Built on flat ground, the towns lacked the individuality of hilltop constructions forced to adapt themselves to a variegated terrain, and they differed only in the number and the shape of the bell towers that announced them from a distance. As the mules traveled at a quickening pace through a denser pattern of small fields and vegetable gardens, Constance could see a huddle of wattle-and-daub huts built under the protective shadow of the city walls, and a party riding out from the gates to greet her. A festive dinner awaited her, fit for an empress but far in excess of what she desired, and then, finally, the relief of lying flat, of stretching out a spine that lamented the hours of jolting and the weight of an already swelling belly.

There is almost no uncultivated land in the Po valley now, and the fields bordering the Via Emilia, much larger than the ones that Constance saw, are well tended by huge mowing machines and tractors and irrigated by long jets of water from mobile irrigation systems. They are still monotonous, however, and rows of poplars still block out the horizon. Worse still, they are poisoned: decades of spraying the earth

It might have been too late in the summer for a threshing
scene like this, but the peasants that Constance saw laboring in
the fields would have been dressed in much the same manner,
with their tunics tucked up while they worked.

with herbicides has polluted the water table, and the cities
keep their municipal water supplies drinkable by raising each
year the level of atrazine that is considered tolerable.

The towns themselves are ringed by suburban sprawl and by
the repetitive sameness of the low and graceless buildings of
small industry, parked in tarred lots strewn with stacked goods
and discarded packing materials, or greened over with
unimaginative landscaping. But they are clean, and light falls
generously on the wide streets of their outskirts, a far cry from
the twelfth century:

Between 1000 and 1300 the European population not only
but became ever more concentrated around the cities

and, for reasons of defense, within the narrow space protected by the city walls. Unfortunately the hygienic and sanitary conditions of the urban centers were what they were. The water in the wells was not always drinkable. Sanitary arrangements were nonexistent, and where they did exist were totally inadequate. Cats, dogs, chickens, horses, donkeys, mules, and other animals dwelled together with the people, making each house a Noah's Ark. The garbage and the sewage of man and beast were piled up at the street corners or in the courtyards. Personal hygiene was preached by the doctors but practiced by few. People didn't wash much. Soap was an expensive rarity, and for many a bath in winter meant the risk of pneumonia. The clothes of the majority of the people were filthy and threadbare. Rats, lice, and fleas flourished everywhere. On the other hand, the intensification of communications and commercial relations meant an increase in the possibilities of contagion. With travelers, merchants, and merchandise, microbes travel as well.[5]

Medical knowledge did not develop as fast as the population did, and by the beginning of the fourteenth century, the problem would become acute. In 1347 the plague known as the Black Death spread rapidly through the crowded cities and countrysides of Europe, killing roughly a third of the population; from then on it was endemic and re-emerged frequently in the following centuries.

Fortunately the problems of sanitation and disease were not yet so desperate in Constance's lifetime, but her first encounter with northern cities must have been dramatic, coming as she did from Palermo, a city with numerous public baths that were open to people of all classes and an Arab tradition of hygiene. One hopes that she had plenty of strongly scented oils and perfumes with her, and that she was endowed with 'that curiously selective sense of smell'[6] that one historian postulates for the people of the Middle Ages.

∼

In retrospect it is hard to believe that Marcella and I arrived in Parma on the same day that we set out from Milan. Even though we had made many detours, we had driven barely a hundred miles, yet we felt as if we had journeyed over the same route twice, once to see the cities and landscapes as they were, and then once again to re-create in our imaginations how they must have looked in Constance's day. It was an incredibly rich way to travel, leaving a feeling of repleteness at the end of the day, as if we had been guests at a sumptuous banquet. It was also very tiring: at six p.m. my energy reserve gave out, and I needed desperately to know where I was going to sleep that night. Each evening we drove a ritual dance around the town where we had decided to alight, rejecting this hotel because it was too expensive, that one because it looked disreputable, and still another because it seemed too noisy.

Once we secured beds, we allowed ourselves half an hour to be horizontal, then went out to look around the town and repeat the same dance, this time in search of dinner. Both Marcella and I belong to a generation of women to whom it does not come easily to eat an evening meal in public without male company, and we usually managed to work up a good appetite before we could settle on a restaurant that looked good, inexpensive, and unintimidating.

In Parma we were planning to splurge. The city is famous for its food: Parmesan cheese, Parma hams, salami and mortadella, egg pasta and rich pastries have turned its citizens into *buone forchette*, 'good forks,' as Italians aptly call those who love to eat. The city has a prosperous and well-fed appearance: the main streets of the old center, now blocked to all but pedestrian and bicycle traffic, are lined with elegantly and expensively understated boutiques, and with delicatessens festooned with hams and sausages and string-tied provolones and stacked with huge wheels of Parmesan and trays of fresh tortellini, tantalizing pastry shops, and grocers selling early and imported vegetables.

We disciplined ourselves to look around before we ate and so pushed on to the Piazza del Duomo. The streets narrowed in the medieval nucleus, and as we walked toward the piazza, we could see only a thin strip of the twelfth-century cathedral. The slender marble columns of the façade, lit by the setting sun, made pillars of golden light against the shadowy arches of the three-tiered loggia. Not until we walked into the piazza itself, however, did we see what we were looking for, Antelami's greatest work, the baptistery.

And what a find! A wedding cake, a masterpiece of confectionery, far more ravishing than anything to be seen in the windows of Parma's fanciest pastry shops. Each of the eight facets of the tall octagonal tower has a high arch on the ground floor, above which rise four orders of deep and columned galleries, and a frieze of blind arches girds the top. Each corner is surmounted by a pinnacled Gothic turret, witness to changing architectural styles during the eighty years needed to complete it. Miracle of miracles, the baptistery had been freshly restored in time to celebrate the eight-hundredth anniversary of its beginnings, and all the soot and grime had been removed from the blocks of white marble that alternate with blocks of pink Verona marble, creating irregular horizontal stripes that run right around the building. We were told that before restoration the baptistery had assumed a dull and almost uniformly orange color, but when we saw it, the cleansed marble glistened and the stripes caught the light, joining with the rows of columns to create a frothy weightlessness in what was basically a quite massive construction.

The light was fading fast, and both the cathedral and the baptistery were closed, so we left them for the morrow and went in search of a restaurant. It was a particularly difficult decision, for we had high hopes for the dinner that awaited us. As we prowled the streets, we wondered what sort of food might have been served to Constance when she stayed here:

cheese, surely, and roast meat, hams smaller and leaner than those produced today but with the sweet and intense flavor of pork raised on a diet of acorns and beechnuts. At the end of the twelfth century, the Genoese and Pisan merchant ships were already bringing dried pasta and marzipan from Sicily, where they had been introduced by the Arabs, to the north of Italy, and what better, greater compliment to the Empress than to serve her costly delicacies from her native land?

Back and forth between centuries and sidewalks, we finally settled on a restaurant that was just down the road from our hotel; the Touring Club Italiano had awarded it three forks in its guide. Our long-awaited dinner was very expensive and so mediocre that I, who can recall the menu from almost every meal I ate on my first trip to Europe at age fourteen, have not the slightest memory of what I ate that night in Parma.

The next morning we retraced our footsteps to the Piazza del Duomo, eager to see the interiors of the buildings that we had been able to admire only from without the night before. The cathedral, basically built of red brick in the twelfth century, is in reality a hodgepodge of centuries and styles: the marble façade is flanked by a Gothic bell tower of dark brick outlined in marble and is decorated with a two-storied porch over the main door, both of which were added at the end of the thirteenth century. Nice lions here, too, but not ones that Constance ever saw.

The cathedral interior is even more of a mix: the walls of the high and handsome Romanesque nave were frescoed in the sixteenth century and topped by a very elaborate vaulted ceiling. In the cupola over the crossing, flights of angels and billows of clouds accompany the Virgin heavenward, the work of the sixteenth-century painter Correggio, delightful but very busy and a bit overwhelming to eyes accustomed to the purity of the twelfth century.

The baptistery was equally lovely in the morning light, and we had the leisure to examine its three carved portals and to discover the bestiary that runs right around it some ten feet from the ground. It consists of seventy marble plaques, each about twenty inches square and portraying a bird or a beast or a man in the most amazing variety of fantasy and reality. Satyrs and centaurs, falcons and griffins, goats and lions, mermaids and mercats and merdogs and every other confusion of species imaginable make their way in an obscurely symbolic dance.

There is a large bibliography of works on the Parma baptistery, for the entire architectural and decorative scheme, inside and out, was inspired by a program of theological doctrine that is said to have come from the cathedral school of St. Victor in Paris. The program centers on the salvation of man through the Resurrection of Christ and the sacrament of baptism:

> The external plan of the baptistery – constructed right over the Great Canal, from which it receives its water – is octagonal because according to Saint Ambrose this shape is the symbol of the Resurrection in as much as Christ rose from the dead on the 'eighth day,' that is, beyond real time identified with the seven days of the week (and baptism resurrects man from original sin). And the number 8 with its multiples (16) and its dividers (4) is a constant of the entire complex. On the inside the facets are doubled, become sixteen, so the shape of the floor plan is almost circular.[7]

The interior was entirely unexpected: smaller and darker, it differed entirely in feeling from the exterior. Between the columns marking the sixteen corners are frescoed niches in which dark blues, deep reds, and ochers prevail. Painted lunettes surmount the niches, while those over the doors have polychromed high reliefs. Above them a double-tiered loggia in brick and marble is crowned by a marble cornice; here the corner columns become sixteen ribs of white marble ascending into a very high dome, which is also completely covered with frescoes.

Apparently at some point in the first decades of the

LEFT: The knight on his way to war brandishes a sickle, neither as a weapon nor as an instrument of physical labor, but as a symbol of the chivalric privilege of feeding his horse on the grass growing by the roadside. CENTER: A peasant harvesting wheat represents the month of June. RIGHT: The month of November: the peasant is pulling turnips, the last harvest of the year. Above him is an archer representing Sagittarius.

thirteenth century the Antelami construction site was closed down abruptly, and it wasn't until the last quarter of that century that the major part of the frescoes was completed, this time by workmen much influenced by the Byzantine style.

Understanding the tightly woven iconography of the dome and the niches and the statues over the lintels is beyond today's layman, but the significance of the fourteen statues carved by Antelami that stand between the columns of the lower loggia is spectacularly clear. They represent the twelve months and two seasons. (Summer and Autumn are missing, perhaps because of the interruption in the construction, or perhaps because of the death of the master himself.)

Spring is a young girl, crowned with flowers, while Winter shows an old man with a long beard, half naked and half cloaked. Behind him a tree, leafy on one side and bare-branched on the other, symbolizes the passage from the last harvesting of November to the enforced and icy inactivity of wintertime.

But it was the figures of the months that totally enchanted me: they represent the cycle of the earth, each month showing a person involved in an appropriate activity, sometimes accompanied by a sign of the zodiac, more often not. June harvests the wheat, July threshes it; August tightens the metal hoops binding the wine casks, while September gathers in the grapes, as a little man stands at his feet and holds up the scales of Libra.

February digs in the fields, the two fish of Pisces swimming past his shoulder as he works. A youthful March blows the horn of the winds. (The medieval calendar begins with this, the month of the Incarnation of Christ.) Poor old January sits gloomily in front of an invisible fire, tucking up his skirts to allow the heat to reach his aching joints.

April is represented by a crowned king holding a palm in one hand and a flower, a fleur-de-lis, in the other, while May is a mounted nobleman brandishing a sickle, with which he will cut forage for his horse, as he gallops toward some military appointment:

> [T]he peasant cycle of agricultural labor is interrupted to make room for the nobility, here promoted to the center of the scene.
>
> Here they are, in spring . . . they incarnate its renewal, in the peace of the flowering forest, in their favorite sport of hunting, or in their professional activity of war. They leave to the peasants the difficult season of summer, the melancholy period of autumn, the freezing cold of the winter; they reserve for themselves springtime, beauty, pleasure, the noble art of war. It is a parenthesis charged with social significance, with the dominant values that they have imposed upon the laborious year of the peasant.[8]

The intricate symbolism, much of it classical in origin, is manifested here in carving of the utmost simplicity and purity of line, a ravishing incarnation in stone of the concentric calendars that dominated medieval life and that in some areas of

Europe still dominate rural life today. Earth and sky, agriculture and zodiac, labor and liturgy, sowing and harvesting according to the waxing and the waning of the moon – all are linked together in an unending cycle of months, a cycle that has disappeared from modern urban life but has been the greatest discovery and pleasure of my life in Sicily.

Wishing to neglect no clue that might lead me closer to Constance, I asked an astrologer in the United States if she could read Constance's horoscope for me. It was a very difficult request: all I could say was that she was a Sicilian queen who was born a few weeks after February 25th, 1154. The astrologer gave me a wide reading, covering a range of possible dates, but it has pleased my vanity to make Constance a Pisces like myself:

The Moon was opposing Uranus on February 25th, 1154. From a personal standpoint, the death of the father/husband critically changed the life of his widow and daughters. This would be more than the usual change that affects a person's life when a spouse or parent dies. If there were sons, their lives would not have changed as much. The moon represents one's home, family, mother, emotions, and habits. Uranus represents change. The opposition represents change being forced by something outside one's self. When the father died, the mother felt as if the rug had been pulled out from under her. If your queen was born during this upset, it is probable that she would always feel like a foreigner in her own family or country.

On the day of her father's death, Mercury opposed Saturn and made a square angle with Pluto. There was quite a bit of serious thinking, especially about where people would be placed in the scheme of things. It was a bad day for communication. Secrets, plots, fear, and control issues interfered with negotiations.

If she was born within a week of her father's death, she would have had strong opinions, but be very frustrated at

150

her lack of ability to be heard. Nobody listened. She would be insightful, mentally combative, and plainspoken. She would also have to deal with a lot of repressed anger and frustration.[9]

It was almost noon by the time we tore ourselves from Antelami and his baptistery and were back on the road again, headed for our next Romanesque cathedral, that of Modena.

The Via Emilia runs through the very center of Modena. In the centuries following the collapse of the Roman Empire and the breakdown of flood control, the original Roman colony of Mutina became practically deserted, but the relics of its patron, Saint Geminiano, were never translated elsewhere, and toward the end of the first millennium Modena began to grow again. Although it did join the first Lombard League, the city was generally pro-empire, unlike its two great pro-papacy rivals, the immensely wealthy and powerful Benedictine abbey of Nonantola, which lies just northeast of the city, and the city of Bologna, some twenty-five miles farther east along the Via Emilia.

In the wake of the Peace of Constance, Modena returned to the imperial pale, and it would have given Constance a warm welcome, even though it had been an independent commune for almost a hundred years. The force of its newly reacquired civic pride can be read in its cathedral, which is older than that of Parma and had been long since completed at the time of her passage.

Work on the cathedral, under the direction of a Lombard architect named Lanfranco, had begun in 1099. The two-storied portico over the main door and the trefoil loggia that runs across the façade and along the sides of the church are from the early twelfth century, but an enormous rose window, inserted in the center during the thirteenth century, lends a Gothic air to the façade.

The guiding spirit of the decoration here was not Antelami but an earlier sculptor, of whom we know even less. His name comes down to us because it is inscribed on a tablet flanked by statues of Enoch and Elijah and affixed to the façade, just to the left of the portico. The inscription announces the date when construction began, and someone, either the sculptor himself in a paroxysm of pride or more probably an enthusiastic fan, squeezed in a few added lines: 'How worthy you are of great fame and honor your sculptures now demonstrate, o Wiligelmo!'

The works that inspired this enthusiasm are still there on the façade, four friezes placed symmetrically on either side of the portico and above the lateral doors. The subject matter is different from that of the Baptistery of Parma: the four reliefs show the Creation, the expulsion from Paradise, the story of Cain and Abel, and the landing of the ark. But the basic theme is the same: man can be redeemed from the damnation of original sin, and one of the principal means of redemption is labor. Here in fact Wiligelmo chose a scene rare in the sculpture of his contemporaries: after the expulsion from Paradise, Adam and Eve are hoeing the earth.

Both the Baptistery of Parma and the Cathedral of Modena were founded and financed by the laity, citizens and townsmen who were both profoundly preoccupied with their own salvation and thoroughly aware of the people in the countryside on whose labor their prosperity rested. By the beginning of the twelfth century, medieval scholars had elaborated a view of society that was based on three orders: the *oratores* (those who prayed – clergy and monastics), the *bellatores* (those who made war – knights and the nobility), and the *laboratores*, the peasants, in uneasy association with the incipient middle class. Labor, in the early Christian view a penitence imposed by Eve's sinning, had acquired redeeming features.

This ambiguity attributed to the countryside, which the city at once despises and honors, is reflected in the person of the peasant himself, emarginated by medieval society, lost in the mass of the oppressed and exploited, who nonetheless achieves a certain esteem within feudal ideology.[10]

If the iconographic program of the Parma baptistery was inspired by the writings of a theologian, that of the Modena cathedral apparently draws on less clerical sources. The Italian scholar Chiara Frugoni sees in the choice and division of scenes, and in the citations inscribed on the background, a very clear reference to the *Jeu d'Adam*, the earliest surviving example of semiliturgical drama.[11]

The Modena cathedral has several other beautifully carved doors with porticoes. One has a calendar of the months reflecting the same themes as that of Antelami, while another contains a charming series of scenes from the legend of King Arthur, their juxtaposition indicating how blurred was the distinction between the sacred and the profane, in that apparently

The double-tailed mermaid seems to have been particularly fascinating to the twelfth century: this one can be found in Sicily, in the cloister of Monreale.

monolithic medieval culture that is so appealing to our splintered present.

With our usual bad timing, we found the Lapidary Museum closed, so we could not see the famous twelfth-century metopes that have been removed from the cathedral walls for better preservation. I only discovered what we were missing at a postcard stand, where a mermaid caught my eye, a stone maiden clutching the extremities of her double tail in her hands, just as her sister does in the cloister of Monreale on the outskirts of Palermo. Afterward I read that there were eight of these metopes, each portraying one of the monstrous beings described in the ninth-century *Liber monstrorum*, which were believed to inhabit the outmost reaches of the earth. This was not, as I had once thought, the mere fantasy of the medieval sculptor: here the church was carved into a *mappa mundi*.

> We do not have, says Saint Augustine, a view from above. We cannot contemplate the entire creation from Heaven, as God does. It is therefore our own insufficiency, the scarcity of our information, that can leave us offended as it were by the deformity of one of its parts, in as much as we ignore its coexistence and its relationship with the whole. Therefore even the geographical unknown can be part of the wonderful work of creation, as Saint Jerome suggests when he relates the dialogue between Saint Anthony the Hermit and a faun, who on behalf of all his fellows asks the saint to intercede with God, that He extend even to them the salvation promised to all men.[12]

This passage speaks to me of the touching humility of medieval man in the face of the natural and the unnatural alike. One mustn't idealize: reckless deforestation is a problem as old as agriculture; nor was sacrifice evenly distributed among the people of the twelfth century. Yet it strikes me that just this sort of humility and respectfulness in the face of what we do not know is required in order to fuel the tiresome tasks of

Lions of the first generation at Modena. To the left of the door is
the plaque singing Wiligelmo's praises, and below it Adam and Eve can
be seen hoeing the earth.

recycling, of forgoing exotic tropical woods for more banal but renewable domestic species, for the laborious pursuit of organic food production.

Here, too, in Modena the king of the beasts presides over this wonderful amalgamation of doctrine and legend. Several pairs of lions guard the different doors to the cathedral, but the ones that sustain Wiligelmo's portico at the center of the façade are very special lions. Not only are they beautiful – they are not crouching but sit tall and proud, with full and wavy and very regal manes – but they are the first to guard a church in the Po valley. The lions that we had seen earlier are their progeny.

Lions first appear in churches at the end of the eleventh century, at the doors of the Cathedral of Modena, and supporting the papal throne of the Cathedral of Salerno, which was consecrated in 1085. This imagery was no coincidence: Pope Gregory VII himself performed the consecration at Salerno, eight years after he had forced the Holy Roman Emperor Henry IV to wait in humiliation before the gates of Canossa.[13] The papacy claimed temporal as well as spiritual supremacy and took for its own the beast that had adorned the throne of the Byzantine Empire and that since the classical era had been the quintessential symbol of temporal power.

Ancient symbols fade and lose their effectiveness as they become divorced from our daily lives, and only by chance can we again experience their primitive force. Some years ago, during the grape harvest, my husband brought home a baby lamb that he had found wandering in the vineyards. It was tiny, only a few days old, and we realized that it must have strayed from the flock belonging to a nearby shepherd, its thin, uncertain legs unable to keep up with those of its mother.

Sicilian sheep are not very attractive beasts; they are raised for their milk and not for their wool, and at the end of the dry summer season their fleece is stringy and dirty and matted with droppings, and their smell travels almost as far as the sounds of their bells. But the animal that I carried in my arms down the road to its fold was so trusting and innocent of fear, so clean and sweet-smelling as I pressed my nose into the warm softness of its tightly curled wool, that the phrase 'the Lamb of God' assumed a potent resonance even for an agnostic like myself.

Lions were also the heraldic device of the Hauteville family. They pranced in gold on Roger II's scarlet robes of state and watched in marble over his throne in the Palatine Chapel; in flesh and blood, they roared in the royal menagerie. Constance had grown up surrounded by lions both live and ornamental. As she walked between the lions of Wiligelmo in Modena, she must have felt the power of their symbolism much more intensely than I or Marcella could. Her family claimed that its right to rule came straight from God: she would have seen in these beasts of stone not a symbol of papal supremacy but an immediate reminder of her own inheritance, which she was on her way to claim, so that she might bequeath it to the child she carried in her womb.

CHAPTER SIX : OCTOBER

Friend, if you had shown consideration,
meekness, candor and humanity,
I'd have loved you without hesitation
   – Castelloza, thirteenth century[1]

I now think it unlikely that Constance would have visited
Nonantola, an abbey founded in the eighth century by
Benedictine monks who drained the swampy countryside
invaded by the Panaro River, a tributary of the Po that cuts
north across the Romagna. In the twelfth century, the abbey
was at the height of its power, firmly placed in the papal camp
and allied with Bologna in the latter's long war for territory
against its rival, Modena.

To Marcella and me, however, any abbey seemed a port in a
storm, and we were determined to see any twelfth-century
church that came onto our horizon. A quick detour, only
seven miles, took us away from the Via Emilia and through the
well-tended fields that eighth-century monks had reclaimed
with hoe and spade for Nonantola. A medieval city had grown
up around the abbey, gained riches and power, and then
declined; it was now a small but flourishing agricultural town,
with streets in which tractors were almost as common as cars.
The abbey church was restored some seventy years ago to its
original twelfth-century Romanesque forms, and the dark red
bricks of the unadorned façade are pockmarked with regularly
spaced holes that must have once sustained the marble swags
and curlicues of the Renaissance or the baroque. The only
marble visible at present decorates a portico that has survived
the vagaries of monastic taste across the centuries, with the

requisite lions guarding a carved portal, the work of a follower of Wiligelmo. We did not linger long but headed once more for the Via Emilia and points south.

～

In leaving Modena, Constance and her company would have had to pick their way along the southern outskirts of the Bosco della Saliceta, the last of the medieval forests of the Po valley to survive into the twentieth century. Having resisted the onslaught of the monks of Nonantola and seven centuries of subsequent attack, the forest did not quite make it into the age of ecology but was cut down less than fifty years before our passing. A *saliceto* is a willow grove: in a photograph from 1934, no willows are discernible, but the wood is flooded, and despite a modern network of drainage canals, the roots of the oaks, the ashes, and the hornbeams are hidden by several inches of water.[2]

We were nearing the delta of the Po now, and the country-side was striped with small rivers running north, so tamed to the requirements of modern wheeled traffic as to be hardly noticeable. No need, as in Constance's day, to hope for the remains of a still-efficient Roman bridge, or for a raft to ferry them across or – since the river waters would still be very low in early October, barely enough to cover a horse's fetlocks – to let their beasts pick their way neatly across the stony riverbed.

Just before entering Modena we had crossed the Secchia, which at that point in its meanderings marks the border separating Emilia from Romagna, which are now united in the single administrative region of Emilia-Romagna but, historically speaking, are two very separate geographical entities – so much so that the differences in the landscape began to make themselves felt even before we passed Bologna.

Bologna was familiar to both of us, and as the thermometer rose steadily, we became less and less willing to tackle a big and noisy city in which the echo of Constance's footsteps would be difficult to hear. She and Henry had held court there in 1186, in 1187, and again in 1191 on the way to their coronation in Rome, but it was traditionally an enemy of the empire, and we decided to pass it by, happy that the arbitrariness of our route could be stretched to accommodate questions of physical comfort.

On either side of the city, the landscape was still relentlessly flat, with no sign of a hill, no geological formation against which to measure our progress. But to the east of Bologna the character of the fields changed, as did their content. Trees were used differently: rows of poplars no longer fenced off the fields, but single large shade trees, elms, perhaps, or oaks, announced the presence of human habitation. Around Faenza we passed miles of fruit orchards, rows and rows of peach trees pruned flat, almost two-dimensional, as if they had been espaliered against a wall that had later been removed. It looked to me as if this was a modern technique, trees forced to conform to the requirements of mechanized modern agriculture.

Not so the vineyards. As we moved east, we saw fewer and fewer vines grown tall and strung between the branches of trees. Despite modernization, a difference is still noticeable between the tall suspended vines of north and central Italy and the bushy grapevines of the South, which are pruned low or supported by a bunch of canes. In my earlier reading, I had made a fascinating discovery: the reason for this difference has nothing to do with climate or grape variety but has everything to do with who first farmed the area in which they grow. The tall vines of the north are an Etruscan heritage, whereas in the South the Greeks introduced the bush technique, known as *alberello*. As we left Emilia, we were in fact leaving behind the land of the Lombards and entering into the realm of the Greeks, the ancient Byzantine Exarchate of Ravenna.

I think it a great shame that guidebooks rarely call their readers' attention to what is happening beside the roads they travel on. A landscape is so much richer, so much livelier to an informed eye that can recognize the plant from which the previous night's artichokes were picked, or notices at what latitude the olive tree enters the landscape, and knows how and when its fruit will be harvested. I was intrigued when I first realized that the history of a landscape can be read in what is growing there, and how – but such an alphabet is not easy to acquire.

After Rome fell to the Goths in 410, Ravenna was appointed the capital of the Roman Empire in the West, and in 493 it was conquered by Theodoric, King of the Ostrogoths. Educated at the court of Constantinople, Theodoric built in a classical and eastern mode, a tradition continued by the Byzantines after their general Belisarius conquered the city in 540 on behalf of the Byzantine emperor Justinian. The Exarchate of Ravenna became a military province of the Empire of the East, the stronghold of Justinian in Italy.

Shortly after Belisarius took Ravenna in 540, the Lombard peoples crossed the Alps and entered the Po valley, gradually creating a division of the Italian peninsula into Lombard Italy – which included almost all of the north, plus the duchies of Spoleto and Benevento – and Roman Italy, which comprised the Exarchate of Ravenna (including the Pentapolis, the five cities – Rimini, Pesaro, Fano, Senigallia, and Ancona – situated along the Adriatic coast), plus the Roman territories and Puglia, Calabria, and Sicily. After two centuries of resistance, Ravenna was conquered by the Lombards in 751, but its distinctive Byzantine character lingered on in the mosaicked monuments that had been built by Galla Placidia, Theodoric, and Justinian.

The countryside as well maintained a different aspect from that of Lombard Italy. Centuries of invasion and unrest had resulted in the depopulation and impoverishment of rural areas throughout the peninsula, and the vast estates meticulously cultivated by the slaves of the Roman Empire fell to pieces. In the north, the fields reverted to the forests familiar to the Lombards and so suited to the raising of their beloved pigs, but in the Greek areas, much of the cultivated land became degraded pasturage for sheep.

The late Emilio Sereni wrote a fascinating study of the parallel development of the agrarian landscape of Italy, so molded by the intervention of man, and of the pictorial landscape portrayed in Italian painting. One of my favorite passages regards Ravenna:

In barbarian Italy – but more particularly in Byzantine Italy, where a more expert social and cultural formalism casts a sharper light – this link between the real landscape and the pictorial landscape becomes particularly evident. . . . The degradation of the agrarian landscape and the net prevalence of shepherding over agricultural activities, is fully matched by the almost exclusive importance that pastoral landscapes assume in Byzantine art. . . . Just as in the real countryside the regular network of roads and fences is falling to pieces and the unity of form proper to an organized and regulated agriculture is disappearing, so in the pictorial landscape the unity of composition breaks down . . . and the landscape motifs, having lost any real point of reference, are transformed into purely decorative and ornamental motifs.

In the splendid mosaic of the apse of St. Apollinare in Classe, in Ravenna, with its stylized images of rocks and plants and animals, an artist of the sixth century illustrates how in Byzantine society these processes of distintegration in the agrarian landscape and in the pictorial landscape accompany each other with rigor and formal perfection. . . . This perfection cannot hide the decadence and the harsh poverty of the contemporary reality, and reveals to us an urban and agricultural society that has declined into a pastoral society, falling apart and at the same time crystallized into a rigidity which mortifies all enthusiasm.[3]

The memory of these very mosaics, the sheep neatly aligned about the apse as they listened to the sermons of Saint Apollinarius, beckoned to Marcella and me as we drove eastward. By the time we reached Forlì, we could see the foothills of the

Apennines on the southern horizon, and we could sense that the sea, although still out of sight, lay ahead of us. We had time enough, we decided, for a quick look at Ravenna, so at Forlì we turned north, leaving the Via Emilia behind us to drive through the fields and marshes surrounding the ancient Byzantine city, catching with pleasure the familiar flight of seagulls busy in the eastern sky.

It had been a long time since Marcella had visited Ravenna, and I myself hadn't been there in over forty years. My memories were of the mosaic sheep in St. Apollinare in Classe, and the watering doves and the starry heavens in the Mausoleum of Galla Placidia, the sort of images that stick with a fourteen-year-old. I had no idea of what to expect from the city in the way of a setting. In the Italian press, Ravenna figures as a port and a center of the petrochemical industry, so I imagined smog-darkened smokestacks and high-rises towering above the vestiges. It was a delight to discover that I was wrong. The ancient port and the lagoon that had protected classical Ravenna from naval attack had long since been silted over; the sea now lay some eight miles to the east; and the ancient walled city was low, light, and airy. Many of its two- and three-storied buildings were painted in creamy colors, and many of its streets, quite wide for a medieval city, were reserved for pedestrian traffic and for a large army of bicyclists of all ages, pedaling easily on the flat paving.

As we walked through the streets, we could admire the prosperity of the citizens, who seemed slightly less opulent than the residents of the fat towns of Lombardy, but somehow less provincial in feel, and at dinner in an open-air restaurant Marcella introduced me to a cheese with an absurd and marvelous name, *squaquerone*, which turned out to be delicious, with the slightly sour, yeasty taste of a *crescenza* or a *stracchino*, but less homogeneous in texture and immersed in a creamy whey.

As I lay in bed that night and thought about the mosaics that awaited us the next morning, I did not feel guilty for having turned aside from the Via Emilia. Constance would have had no reason to take the same detour, unless (and I think it unlikely) she had been asked to make an appearance, a reminder of imperial rule, in a town that had not seen Henry VI since he became emperor. She had paid a visit there, however, exactly eight years earlier, when Henry sat in court in Ravenna on the sixteenth and seventeenth of October, in 1186, and even if in 1194 she passed no closer than Forlì, Constance would have remembered Ravenna.

Her memories would have been ambivalent at best. The royal couple had spent the ten months following their wedding on the road: making a longish stay at Pavia, then going to San Donnino, and then heading southward, possibly along the Via Francigena, reaching Orvieto in June. Back up through Umbria to Gubbio, then west again to hold court in San Miniato during the first week of September. A whiff of the sea at Pisa, and then they had turned inland again to Prato, crossing the Apennines to Bologna, and continuing on to Ravenna. They traveled slowly: Henry and his knights advanced ruthlessly where they encountered opposition but elsewhere were entertained lavishly, if grudgingly, by the princes of the land and the Church. They had stopped to participate in religious festivals or the hunting parties that their hosts arranged for them, knowing that Henry would have his hawks and eagles with him.

It must have been an interesting time for Constance. However much the Queen was expected to take the postilion in these travels, a whole new world, so different from her own Sicily, was unfolding before her. The Italian men of the twelfth century were likely to be just as attentive to women as they are today, and perhaps for much of this journeying she had had the solicitous attentions of Frederick von Hausen as well.

She had made other discoveries then, too, for the months she passed in traveling with Henry could not but reveal more and more of the character of the man to whom she had just been given in marriage.

Like most major historical figures, Henry VI is a victim of

Real sheep are far too stupid and pushy to stand in such a neat line,
but these well-disciplined beasts do make a splendid mosaic.

The Arab craftsmen of southern Italy were famous for their work in ivory: this intricately carved 'oliphant,' or hunting horn, is fit for an emperor's pleasure.

appropriation. Each historian who writes of him describes him in the light of his or her own national or political viewpoint, judging his ambitions and his statesmanship by subjective parameters. (I should perhaps add here that I am fully aware that I write in a glass house.) Yet if scholars have come to little agreement as to his statesmanship, none make the case that Henry's character was a pleasant one. Even the German historian Ernst Kantorowicz, writing at the height of his enthusiasm for the Hohenstaufen emperors, paints a grim portrait:

[H]e had nothing of the genial *bonhomie* of his family, nothing of their gracious exterior. His body was gaunt and frail, his sombre countenance, dominated by the mighty brow, was unvaryingly stern. His face was pale, his beard was scant. No man saw him laugh. His personality completely lacked the amiability and the compelling charm of Barbarossa. He had a gloomy autocratic way with him; in later days he might almost have been of stone. His policy was ambitious and all-embracing, but hard and uninspired. Hardness was indeed the keynote of his being, a hardness as of granite, and with it a reserve rare in a German. Add to this a mighty will, a passion immensely strong but cold as ice, an amazing shrewdness and political acumen.[4]

He was no soldier: falcon hunting was the only physical activity that he was known to enjoy. In answer to a courtier who reproached him for neglecting his health and eating only late in the day, a Byzantine author quotes him as saying: 'For an ordinary man any time is appropriate for eating, but for a king, distracted by his many affairs, if he does not want to betray his role, it suffices that he think of his body in the evening.'[5] Given Constance's years of barrenness and the absence of any recorded bastards, we may well wonder if he even took pleasure in sex.

His contemporaries admired him for his intellectual pursuits. Theology, history, and statecraft were his great passions, and he was an accomplished poet, although even in the world of chivalry and courtly love, power remained his only metaphor.

I greet my Beloved with a song –
I could nor would not shun her.
Since I last greeted her with my own lips
Many days, alas, have passed.
Whoever shall sing this song in the presence
Of her whom I must abandon so abruptly,
Be ye lady or lord, give her my greeting.

Kingdoms and nations are under my dominion
When I am together with my Beloved,
But when I must take leave of her,
Then all my powers and riches disappear
And I count only sorrow as my lot.
Thus am I raised in joy only to descend
In changing fortunes that I will suffer until the grave.

And since I now love her so with all my heart,
And do not doubt her even for a moment
But carry her in my heart and thoughts even when it pains me,
How shall love repay me, with what reward?
She is reward enough, repays me so well, with so much beauty,

That rather than give up my love, I would renounce my crown.

He does me wrong who believes me not,
For I could live my days in joy
Even without a crown upon my head;
And yet without my love I'd have not even that,
If I should lose her, what would I have left?
I would not delight in the company of man nor woman,
And banishment would be my greatest comfort.[6]

Above all, in an age characterized by strong and violent emotions, Henry VI is remembered for his cruelty. The full extent of his ruthlessness would manifest itself in his later years, but even during these first months of marriage, it must have been revealed to some degree. The Pope who had ascended to the throne of St. Peter just a few weeks before the royal wedding was Urban III, former Archbishop of Milan and an implacable enemy of Frederick Barbarossa. Immediately he began to incite northern and central Italy to rebel against imperial rule. Barbarossa returned to Germany, leaving his son to put the situation to rights. According to one British historian, 'Henry carried out his task with a thoroughness which characterized all his actions; he devastated the country to the frontier of Apulia, received the oaths of allegiance from the towns and nobles of the Campania and Romagna, and by the end of the year 1186 almost the whole of northern and central Italy were under imperial control.'[7] In this same period, Henry is said to have cut off the nose of a papal legate who had angered him, an intriguing episode that lacks, alas, any substantiating footnote.[8]

Nicetas Acominatus, the Byzantine author already quoted, goes on to describe how some German knights, sent by Henry in 1195 to demand tribute from Constantinople, were received by the Byzantine emperor Alexius III, who hoped to intimidate the Western barbarians with the pomp and ostentation of his court. Nicetas encapsulates in one brief moment the clash of two opposing empires, of two irreconcilable civilizations:

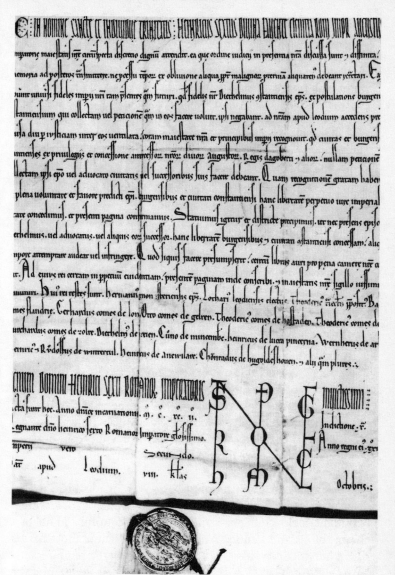

Henry VI was a learned man, but such an elaborate signature as the one
on this document was probably the work of a chancellery clerk.

On the solemn feast of Christmas the Emperor [Alexius III] put on a robe encrusted with gems and commanded all the others to dress in cloth of gold. But rather than stupify the Germans, the spectacle of their enemies' pomp and luxury fired them with greater cupidity, and they yearned to subjugate the Greeks at the first possible opportunity, considering them to be abject creatures dedicated only to slavish delights.

When the members of the imperial court exhorted them to admire the splendor of the gems with which Alexius glittered like a flowering meadow, and to behold the sweetness of springtime in the midst of the winter, the Germans answered that they were far from desiring such spectacles, nor were they accustomed to marvel at feminine ornaments, the splendid jewels and sparkling earrings with which lustful women try to please the virile sex. In order to intimidate their hosts, they added that the time had come to banish womanly adornments and to exchange gold for iron.

For should their embassy prove vain and the Emperor decline the proposals of their King and lord, the Greeks would be forced to cross arms with Germans, men who did not shine with gems like a meadow, nor seek courage in the roundness of their pearls, nor glorify – almost like peacocks – in their amethysts interwoven with purple and gold. For the Germans are the pupils of Mars, their eyes flaming with ire shoot rays similar to those of jewels, and their bodies daily dissolve in beads of sweat more resplendent than pearls.[9]

Constance's first and certain visit to Ravenna in 1186 took place little more than a year after she had come north, leaving behind her beloved nephew and his bride. Beautiful and full of charm, pious and gentle, William II and Johanna must have ruled her memory like Arthur and Guinevere, reigning in harmony over Camelot, the differences in their geographical background and education an endless font of delighted surprise and discovery. That Henry would remain forever a stranger to Constance must have been clear to her long before they reached Ravenna, but how much harsher it must have been to contemplate her own situation within the walls of a city that, in its lingering Byzantine flavor, was so much more familiar to her than any she had visited so far, so profoundly and nostalgically evocative of home.

∾

Marcella and I were off early the next morning for a lightning visit to the mosaics. The monuments belong to the Archdiocese of Ravenna, which takes care of them with good organization – one ticket entitled us to three basilicas, a museum, a mausoleum, and a baptistery – and with tolerant good humor as well. In search of the Neonian baptistery, we approached a small Romanesque church. The wooden door was locked, but on it was posted a sign that read, 'This is the church of San Giustiniano. NOTHING TO SEE. The baptistery that you are looking for is next to the Duomo bell tower.'

The same delightfully forthright approach was evident in the Basilica of San Apollinare Nuovo. Here virgins and martyrs proceeded down the walls, the first toward the Madonna, the others toward her son, and it was a pleasure to rediscover the Magi looking like French revolutionaries in their red Phrygian caps, and the imperial palace with fringed and embroidered curtains hanging in the archways. The apse, however, was invisible, closed off by a rough wooden partition that hid the restoration in progress. We could hear the restorers chatting as they worked, and evidently they were tired of being interrupted by tourists, for one of them had writ large on the wood with a pencil: 'Apse destroyed by an earthquake. There are NO mosaics in the apse.'

But we were more than content with what we could see. In striking contrast to the cathedrals that we had been visiting across the Po valley, in which every stone, from first to last, on the outside and on the inside, preaches to the layman, the message of the Ravenna mosaics is a totally unexpected glory hidden within a humble brick exterior. My taste had not grown more sophisticated during the forty years since my last visit, for those mosaics that I remembered best were the ones I still found the most enchanting. The Mausoleum of Galla Placidia, sister to the Emperor Honorius, is the earliest, built sometime before 450, and its charmingly frivolous mosaics, the ribbons and garlands of fruit and the doves in a birdbath, were the ones that had so appealed to me as a teenager. Overhead the deep blue vault of the firmament was studded with stars like a flowering meadow. This time, armed with Emilio Sereni's insights, I took notice of the lunette of the Good Shepherd, who sits on a real stone, patting a real sheep in the middle of a real and luxuriant landscape, a paradise already lost in the apse of St. Apollinare in Classe, built just one century later but mirror of a much impoverished world.

St. Apollinare in Classe stands in open fields a few miles south of the city, surrounded by a few trees, a much later cylindrical bell tower, and excavations of the old Roman-Byzantine port. (The name *Classe* comes from *classis*, the Latin word for 'fleet.') After we had refreshed our memories of the saint and his sheep, Marcella and I sat down outside the basilica in the shade of an umbrella pine and ate the lunch of *squaquerone*, bread, and early peaches that we had bought in Ravenna. Mosaics were much on our mind: those we had seen that morning, and the famous mosaics of Palermo that Constance had either known from childhood or seen in the making.

Aside from the Palatine Chapel, where Constance had probably been baptized and where she must have felt completely at home, Palermo houses two other churches that are famous for their mosaics. The earliest is the Church of Santa Maria dell'Ammiraglio, built by Roger II's admiral, George of Antioch, who was himself a Greek. It stands only a little farther down the Cassaro from the Convent of San Salvatore, and I like to think that Constance often begged her nurse to take her there, to see the mosaic just inside the door. Here she could look upon the face of her father, dressed in the full regalia of a *basileus*, a Byzantine emperor, in the moment of being crowned by Christ. The mosaic is heavy with political and theological implications, a claim to divine anointment that would have been lost on a little girl in search of the father she had never known.

The other church is the magnificent Cathedral of Monreale, perched on the mountainside just behind the city. It was dedicated to the Madonna by William II, in answer to a dream in which she had commanded him to build her a church and also in answer to the ambitions of the Archbishop who was rebuilding the Palermo cathedral and getting too big for his vestments. As part of an extremely well-endowed Benedictine abbey that followed the Cluniac rule, the Monreale church would have lain outside the authority of the Palermo hierarchy; at William's insistence, the Pope endowed its abbot with the rank and regalia of an archbishop.

Construction began shortly before 1174 and was largely completed by the time Constance left Sicily. She must have often accompanied William and Johanna on the short ride up to Monreale to visit the site and watch the hundreds of workmen scurrying up and down the ladders of the scaffolding, pressing the small glass tesserae into the wet plaster with deft and rapid movements.

Piece by piece, the walls were completed and the scaffolding was removed. The scenes of the Old and New Testament lining the naves and transepts shone out in a glitter of light: the perfect circle of the newly created firmament, the expulsion from Eden, the sons of Noah welcoming the animals into the ark. The lower walls were faced with slabs of marble surrounded by colorful geometrical designs in the Arabic fashion, but above that – bit by bit, but in the arc of only seven years – the entire church, over 9,000 square yards of walls and vaults, was gilded and colored by tiny glass squares: the Nativity, the miracles of Christ, Saint Paul escaping from Damascus in a basket lowered from the ramparts, saints and seraphim surrounding the enormous head of Christ Pancreator in the apse.

One can imagine that William, a very learned young man, liked nothing more than to point out the saints (near the altar stood Thomas à Becket, an homage to his English bride) and to explain each scene to his ladies, lecturing them on its relationship to the whole and to the message that he wished to proclaim to his people.

An American scholar, Eve Borsook, has recently made a detailed study of the Palermo mosaics, analyzing the choice and setting of each scene or saint and the accompanying texts, and has come to the conclusion that both the Palatine Chapel and the cathedral in Monreale reveal a much more unified and complex iconographic program than heretofore has been believed. Hers is an awesome job of interpretation, far too complex for summary here and perhaps even for Constance to follow in all its details. But if Borsook is right, then William would have explained to her and Johanna that 'the underlying theme . . . in the Monreale Genesis cycle is Paradise created, Paradise Lost, and the promise of Paradise regained.'[10] The Christological sequences in the transepts and apse confirm this promise of a new Jerusalem, ruled by the Norman king of Sicily, who sits on the throne of David both by right of divine anointment and by hereditary claim.

William actually had inherited a claim to the Crusader state of Jerusalem, through the second marriage of his great-grandmother, Adelaide of Savona, with the Frankish king of Jerusalem, Baldwin I. The marriage agreement had stated that in the absence of offspring, the crown would pass to Roger II, Adelaide's son by her first marriage, but Baldwin rather brutally repudiated Adelaide in favor of a younger woman. In any case, 'the Norman kings had used their hereditary claim to Jerusalem as a means of bolstering and exalting a new monarchy. Rather than actively pursuing the claim, the Normans employed it as a propagandistic ploy in which . . . the realm was spiritualized and thereby the Norman state assumed a sacred nationality.'[11]

Constance had little reason to be sympathetic to the Byzantine Empire. It was to fight against its troops that her Norman ancestors had been called into southern Italy; her father had waged successful campaigns to conquer Byzantine possessions in the eastern Mediterranean; and she herself had seen and shared the mortification of William, waiting on the dock for a Byzantine bride who never arrived. Nonetheless, Marcella and I concluded, despite the differences in century and style and content, the gilded glow of the Ravenna basilicas must have made her feel very, very homesick. In that first visit, in 1186, her nostalgia might have been for a paradise lost; when she and her unborn child passed Ravenna on the journey south eight years later, Constance was looking to the future. She was heading toward the throne of David, toward an earthly paradise that still might be reclaimed.

~

With that we brushed off the crumbs, picked up our trash, and started south, returning to the Via Emilia again at Cesena, some fifteen miles to the east of where we had left it at Forlì. To the south, a small mountain, topped with a tower, was the first real interruption in the flatness that we had been looking at for days, but it was a false alarm, and the plain of the Po delta continued relentlessly on either side, all the way to Rimini, where the Via Emilia runs into the Via Flaminia.

We were near the sea by this time, but the Flaminia passes inland, conceding us only the smell of salt and an occasional seagull gliding overhead, but offering no view of the famous beaches of the Adriatic, which spread from north of Rimini down through Riccione to Cattolica. In early June the beaches would have been fairly empty, and the locals hard at work repainting the cabanas and the boardwalks and setting out the beach umbrellas, each shading a pair of deck chairs, to march in regimented rows for miles and miles and miles. In a week or so, the tide would begin, a trickle of early vacationers to pave the way for a river in July and then a deluge in August, when the factories close and a good part of northern Italy empties out onto these beaches, struggling for space against an army of Germans. A Teutonic invasion far more peaceable and far more numerous than that which accompanied Constance's comings and goings, these hordes from the north spill across the Alps each summer in search of the sun and a taste of *la dolce vita*.

After Cattolica the road began to climb. We had left Romagna behind, and the green hills of the Marche crept down to the edge of the Adriatic, leaving barely enough room for a small coastal road to wind its way between woods and waves. The Via Flaminia does not attempt this narrow passage but climbs up through the hills behind Cattolica and Pesaro, through a landscape that is softer and greener, alternating woods and pastures.

After Pesaro we finally arrived at the coast, close enough at last to see the sea. The water playing in the sunlight and reaching out beyond our sight to Dalmatia was a balm after the claustrophobic landscape of the Po valley, where the horizon is never more than a few fields away. For Constance it would have been her first glimpse of the sea in almost three years, a

William of Normandy set out to cross the Channel and conquer England just six years after Constance's grandfather, using similar boats, crossed the Straits of Messina to conquer Sicily.

long stretch to be landlocked for someone who had grown up in a port city, who had been able to see the waters of the Mediterranean – greener, bluer, brighter than these – from her palace windows.

Once they left their longboats beached on the coasts of the North Sea and settled in France, the Normans had forgotten their seagoing skills, and when the Great Count Roger, Constance's grandfather, conquered Sicily in the eleventh century, he had done so by land, commanding a cavalry of one thousand Norman knights who had been ferried across the Straits of Messina, just as the trains and cars from the continent are loaded onto ferryboats today – a quick trip, the merest illusion of a sea voyage.

But with their customary ability to size up a novel circumstance and turn it to their own use, the Norman kings had been quick to realize that for the Sicilian Kingdom, the sea meant commerce and conquest. Under the command of a series of remarkable admirals, the Norman fleet had ruled the better part of the eastern Mediterranean. Constance herself had made at least three longer voyages to the mainland and had probably sailed often along the coast as the court moved back and forth from Palermo to Messina. Life in southern Germany, with only the waters of the Rhine to watch, must have been a trial to her.

The Via Flaminia turns inland at Fano, and although my map of Roman roads shows a major road continuing down the coast, it didn't seem to rate a name. Whatever it was, it was nasty: here again our decision to avoid the superhighway brought Marcella and me into a morass of intersections, billboards, and long strings of noisy, smelly trucks that were difficult to pass. We drove with determination where Constance would have moved slowly, the mules carrying her litter picking their way slowly along the hillside and along the narrow coastal plain. She saw less woodland here, and more pasturage for those Byzantine sheep: vineyards fenced in by stone walls, Greek fashion, to protect the tender shoots and the ripening fruit from goats and wild boars. A few late apples and pears still hung on the trees, too, although in the medieval countryside the fruit tree was much rarer than it is today, for fruit was a luxury destined for the lord's table, and peasants had a healthy resentment for a tree that required space, water, and labor with no return to themselves, an attitude that persists among Sicilian countrymen today: the fruit tree is 'useless.'

Just before Senigallia we crossed the border between Umbria and the Marches. Fifteen more miles of coastal road separated us from the fork where Constance and her escort had turned into the rolling countryside that joins the sea to the foothills of the Apennines, inland toward Jesi.

Many historians write of Constance's having given birth in Jesi as if it were pure happenstance, along the lines of 'I was just passing through when the labor pains began.' On the contrary, I am convinced that Jesi was chosen carefully, in terms of both its politics and its position.

Now an attractive walled city full of sixteenth-century palazzi, Jesi at the end of the twelfth century was one of the key communes in the disputed central Italian territories. Papal and imperial claims conflicted here; just as Ancona, down the road by the sea, was generally favorable to the papacy, Jesi tended to support imperial interests.[12]

The choice of Jesi was not only politically correct but geographically appropriate: at 318 feet above sea level, the town could be approached from the coast by an easy climb, hardly noticeable in a litter and relatively comfortable for a traveler in an advanced state of pregnancy, whereas beyond Jesi the road rises abruptly and tortuously through mountain passes that are narrow, easily ambushed, and probably not negotiable in the twelfth century except on horseback. As October drew to a close and Constance completed her seventh month of preg-

In the great hall of the Zisa palace is a fountain whose waters, it is said, bore
tiny amphorae of cooled wine across the room to the banqueters.

Constance waits until the very last moment, when she is
already mounted on her horse, before she hands her baby over
to the Duchess of Foligno for safekeeping.

This crown, of a type reserved to men, was found in the tomb of
Constance's daughter-in-law. It has been suggested that Frederick himself
cast it therein, in despair over his wife's death.

The magnificent state mantle of Roger II was probably carried off to Germany by
Henry VI and was later transferred to the Imperial Treasury in Vienna.

The wax seal from a letter of Frederick II, dated 1239
and addressed to the imperial princes, expressing his opposition
to the claims of Pope Gregory IX.

Roger's room in the royal palace of Palermo: "this enchanting room, this gorgeous bestiary in blue and green and gold."

Wild beasts, musicians, and dancing houris decorate this fragment of silk woven in the royal *tiraz* in Palermo.

William II presents the Virgin Mary with the Cathedral of Monreale.
She had appeared to him in a dream in which she commanded him to build her
a church on the site of a small chapel on the mountainside above Palermo.

The creation of the firmament is the first mosaic in the Monreale cycle representing the stories of the Old Testament, an extraordinarily beautiful way for worshipers to learn about their religion.

Christ crowning Roger II—perhaps the only portrait in which Constance could see the father who had died before her birth.

nancy, she knew that her destination was Jesi, where she was expected and where, as she had ordered, she might repose in cosseted privacy until the moment when she would give birth.

~

At the fork, we did not turn inland toward Jesi in Constance's footsteps – not yet – but continued south toward Ancona, the enemy camp. My son Francesco had two pieces of sculpture in a contemporary art exhibition there, the Premio Marche, and I was eager to see them in situ and to report to him. This was his first appearance in a major show, but he would not see it: he had been living in New York since the previous September, and the show would be closed before he returned to Italy.

Our arrival in the city did not endear Ancona to us. It is situated on the inner curve of a mountainous promontory that hooks out into the Adriatic: approaching from above, we were swept down in the early evening traffic rush along one-way streets that precipitated toward the harbor and brooked no stopping, no parking, no moment of hesitation. We drove down and around again several times before we found a hotel and a parking place, then circled at length on foot before we found a restaurant. By then the traffic had gone elsewhere and the streets were deserted, and we had no comforting parade of solid citizens taking the air to mingle with as we looked the city over. Moreover, it seemed all skewed around: an angry red mist hid the western side of the harbor from view, so that the sun seemed to be setting in the sea, something we knew could not be happening on the Adriatic coast.

Marcella and I were arguing – the closest we ever got to a heated discussion on the entire trip – about what it means to have a child leave home. In Sicily I had long been considered a *madre snaturata*, unnatural and unmaternal in the typically American way in which I pushed my children out of the nest, first into summer camps and travel, then to study on the continent. And now I was finding myself with one child living in the

States and the other studying in central Italy, neither of them likely to return to Sicily to stay. Now I had not only the empty nest but the syndrome as well – something I had blithely assumed that intelligence and forewarning would spare me. Yes, it was natural, but no, it was not nice. Nor did it look curable.

Marcella, more relaxed than most Italian mothers, told me I was exaggerating, that it was natural and *basta*. We reached no conclusion, and I refrained from telling her that she didn't know what she was talking about: of her three children, one was still at home and two lived just on the other side of Rome!

We left the hotel early the next morning, in a vain attempt to avoid the heat, and picked our way along the harbor to the Mole Vanvitelliana, a huge and handsome pentagonal fortress sitting on an islet in the middle of the harbor. Built in the second half of the eighteenth century as a fort and quarantine, it had recently been restored and reopened as an exhibition space. The Premio Marche exhibit was on the lower floor, in the storerooms and dungeons. Francesco's big piece, a figure of a man three feet high cast in red fiberglass and standing with arms widespread as if at the tip of a diving board, was bolted to a metal axle on stanchions. A specially geared crank allowed you to rotate the axle and stop it at any point, so that the man could describe a complete circle around his axle, swooping in a rapid dive or hovering in whatever position the onlooker desired. It was very well installed, set at the far end of a long, barrel-vaulted room of rough-hewn stone, and lit so that the bright red figure caught the eye. The guard told us that it was hard to keep visiting children away from the crank, so all was as Francesco would have wanted. I missed him acutely as I looked at it.

This detour to Ancona had been a totally maternal affair, ostensibly far removed from my preoccupations with Constance. Once more a big city, much of it rebuilt after the terrible bombardments of World War II, had disrupted our mood with its noise and dirt and confusion. And yet it was all one, I reflected: it was the cross-cultural marriage, the bringing up of children suspended between two cultures, that was at the root of my obsession with Constance, although I had been a great deal more fortunate than she. Constance was about to give birth to a child half-German and half-Sicilian, just as my children were both Sicilian and American, and she would have to decide – or to deceive herself into thinking that she *could* decide – to which of these two cultures her child would belong. Herein lay her fascination for me; this was our true affinity.

CHAPTER SEVEN : NOVEMBER

She stayed alone, often
Clutching at her throat, wringing
Her hands, beating her palms,
Reading psalms from a prayerbook
Illuminated in letters of gold.
— *Yvain, The Knight of the Lion*
Chrétien de Troyes, c. 1177

A few miles inland, the road to Jesi passes through a town called Chiaravalle, its name alone making it imperative that we stop. Here as elsewhere the Cistercian abbey had been swallowed up by urban development. According to our guidebook, the abbey church, which dates from 1126, is the earliest Cistercian-Gothic church in Italy: the interior was imposing but not particularly interesting to our untutored eyes. There was a park behind the church, almost empty on a Saturday noon except for a young mother spooning yogurt into the mouth of a small child in a stroller. The heat had been increasing steadily as we moved south, and the lush lawns shaded by large trees in the fullness of their June foliage were an invitation to sit for a while and admire the intricate brickwork on the exterior of the apses.

The trees above us looked like chestnuts, *castagni*, and the name of the abbey was Santa Maria in Castagnola, a clue that the monks had planted chestnut groves in their work of reclaiming the land. A great many chestnuts were planted in the twelfth century, and would continue for centuries to provide the half-starved Italian peasantry with basic nourishment in times of famine.

Conceivably, Constance might have spent her last night on the road at Santa Maria in Castagnola, but she would surely have been as anxious as we were to get on with it, to travel the last few miles that would bring her to Jesi. It was an easy trip along a country road lined with robinia trees, which were past their bloom at sea level but still in flower around the walls of Jesi. The old city, which sits on the long and narrow crest of a hill overlooking the valley of the Esino River, is surrounded by fortified walls and towers built of brick. We left the car in the shade of the robinias and entered the city gates on foot, passing by deserted streets and shuttered stores in search of a bar that remained open at siesta time and could furnish us with a sandwich to fuel our walk about the town.

It was very unfair but unavoidable: as a Constance buff, I was hard put to appreciate Jesi. Its walls were handsome, its narrow streets and wide piazzas had charm, the palazzi and the churches were interesting if not exceptional, but the walls and all that stood within did not appear to contain one single stone that dated from the twelfth century, nor one single contemporary reminder of the town in which Constance had chosen to give birth. It seemed wrong to give up too easily and leave while everything was closed, so we decided to return to the car to wait until four o'clock, when the tourist office would reopen for the afternoon.

We were beginning to feel very at home in the little Fiat. Our suitcases and the computer were stuffed into the trunk, which we never opened on the road, while the backseat was crowded with shoes and jackets and cartons: one holding emergency rations of water, fruit, cookies, flashlight batteries, and toilet paper, the other a traveling library of guidebooks, road maps, guides to trees and wildflowers and ancient Roman roads, and books on Sicilian and German history and medieval travel and architecture, which spilled out all over the seat every time we rummaged to check up on something en route. No one would ever take it for a local vehicle, but at least – we hoped – the jumble of books and rumpled rain jackets had no tempting air of affluence.

So it was no hardship to sit in the tree-shaded car, a book open but unattended on my lap. Marcella fell asleep, but my thoughts kept me awake: if Jesi could give me no visual clues, I would have to rely upon my imagination to re-create Constance's stay here.

In what frame of mind did Constance reach Jesi? Relief must have been foremost in her emotions, for she had been on the road for two and a half months by my calculations, rarely spending more than two nights in the same bed, enduring hours of trying to adjust her body to the irregular movements of the litter as the mules moved slowly along. The roads were nothing in comparison to what she had experienced in her Alpine crossings, but they nonetheless afforded frequent opportunities for stumbles and jerks, a discomfort that grew as her pregnancy advanced and her belly expanded. Upon reaching Jesi, the first lap of her journey was over, and the perils that had tormented her imaginings since she left the safety of Meda – storms and floods, an ambush or a roadside miscarriage – had been successfully avoided. She was weary, and she could rest. And yet, deprived of the distractions of travel, of changing scenery and new faces, she would find the waiting burdensome, alone with her fears for the future and the ghosts of her past.

Not so many decades earlier, the Cistercians had decided that the first days of November should be devoted to the commemoration of the dead: All Saints' Day on the first and All Souls' Day on the second. It was an attempt on their part to Christianize the Samain, the feast at the beginning of November in which the Celts had celebrated the start of a new year and commemorated their warriors and their ancestors. In the Gallic tradition a wintertime Lent began on the eleventh, with the feast of Saint Martin, a saint dear to the Normans as well, a period of penitence in which to prepare for the coming of the Christ Child. The Church thus gave its blessing to a period that had long been sacred to the dead, the moment in the ancient calendars when the nights grew long and the seed was sown in the darkness of the earth. To quote a sentence that I love and have used before:

> In October the sowing of the wheat begins, and November honors that which lies beneath the ground awaiting rebirth; the dead return in a ritual visit to the living, just as the living celebrate the cult of the dead, and the whole period between the beginning of November and Epiphany is a *tempus terribile*, in which the gates to the Afterworld remain open.[1]

In the medieval period it was the women, according to Georges Duby, who had particular responsibility for the cult of the dead (a condition still true in Sicily today). They were the chief mourners, they walked at the head of the funeral processions, and they organized such rites and remembrances as were celebrated outside the church and within the walls of the family. It was an important responsibility:

> The ancestors were, in the precise meaning of the term, revenants; they resumed their place within the family circle every time that their surviving descendants gathered to recall their acts and their 'deeds.' To commemorate them solemnly on certain dates was an act that was strictly speaking vital because it served to revitalize the sap of the family tree. . . . What indeed was *nobilitas* if not the capacity to claim for oneself very distant and valorous ancestors?[2]

How desolate a scene must have appeared to Constance as she prepared to commemorate her dead, so many many dead. She alone remained to perform the rites in memory of the mighty house of Hauteville, to charge the monks of Chiaravalle and the priests and canons of Jesi with saying masses for the souls of her father, her brothers, her nephews. If she were to die in childbirth, if the child were stillborn, their seed would vanish and their lineage come to an end.

Who was this father, for whose soul Constance prayed and whom she had never known? His contemporary, Archbishop Romualdo of Salerno, describes Roger II as 'tall, corpulent, regal in aspect, and harsh of voice. . . . Proud in public, benign in private, he dispensed honors and prizes to those faithful to him, and insults and punishments to those who betrayed him. In his subjects he inspired terror rather than love.'[3]

Constance may have seen her father's image impressed on the seals of chancellery documents or in other effigies that have since disappeared. Surely she knew the mosaic in the Church of the Martorana, where he is portrayed in a very Christ-like fashion, dressed in the robes of a theocratic king, a 'living icon of Christ,' as Byzantine emperors were described.

Lord Norwich has used this portrait as a pretext for summing up the man:

Even in something so hieratic and formalized as the Martorana mosaic, there are certain inspired touches, certain infinitesimal adjustments and gradations of the tesserae, that bring King Roger to life again before us. Here, surely, is the southerner and the oriental, the ruler of subtle mind and limitless flexibility whose life is spent playing one faction off against another; the statesman to whom diplomacy, however tortuous, is a more natural weapon than the sword, and gold, however corrupting, a more effective currency than blood. Here is the patron of the sciences, the lover of the arts who could stop in the middle of a desperate campaign to admire the beauty of Alife, stronghold of his archenemy. Here, finally, is the intellectual who has thought deeply about the science of government and rules with the head and not the heart; the idealist without delusions; the despot, by nature just and merciful, who has learned, sadly, that even mercy must sometimes be tempered in the interests of justice.[4]

A hard act to follow, both for Constance as his daughter and heir and for me as a writer. I find it difficult to believe that as a young girl she could have discovered much more than sad and distant attention in this mosaicked face, let alone seen any of the love, approval, and ambition that a young girl needs to find in her father's eyes, if she is to have a strong sense of herself as a woman.

Not that Roger would necessarily have paid much attention to a daughter, had he lived on after her birth. Of the five sons that his beloved first wife, Elvira of Castile, had borne him, by 1149 only William (the future William I) was still alive, and Roger, fearing for the future of his dynasty, remarried. After fourteen years as a widower he took as his second wife Sybil of Burgundy, who died two years later, most probably in child-birth, and then in 1152 he married Constance's mother, Beatrix of Réthel. Both of these later wives came from north-ern Europe, chosen perhaps through the offices of the French king Louis VII, with whom Roger had just had a successful meeting, or dictated by Sicilian interests in the prosperous Flemish wool trade. Neither was able to produce the male heir that Roger had expected of them.

About Beatrix we know nothing except that she was the daughter of Gunther, Count of Réthel, and of yet another Beatrix, the daughter of the Count of Namurs. Réthel lies in the forests of the Ardennes, just northeast of Rheims, a little over sixty miles west of Trifels and Haguenau. Marcella and I had not taken the time to make the detour, for the town of Réthel was the scene of very severe fighting in both world wars, and little vestige of the Middle Ages remains. Beatrix was most likely in her late teens or early twenties, the height of her fertile years, when she made the trip south to marry the King of Sicily, and although it has suited me to think otherwise, the fact that she remained in Palermo after his death in 1154 and was not packed off to marry someone else may mean that she very soon entered the convent.

In the light of her own adult experience, Constance would

come to have great sympathy for the loneliness and foreign-ness of her mother at the Sicilian court, and if, as some sources say, her mother lived until 1185, one hopes that her death came in the spring, before Constance left for the north, so that as she prayed for her mother's soul, she did not have to bear the guilt of having abandoned her on her deathbed.

She must have felt a certain envy, too. Fate had allowed Beatrix to escape from what had probably been a loveless mar-riage and an alien court, to find peace, safety, and solace in the company of women, a company whose habits and rituals would have differed only in minor matters from those of the cloistered women she had known in her northern home. How often in recent years Constance must have contemplated her own impotence and wished that she could follow in her mother's footsteps.

Entering a convent was by no means the drastic step that we consider it to be today. For a woman, it represented first and foremost her surest path to eternal salvation. The fragility of women, their physical and moral weakness, their acknowl-edged inferiority were best protected, their congenital lasciviousness best held at bay, behind high walls and barred windows. The routine of prayer and contemplation, undis-turbed by worldly distractions, offered the pious the possibility of a mystical union with God. Yet religious vocation was not the sole motive urging twelfth-century women to take the veil:

[Convents] were also important social institutions. They took in girls from families with so many sisters that there was simply not enough property to give each a dowry appropriate to their rank; they sheltered daughters who suf-fered from physical or mental handicaps that made marriage impossible. Convents fulfilled many other functions: they were educational institutions, orphanages, homes for widows, shelters for abandoned wives.[5]

They also offered capable and well-connected women, like the Abbess Letizia of Meda, opportunities to exercise talent and authority, although as the twelfth century came to an end, the role of women both within the Church and without was becoming more and more circumscribed. To Beatrix, the Convent of San Salvatore must have offered an oasis of serenity after the intrigue and violence of the Palermo court, one that her daughter could now appreciate.

In her prayers during the early days of November 1194, Constance would have remembered not only the dead of the house of Hauteville but her maternal ancestors, and she would have been obliged to pray for their enemies as well. Beatrix had doubtless told her of the glories and the noble deeds of her forebears, but the only recorded contact that we have between Constance and her relatives in Réthel was over the question of the Archbishopric of Liège, a complicated story that is relevant, I believe, because of the damage that it wrought on Constance's self-esteem.

Liège was one of the important centers of power in the Duchy of Lower Lorraine, which lay within the western borders of the Holy Roman Empire, and its archbishop had the status of an imperial prince. The election of the ecclesiastical princes was carefully controlled by the emperor, who thus ensured their loyalty and collaboration in keeping the local nobility under control. In August of 1191, while Henry was in Italy on his first ill-fated southern campaign, the incumbent Archbishop of Liège died. The question of a successor unleashed the rivalry of two local lords, Duke Henry I of Brabant and Count Baldwin V of Hainaut: Henry of Brabant championed the candidacy of his brother, Archdeacon Albert of Louvain, while Baldwin backed a cousin, Provost Albert of Réthel.

Albert of Louvain was a pious and capable man, who also seems to have been legitimately elected, but the other Albert had, if nothing else, his family going for him: he was Constance's maternal uncle, and she is known to have pressed her

The murder of Thomas à Becket had much the same shock effect on medieval Europe as Kennedy's assassination had on the world of the twentieth century.

husband to have him elected to the vacant see of Liège.

When a committee of ecclesiastical princes put the disputed election into the Emperor's hands, Henry chose to please neither faction and decided for a third candidate. From Constance's point of view, the problem was not solely the defeat of her uncle but also the fate of his rival. Albert of Louvain journeyed to Rome, where he made a successful appeal to the pope, and on his return he was consecrated by the Archbishop of Rheims, in whose city he took refuge. The following month he was befriended by three German knights who claimed they were hiding from the Emperor's wrath, and on the twenty-fourth of November they invited him to ride outside the city walls. 'The three knights fell upon Albert with their swords. The first blow crashed into his skull and he slipped to the ground without a word. Having lacerated his body to make sure of his death, the knights seized the bishop's horse and galloped off towards the east. All efforts at pursuit proved futile.'[6]

The parallel with the murder of Thomas à Becket, just twenty-two years earlier, was immediately obvious. The knights were never brought to justice, and many believed that they had acted on Henry VI's instigation. The scandal united the nobility of Lower Lorraine in rebellion against the Emperor, jeopardizing his hold upon the throne, and peace was restored only through the good offices of Richard the Lionheart during the last months of his captivity. In the opinion of one scholar, Henry was probably not guilty: 'Undoubtedly the plot against Albert originated in the emperor's entourage, but not necessarily with his foreknowledge'[7] – but the whole affair caused him substantial damage.

Albert of Louvain was canonized shortly afterward as a saint and martyr, and claims were put forth as to the miraculous powers of his relics. An attempt seems to have been made to launch a cult comparable to that which had sprung up spontaneously around the martyrdom of Thomas, but perhaps because Albert was not well enough known beyond the borders of Lorraine, it never flourished.[8]

For Constance the parallel must have been most distressing. Through the piety of Johanna, Thomas à Becket had come to be revered in Palermo, not only in his portrait on the walls at Monreale but in the hearts of the people as well. (In his *Vita S. Thomae*, William of Canterbury related the story of how the saint appeared in a dream to a Saracen of Palermo, who upon awakening decided to convert.[9]) Not only had Constance failed to advance the interests of her mother's family, but by interceding on their behalf she shared, although very indirectly, in the responsibility for a crime that seemed similar to that committed by Johanna's father, Henry II, one that had caused her beloved niece such grief.

By the time of Constance's marriage, the powers of the queen consort were severely limited and indirect. One of the few powers remaining to her was that of intercession with the king on behalf of others, an intercession most often acted out in the intimacy of the royal bedchamber. In the case of Constance and Henry, the evidence points to a rather limited and low-key intimacy, and the Liège debacle, provoked in part by her attempts to intercede in favor of her uncle, may well have seemed further proof of her inability to function in the role to which fate had destined her.

～

Constance's days of mourning at Jesi were followed by the feast day of Saint Martin, on the eleventh of November. As the patron saint of the Frankish and Norman monarchies, he was the most likely advocate for the well-being of the child and heir who was soon to be born. His feast day ushers in a brief season of mild weather, that 'summer of Saint Martin' which Americans know as Indian summer, when the sun shone to warm the sainted soldier-turned-bishop after he had divided his cloak with a half-frozen beggar.

Per San Martino ogni mosto è vino. By the eleventh of November the grape must has finished its fermentation, and the new wine is ready to be decanted from the dregs. One would like to think that Constance was able to enjoy a brief respite – fair weather and a restorative glass of wine, perhaps a raisin wine, the kind my husband is making as I write, and which a twelfth-century English cleric described with rapture:

> [A] raisin wine . . . is clear to the bottom of the cup, in its clarity similar to the tears of a penitent, and the color is that of oxhorn. It descends like lightning upon one who takes it – most tasty as an almond nut, quick as a squirrel, frisky as a kid, strong in the manner of a house of Cistercians or gray monks, emitting a kind of spark; it is supplied with the subtlety of a syllogism of Petit Pont; delicate as a fine cotton, it exceeds crystal in its coolness.[10]

Constance's sojourn in Jesi strains the imaginative powers, for we do not know where she was lodged: in the bishop's palace, or at the house of some local seigneur? Perhaps she had a garden where she could walk in the good weather and feel the autumn sunshine on her weariness. Imagine such a garden, its walls sheltering her from the public eye, tended at most by a peasant dressed in belted tunic and leggings. It was the season for pruning back the summer growth on the thyme and the oregano, the lavender and the roses, for setting out a crop of cauliflower and fennel for spring harvesting, or, if the owner was wealthy, moving the potted orange and lemon trees under shelter for the winter. The calendulas would be in flower, bright yellow and orange, although perhaps smaller than the ones we know today, and maybe the last apples would be hanging from leafless trees. Pomegranates were waiting in ripe abundance, prized not only for their beauty but for the acid sweetness they gave to sauces, and quinces, fully yellow and fuzzy, to be cooked in stews or – an extravagance to tempt the Empress's appetite – boiled down with sugar into a paste.

Quince paste, sugar-coated almonds and anise seeds, and marzipan tortes were luxuries that the Normans had inherited from the Arabs, who first introduced the cultivation of cane sugar into Sicily. Childhood treats for Constance, they would have been rare in Jesi, but maybe someone had had the fore-sight to order them sent up from the South to satisfy her pregnant cravings.

Time passes slowly in the last weeks of pregnancy, and even if darkness came mercifully early in November, Constance had many hours to fill. If new books were available, to alternate with the few well-read volumes that had traveled with her, reading would have helped, as would the chance to sit and gossip with the ladies of the house. To see the same faces more than three days running, and to finish a conversation once begun, would have been a welcome change from life on the road.

Chess and checkers she undoubtedly knew; they had come to Europe from Islam through Sicily, and in less than two cen-turies they had gained great popularity. The Muslims played with red and black pieces, on a monochromatic board of white squares divided by incised lines. But where Muslim culture saw a great contrast between the colors red and black, no such opposition existed in Western minds, and the color of the pieces gradually changed. Constance would have played black against white on a white board, and since she was royalty, her pieces would have been carved of precious ivory.[11]

There are ivory checkers from twelfth-century Sicily in the collection of the Bargello Museum in Florence, and chess pieces from northern Europe. It would have been painful indeed to lose these pieces to one's adversary, for they are beautiful, finely carved with dragons and hunting scenes. In the Walters Art Gallery in Baltimore, there are more of these round draftsmen for playing checkers and backgammon, as well as exquisite Sicilian ivory caskets. Dating from the twelfth century is a cylindrical box with gilded copper fittings, incised with arabesques that are quite Persian in character: birds, gazelles, and figures drinking, with an inscription that reads: 'To its owner the enduring blessing, the enduring, all-inclusive

The dedication inscribed on this box suggests that
it was made for someone of very exalted rank.

blessing.' In the same display case is a double comb of ivory, in
the shape of a wide H, with teeth on either side of the crossbar,
on which is carved a bird and a lion. I have stared at these
objects of daily use from behind the glass, yearning to learn the
feel of them through my own fingers and wondering if on any
of them, ever so faint and rubbed by time, Constance's finger-
prints endure.

She would have had entertainment in the evenings – not, of
course, the dancing girls and the Arab musicians of Palermo's
court, nor the courtly poets of Haguenau, but some local
flautist and drummer, or a singer with a lute. The road that led
past Jesi was not a major route, but surely passing *saltim-
banchi* and jugglers, mimes and puppeteers could be found
and called in for the Empress's distraction, and no doubt the
news of her presence there spread, a magnet for any enter-
tainer traveling in the region.

~

It is difficult to know how closely Constance in Jesi was able to follow her husband's progress southward. The extremely efficient system of postal couriers that the Arabs had established in Sicily during their occupation of the island was already in decline when the Normans invaded, and nothing was done to revive it until the thirteenth century, so that messages took an uncertain and often surprisingly long time to travel from one part of the kingdom to another. But before too many November days had passed, she must have learned that Naples had opened its gates in welcome to the Emperor, and that the city of Salerno, in punishment for its betrayal three years before, had been razed.

The events of that betrayal, during the first expedition in 1191, still burned vividly in her memory. That time they had left Germany much earlier in the year: Henry and his army, with Constance in attendance, had passed the Alps via the Brenner Pass – more easily negotiated in the winter months – at the end of December. By the end of January, they had been in Lodi, where they encountered Eleanor of Aquitaine, and then, following the Via Francigena, they had crossed to Pisa and proceeded south to Rome. There the newly consecrated pope, Celestine III, officiated at the imperial coronation on Easter Sunday, the fifteenth of April. It was rumored that the new pope, unfriendly to the imperial cause, had put off his own consecration for two weeks in order to delay the crowning of the Emperor, and a contemporary chronicle reports what appears to be a marked ambivalence on the part of the pontiff:

> Our lord the Pope then led them into the church, and anointed him emperor, and his wife empress. The Pope sat in the pontifical throne holding the imperial crown of gold at his feet, and the Emperor, kneeling with bared head, received the crown, and in like manner the Empress received hers. Suddenly our lord the Pope struck the crown of the Emperor with his foot, causing it to fall on the

ground, to indicate that the pope possessed the power of casting the emperor from his throne, should he show himself unworthy. Immediately the cardinals picked up the crown and replaced it on the head of the Emperor.[12]

The crown in question is probably the one now on display in the Schatzkammer of the Kunsthistorisches Museum in Vienna. Eight vertical panels of gold form a circle decorated with enameled plaques and encrusted with huge cabochon gems and pearls. An arch of gold filigree and pearls joins front to back, and a gold cross surmounts the central panel. Originally made for the coronation of Otto the Great in 962 – the arch and cross are later additions – by the time of Henry's coronation the crown must have looked much as it does today, weighty and ostentatious but very impressive. It would have required quite a hefty kick on the part of the elderly Pope (he

The idea of the Pope kicking this very solid crown off the Emperor's head hardly coincides with our present-day concept of a ceremonious and dignified coronation.

was eighty-five) to knock it off Henry's head, and the wincing dismay of the cardinals as the heavy gold crown crashed to the floor must have been audible throughout the basilica.

Be that report truth or gossip, the Emperor and the Pope appear to have parted on good terms, and the Emperor and Empress continued to advance slowly southward. The siege of Naples began at the end of May. Salerno, some thirty miles south, proclaimed its loyalty to the Emperor and invited the Empress to spend the summer in the palace that had belonged to her father.

Salerno had been founded in the eighth century by the Lombard prince of Benevento. In addition to being an excellent port, the city marked the crossroads of traffic passing between Naples and Calabria to the south, and that moving inland toward Benevento. It soon became a capital and a rich commercial center, so much so that by the mid-eleventh century it was known as *Salerno opulenta*. The Lombards were less responsible for this economic growth than the merchants and the artisans belonging to the strong ethnic minorities in the city: large numbers of fortune-seekers from nearby Amalfi, Greek Sicilians who had fled the Saracen occupation, a large Jewish community, and an Arab community as well.

Salerno was conquered by the Normans under Robert Guiscard in 1077, and with the coronation of Roger II in 1130, it became, together with most of southern Italy, part of the Sicilian Kingdom. The Norman rulers pursued the same policy of tolerant coexistence as their Lombard predecessors. They built a large and handsome cathedral and took over the Lombard palace next door. It was in this palace, rebuilt to his own taste by Roger II, that Constance was to spend the hot summer months of 1191.

As she rode through the streets, she must have felt herself in Palermo: the same polyglot conversations on all sides, the heaping abundance of the fruit and vegetable stalls, the magnificent displays of copper, silks, and ceramics, the contrasts in dress and custom as she passed from one neighborhood to the next.

When Constance arrived at the Lombard palace, she must have felt that she had come home. Although the rooms that had been prepared for her were considerably simpler and less dazzling than those of the palace she had grown up in, they were furnished in the same style. The dinner table offered her the same foods she had eaten as a child: dates and sugarplums, citrons and spices and sugared almonds. Shrimp and octopus and fresh fish had the intense flavor of the salty Mediterranean waters, and there were squashes and zucchini and cucumbers in all shapes and shades of green. (It's hard to imagine a summer in southern Italy without peppers and tomatoes, still hidden away in the New World, and without eggplants, which were due to arrive from the Arab world via Spain in the next century.) Constance was in her own kingdom, and her husband's mighty army was besieging Naples and had surrounded Tancredi's lieutenant and brother-in-law, Count Richard of Acerra. Palermo was but a few days' sail across the sparkling turquoise waves that she could watch from her bedroom window. Victory had seemed very close indeed.

~

Salerno today is still an unexpectedly enchanting town. My husband and I spent a few days there in 1999, a visit prompted more by my sense of duty toward Constance than by any real desire to see what we thought would be a southern seaport in decline, eclipsed by the vast Neapolitan port to the north and beset by poverty and unemployment. We approached it from the hinterland, on a trip that had taken us from Naples to Benevento to Bari, then back along a more southerly route along the valley of the Basento. The last leg had been through wooded mountains, past Eboli, a region impoverished in economic resources but rich in landscape and lush June foliage, to which the outskirts of Salerno – high-rise housing projects and chaotic traffic – were a rude contrast. But once past the periphery, we were entranced.

With banners and flowers, the noblemen of Salerno and their wives
welcome Constance into the city.

We stayed at the Jolly Hotel, the best that Salerno offered,
and its location was worth every penny of its hardly exorbitant
price. The hotel stood at one end of a long sweep of palms and
flowerbeds that followed the curve of the sea, the waves to one
side, a row of elegant turn-of-the-century buildings to the other.
Cars were banished here, and as the day ended, the Salernitani
were escaping the small and stuffy quarters of the old city,
baked by an early heat wave. Every bench was full, the paths
bustled with bicycles and dogs on leashes; pensioners gossiped
as they gathered about checker-topped tables and shuffled
cards, tired housewives rested swollen feet, and young couples
strolled arm in arm. A low wall held back the sea: leaning over,
we could look down to the water's edge and a strip of rocks
where a convention of cats was in progress. Turning and

leaning back, we could look up over the rooftops to the hill above the city, guarded by a fortified castle, and to the mountains beyond.

A few blocks away the wrought-iron gates of a large and beautifully maintained botanical garden were open until late in the evening, and it was crowded with people who seemed to feel totally at ease there even though darkness had fallen. The same sense of security reigned in the narrow streets of the medieval city, just a short walk inland. Confused by the labyrinth of alleys and archways, we were unable to find the few remaining vestiges – hardly more than a cornice and a window – of the royal palace, but the cathedral was resplendent, even seen through the green netting that swathed the last of the restorations in preparation for the coming jubilee.

First of all the lions, a lovely pair sitting proudly before the portal, their forelegs straight, their heads bent in deference. The one on the left is a she-lion, suckling a small creature

A gentle lioness suckling her young guards the
doorway to the Cathedral of Salerno.

sitting beneath her belly and stretching its mouth to the milk. It is a gentle family scene, not fiercely guarding but welcoming the faithful into their home. The Portal of the Lions leads into a large square atrium that is surrounded by an arched portico and by an upper gallery of smaller arches decorated with inlaid medallions of different geometric designs in red, black, and white stone. This play of colors is repeated in the stones of the campanile, a square tower topped by a round drum of overlapping arches, with a cornice of inlaid white stones that looks from the distance like a chain of daisies.

Much has been changed in the interior, but it is still dominated by two large pulpits and a marble iconostasis with traceries of mosaic and marble inlay so similar in style and decoration to some of the work in Monreale that Constance must have gaped the first time she saw them.

We too found sweets to delight us in Salerno, in a glorious pastry shop in the Via dei Mercanti, the main street of the medieval city, where the late spring speciality was a *scazzetta*, a 'skullcap' of sponge cake, low and domed and covered with strawberry icing in a bright cardinal pink.

~

Alas, the expedition in 1191 had not gone as planned, and the victory that had seemed so close, as Constance waited in Salerno, turned into profound humiliation. Laying successful siege to Naples required control of the sea, but having no fleet of his own, the Emperor was forced, like his father before him, to rely on the fleets of the maritime republics of Pisa and Genoa. While Henry had visited Pisa in person on his way to Rome, signing with his own hand the treaty that enlisted their aid, his negotiations with Genoa had been entrusted to envoys, and this treaty was not signed until the end of May. Harried by the Sicilian fleet, the Pisan ships alone were insufficient to blockade the port of Naples and prevent fresh supplies from reaching the besieged city.

The heat of the southern summer set in, malaria and dysentery raged through the German camp, and the Emperor himself fell seriously ill. On the twenty-fourth of August the siege was lifted. Henry gathered the remnants of his defeated army about him and started north, leaving his wife in Salerno to await his return with reinforcements the following spring.

The siege of Naples had truly been a disaster for the empire. According to Gislebert of Hainaut, who was sent to Italy by Duke Henry of Brabant to plead the Emperor's support for Albert of Louvain, 'the most powerful Archbishop Philip of Cologne, and the Duke of Bohemia, an illustrious, upright, wise and most learned prince, died, together with many other princes, archbishops, bishops, abbots, dukes, marquis, palatine counts and many other nobles, so many that scarcely a tenth part of the entire imperial army escaped death.'[13]

A rumor that the Emperor himself was dead reached the people of Salerno, who were taken by panic, fearing the wrath of Tancredi – usurper of the Sicilian throne to which the city belonged – for having given support to the Emperor and hospitality to Constance. A mob stormed the royal palace and took the Empress captive: she might have been killed had it not been for the intervention of a cousin of Tancredi, Elias of Gesualdo, who rescued her and bundled her off to Tancredi in Messina, thus avoiding a murder that would have outraged Christendom. Besides, a live empress taken hostage was far more valuable than the dead wife of an extremely vindictive man. Tancredi found himself in a very powerful position.

Constance spent the next four months in Palermo under the watchful eye of Tancredi's queen, Sybilla of Acerra. The poet Pietro of Eboli claimed that she was even made to sleep in Sybilla's very own bed, although it is not clear whether he considered this to be a treat or an imposition. The Empress was received as an honored guest, made welcome by the townspeople in the streets and by the rulers at court. Perhaps she went with the royal couple to see the architectural progress that had been made since her departure: the completed

Supported in the saddle by his knights, a sick and defeated
Henry VI returns to Germany in 1191.

Constance kneels in prayer as her knights attempt to defend the royal palace from the attack of the Salerno townspeople.

mosaics at Monreale and the finely carved capitals of the cloister next door, in place now upon their slender double columns wrapped with swirling mosaics.

Maybe she banqueted with them at the finally finished palace of the Zisa, the enchanting pleasure pavilion set in the gardens of the Genoard, where a fountain in the big hall splashed down into a channel patterned with mosaic fish that seemed to wriggle under the current. The channeled waters bore tiny amphorae of wine across the hall to the banqueters, then ran out into the reflecting pool that mirrored the sky, the façade, the palm trees, and the oranges. Construction of this palace had been undertaken by William I, who fled from the cares of court and family to the harem he kept there, and it had been completed by his son, who is thought to have used it for more innocent pleasures.

But wherever Constance had gone, however well she had been treated, and however much she had tried to believe that she was home again, she had been a prisoner. She had been in the company not of her beloved William and Johanna, but of Tancredi and Sybilla, and he was an ancient menace and a present usurper. The throne on which he was seated when he held court belonged rightfully to her, and the kingdom that he ruled was rightfully hers.

Even were she to regain the throne, however, she had yet to provide it with an heir, whereas Tancredi and Sybilla had not one but two sons, and three daughters as well. The humiliation must have been almost beyond endurance, aggravated by the fact that Henry had refused to make any sort of concession in order to have his wife back.

It was Celestine III who had broken the stalemate. Although his sympathies lay with the Norman king, the Pope had been unwilling to see either side gain too much of an upper hand, and he had proposed himself as mediator, convincing Tancredi against his better judgment to give Constance over to papal care.

In January of 1192 the Empress had set sail for Gaeta, on

the coast north of Naples, in the company of three cardinals. From Gaeta they had proceeded on horseback, up over the Arunci mountains and down into the valley of the Liri, a gentle river which even today bends back and forth through wooded glens, small fields, and farmhouses.

Picture Constance, the cardinals, and a small escort of Norman soldiers, riding single file on a dirt track through these woods. Imagine the thoughts of the captive Empress as she prepared to exchange one golden prison for another, much as she had on her first ride north as a bride-to-be, in truth, but with less personal freedom and certainly with less dignity.

Hoofbeats on the track ahead, and coming toward them a party of German knights, members of the imperial guard. A moment's hesitation, and Constance declared herself: 'I am your Empress. I place myself under your protection.' And off the knights had borne her, eastward to Spoleto, avoiding the Papal States, and on to Germany, leaving the infuriated cardinals to continue empty-handed toward Rome.

Her rescue was a tremendous coup, an obvious success, yet I have never been able to believe that in the moment in which she declared herself, Constance was wholeheartedly happy with her choice. I think she did hesitate, and that on some sub-conscious level she knew that in identifying herself as empress, she was admitting that there was nothing left for her in Sicily. It was but a partial victory, mixed with profound alienation: a return to exile.

~

On this second expedition of 1194, Henry was determined not to repeat the mistakes of 1191. After leaving Constance in Meda, he had gone first to Genoa and then to Pisa to negotiate in person for the support of both fleets. He spent the month of July in Pisa, and probably both Naples and Messina sent ambassadors to surrender to him there. The situation in the

Henry on horseback urges his troops on in their 1194 attack on Salerno,
as the women and children of the city huddle in terror in the main square.

South was very different now: Tancredi was dead, and the throne was occupied by a small child, for whom Queen Sybilla was hardly equipped to be an effective regent. A change of loyalties was the wisest course.

Determined to avoid the deadly effects of another long siege, Henry planned to make a very rapid descent on Sicily. On the twenty-third of August the combined fleets of Pisa and Genoa, under the command of Henry's closest advisor, Markward of Annweiler, entered the Bay of Naples without meeting opposition, and from there they sailed south to Messina, arriving on the first of September to take command of the straits and establish their winter base.

Meanwhile Henry and his army continued south by land, stopping to punish Salerno for its treason, and then moved inland, avoiding the narrow valleys of the Via Popilia, where Richard of Acerra was waiting for them, and going east through Melfi and Venosa to Spinazzola, then south to the instep and across to Calabria. Although one or two Norman strongholds were razed, the Emperor encountered very little hostility, and before the end of November, Constance received the news that Henry had crossed the Straits and was successfully encamped in the Sicilian city of Messina.

Just to what degree his forces destroyed the city of Salerno is an open question. Norwich claims that the 'city was taken by storm and given over to merciless pillage. Such of the population as escaped massacre had their property confiscated and were sent into exile. The walls were reduced to rubble; by then there was little left for them to enclose.'[14] Contemporary accounts of sack and destruction tended to exaggerate, however; in reality, it was often a city's defenses that were razed rather than the city itself. A study of the economic history of Salerno in this period speaks of a prosperity that continued into the thirteenth century and does not consider the effects of Henry's vengeance worth mentioning.[15]

But pillage and bloodshed there surely were, and it is difficult to imagine that Constance received the news of Salerno's destruction lightheartedly. The first months of her stay had been happy ones; people there had befriended her, and some had attempted to protect her from the panicked crowd. She would not know who among them had now fallen to the fury of the German swords, and who had escaped. After all, they were – traitors and not – her people, citizens of the crown she claimed as her own.

I have often rendered thanks that as an expatriate I have never had to choose sides in anything more serious than a soccer match. I don't know how I could endure being in such a position. The great-grandmother for whom I was named barely escaped insanity when her father and her brother died fighting for the Confederate Army, while her husband was killed as an officer in the Union Army. It is said that a medieval man's loyalty went to his family and his liege lord, yet no less an authority than Georges Duby believes that 'the sentiment of belonging to a people, "Franks" or "Angevins," was very strong at the end of the twelfth century.'[16] Constance's loveless marriage and lonely years abroad can only have accentuated her sense of identification with her Norman origins. I cannot think that she rejoiced that Normans should die at German hands, or that as she waited her time in Jesi, these conflicting loyalties did not lie heavily upon her.

CHAPTER EIGHT : DECEMBER

I have a relative in Salerno . . .
She's practised the medical arts for so long
that she's an expert in medicines.
She knows herbs and roots so well
that if you want to go to her
bringing a letter from me with you,
and tell her your problem,
she'll take an interest in it;
then she'll make up such prescriptions
and give you such potions
that they'll fortify you,
give you lots of strength.

                    – *Les Deus Amanz*
         Marie de France, twelfth century[1]

I t was not only the shocking news of sack and destruction that reached Jesi from Salerno, or so I like to believe. Salerno was the home of the *mulieres salernitanae*, the women of Salerno, empirical practitioners of what we might call popular medicine, as well as trained women doctors who specialized in (although they were not limited to) gynecology and obstetrics. Salerno had long been famous as a center of medical arts, and although in the twelfth century the famous school of medicine had not yet taken institutional form, there were numerous private schools where learned doctors passed on their knowledge to their followers. Among these were women, women whom Constance would have met during her ill-fated stay there in the summer of 1191, and to whom she had surely applied for help to cure her sterility.

What would have been more natural for Constance, as soon as she realized that at the late age of forty she would be facing her first childbirth, than to send to Salerno, ordering that a *medichessa* be brought to Jesi to assist her in her ordeal?

Common sense and empathy are the only reasons for thinking that she did so, but nonetheless I have chosen to create such a figure, just as I have created the figure of Nahid, to bring Constance comfort. I shall call her Polisena, a name chosen at random from a list of women to whom the Salerno school granted surgical licenses at the end of the thirteenth century.

What can we hypothesize about Polisena? First of all, she was not a mere midwife, operating in the shadow of learned male doctors, but a proper surgeon, trained in various branches of medicine and licensed to treat both men and women. Probably of noble birth, she was quite possibly a professor at one of the Salerno schools. Much if not all of her medical knowledge, at least in regard to obstetrics, was encompassed in the famous treatise *On the Diseases of Women, Before, During, and After Childbirth*, written a century earlier and attributed to her predecessor, Trotula de Ruggiero.

The story of Trotula is both fascinating and emblematic. Some scholars claim that Trotula was the daughter of a Salerno nobleman, the same Ruggiero who donated part of his land for the construction of the Cathedral of Salerno, and that she practiced and taught at the school during the eleventh century. They say that she was the wife of Giovanni Plateario and the mother of Giovanni Junior and Matteo, both of whom were doctors in their turn, and both of whom cited their mother's work in their own writings.[2]

Only a few centuries later, she would be delegitimized: with the increasing professionalization and above all masculinization of medicine, it became inadmissible that a woman should have a place in the Olympus of scientific knowledge. Trotula became Dame Trot of Chaucerian fame: a midwife, a witch, an old wives' tale. She even became a man, Trottus by name. An analysis of a manuscript recently discovered in Madrid, containing three treatises by a woman of that name, seems finally to demonstrate that Trotula did exist as a historical figure, although more probably in the twelfth rather than in the eleventh century. Even if the correct attribution of the various works that go by her name remains uncertain, these writings do give us an idea of the medical theories in vogue in Constance's lifetime.[3]

The clouds of prejudice that have obscured the figure of Trotula extend to medieval medicine in general, making an unwarranted distinction between unlicensed female healers and trained male doctors that is only now being dismantled. 'Although they were not represented on all levels of medicine equally, women were found scattered throughout a broad medical community consisting of physicians, surgeons, barber-surgeons, apothecaries, and various uncategorizable empirical healers.'[4]

Childbirth in the Middle Ages; once again
Bathsheba is the protagonist.

213

The medical knowledge that Polisena, if my readers will accept her, brought with her to Jesi in the last weeks of Constance's pregnancy had its foundation in classical medicine, particularly in the theories of Hippocrates and Galen. To this corpus Salerno had added the study of the Arabic medical texts translated in the eleventh century, especially by the hand of Constantine the African, a convert from Islam who traveled there from Carthage and spent ten years working at the nearby Monastery of Monte Cassino.

At the basis of this corpus lay the Hippocratic theory of the four humors, which Galen linked to the four elements. All matter is composed of fire, air, earth, and water, with which are associated the four qualities of hot, cold, dry, and humid, and the four humors of the human body: blood, phlegm, yellow bile, and black bile. Good health depended on an equilibrium among the four humors, each of which governed both a temperament and a season. Springtime, both of man and of the year, was dominated by airy cheerfulness, summer by the fire and anger of youth, and autumn by earth and melancholy, while aged winter was the phlegmatic season of water.

Medieval scholars elaborated upon this seemingly simple scheme in many directions and to a great degree of complexity. Nutrition was one of the most important areas – proper attention to the qualities of the diet would contribute to the desired equilibrium of the humors. Perhaps the theories of Galen concerning diet survived at greatest length. People in Sicily today are still convinced that certain vegetables – cabbage and other *brassicae*, for instance – are hot and therefore irritating, while summer squashes on the other hand are cold and 'refreshing' to the intestines.

Hildegard [the German mystic of Bingen] is the only medieval woman who defines the humours and applies the characteristics of each specifically to her own sex, with special emphasis on their effect on female sexual behaviour. Women were usually considered to be naturally melancholic

214

and Hildegard certainly placed herself in that category. Such melancholic humours were generally believed to encourage women in what might now be termed neurotic behaviour. Certainly, since medieval women were so constantly lectured on their natural inferiority and their inheritance of Eve's guilt, as well as hedged by so many prohibitions about their behaviour, their level of stress must often have been unbearably high. Because they were felt to be primarily influenced by cold and dry humours which pushed them towards death, the coldest and driest state of all, it was taken for granted that they died sooner than men who generally were of the more healthy sanguine type.[5]

When carried to extremes, such a theoretical construction appears ridiculous to us today, yet it is in some ways an intuitive forerunner of modern holistic medicine and must have offered some reassurance to people who could not hope for a satisfactory biological explanation for the state of their health. The medical practice of Salerno differed from that of the great schools of northern Europe in that it was less fettered to the classics. A greater familiarity with Arab and Hebrew sources, and perhaps the leaven contributed by the presence of female practitioners, gave it a more empirical cast, a greater interest in concrete observation. Yet the distinctions between empirical knowledge, occasionally quite contradictory classical theories, and downright magic are very blurred, and some of the treatments that Trotula suggests sound absolutely revolting and quite lethal as well.

What would have been the advice of Polisena at her first meeting with Constance in Salerno in the summer of 1191, when Constance, still barren then, applied to her for help in conceiving? She would at least have given Constance the benefit of doubt, for she knew that 'conception is impeded by defect both in the man and in the woman.'[6]

In order to understand which member of a couple was sterile, a urine test was necessary: a sample of urine from each was mixed with bran and left to sit in a pot. At the end of ten days, the one with the most worms was the guilty party. In the summer of 1191 Henry was off besieging Naples, so his urine would not have been available, and Constance would have had to take the responsibility upon herself. Given the general condition of her life, and the ill tidings that were beginning to arrive from her husband's disease-ridden army camp, it is reasonable to assume she was suspiciously tearful:

> If her inability to conceive is in truth due to excessive humidity in the uterus, the symptom will be her constantly lachrymose eyes. Since the uterus is connected through the nerves to the brain, it is inevitable in fact that the brain suffer together with the uterus. Thus if the uterus contains an excess of humidity, this will fill the brain and overflow towards the eyes, forcing them to emit involuntary tears.[7]

The remedies for sterility were varied and, on the whole, repellent: fumigations, purges, and doses of powdered animal testicles dissolved in wine. If, as in the case of Constance and Henry, it was important that a male child be conceived,

> the man should drink the uterus and the vulva of a female hare that has been dried, reduced into powder and dissolved in wine. And the woman should do the same thing with the testicles of a hare, and after the end of her menstruations lie with her man, and thus she will conceive a boy.[8]

By December of 1194 Constance had left the problem of sterility behind her, and Polisena's chief preoccupations in the first weeks after her arrival would have been with diet and care in pregnancy. She would have considered it important – and this sounds familiar to us – that no one name a food that could not be procured, lest the desire for it provoke a miscarriage. The expectant mother should, on the other hand, eat light and easily digestible foods, and finish her meal with the meat of fowl, and quinces and pomegranates – both fortunately in season and produced abundantly in the neighborhood.

If Constance's feet were swollen, Polisena would have massaged them with a mixture of oil of roses and vinegar, and she would have encouraged the Empress to take frequent baths, after which she would soften her lady's belly by rubbing it with the oil of olives or violets. If it were distended with flatulence, she would take

> celery seeds, cumin seeds, and mint, 3 drachmas each, Mastic, cloves, cardamom, *Rubea maior* root, of each 3 drachmas; beaver musk, ginger, orrisroot, 2 drachmas each, and 5 drachmas of sugar. This . . . if taken as prescribed, removes the flatulence from the food and impedes miscarriage.[9]

The days were growing shorter and shorter, the hours longer and longer as the three women sat – Constance, Nahid, and Polisena – waiting for the Empress's time to be fulfilled. I doubt that tact was in any greater supply in the twelfth century than it is in twentieth-century Sicily, where the women who gather around an expectant mother cannot refrain from spinning off a litany of difficult childbirths and disastrous deliveries, intended, I suspect, to ward off such evils from those present, but nonetheless – speaking from personal experience – somewhat discomfiting. Polisena surely had many such tales to tell, and I hope Constance had the good sense to shut her up.

On the thirteenth day of the month, the women would have invoked the help and blessings of Lucy, a Sicilian saint, the virgin martyr from Syracuse who tore her eyes out and offered them on a plate to her pagan suitor. Patroness of eyesight, bringer of light in the darkest days of the year, she promises rebirth and the return of spring. She would surely intercede for the nascent heir to the Sicilian throne.

I suspect that the women's pastimes grew more private,

These late-twelfth-century thimbles are made of copper;
Constance surely sewed with one of gold. Nowadays thimbles are usually
plastic, but the medieval design has not been improved upon.

more intimate, as the time approached. Polisena had brought
most of her medicaments and dried essences with her, but
there were fresh herbs to gather, to pound with pestle and
mortar, and to brew into tisanes and soothing balms. Constance most likely spent the daylight hours embroidering the
last stitches onto the tiny caps and scarlet swaddling bands that
she had been preparing since Meda.

As the days passed, it became more and more obvious that
the birth of Constance's child would come close to, or even
coincide with, the birthday of the Christ Child. In a world
accustomed to seeking symbols in all natural phenomena and
to reading omens into every event, such a coincidence would
not have passed unnoticed. Indeed, Constance would have
rejoiced in the analogy and prayed to the Virgin that she might
be delivered on Christmas Day, that she might give birth to a
savior for her kingdom, just as Mary had given birth to the
Savior of the world.

The precise day of December 25th was not so important,
for Christmas was a solar festivity, close to the winter solstice
and the ancient Roman Saturnalia, a feast of twelve nights, one
for each month of the year. The entire period was of great
prophetic significance. (Sicilians still say that you can predict
the coming year's weather by marking how the rain and sun

218

alternate during the twelve days of Christmas.) This dignified religious festival had no Santa Claus, no tree with presents underneath, at most a Yule log, hefty enough to burn for twelve nights, becoming ashes that would be carefully preserved for their particular powers of fertilization.

> The log burning on the hearth is the old sun that dies in the winter solstice, only to rise again, renewed: it is the Child of Bethlehem, who springs from the grotto of the Nativity as from the womb of the Virgin. The traditional scene of the divine birth is an awesome theophany. The grotto, symbol of mystical secrets and subterranean depths, is a gaping gateway to the Netherworld where, in the heart of the darkness, the light of the new sun bursts forth. The Virgin who gives birth to the Son of God, intact and perfectly pure Nature, is primordial in the biblical sense that she is untainted by original sin, while the old man symbolizes ancient humanity bent by the guilt of Adam and weighed down by the millennial load of sins. The ox and the ass represent inferior dispositions of the human soul. . . the shepherds with their flocks are all mankind. The Magi signify the nations of the world and of postdiluvian humanity, *primitae gentium*; the star the entire astral universe which moves towards the Lord and orders itself about Him.[10]

How could Constance not have seen the birth of her own child as charged with portent? How could she escape a sense of mission? As an Hauteville, she would have remarked yet another significance: her father, Roger II, had been crowned on Christmas, a fact commemorated in the mosaics of the sanctuary in the Palatine Chapel, where many of the subjects and inscriptions are taken from the Roman and Byzantine liturgies for Christmas Day.[11] Constance's family tradition resonated with the regality of this festivity.

~

A grotto was out of the question, but where exactly was the child to come into the world? In the normal way of things, Constance would have given birth in the big bed of the great chamber of the castle or palace in which she was lodged. But nothing as grandiose as the palace in Palermo would have been available in Jesi, however. Most domestic space in the twelfth century was quite unarticulated. Georges Duby gives us an account of the castle of Arnold, Lord of Ardres, at the beginning of the thirteenth century:

> In Arnold's house, the main story was divided into two. On one side were the quarters of the men, the open area of conviviality, the hall where the lord, seated in majesty, eating, offering food to others, welcomed his guests, and where his companions and servants lay down at night to sleep. On the other side were the women's quarters, enclosed, arranged around the 'great chamber,' around the bed where the master and the lady slept together, 'the secret part,' flanked by a cubbyhole for the maidservants, a dormitory for the children and a nursery for the babes-in-arms.[12]

Arnold's castle was probably far fancier than anything to be found in Jesi, but the division between hall and chamber was everywhere the norm. A lady gave birth in the bed where she had conceived, in a chamber whose walls were decorated with embroidered cotton or wool hangings. Constance's baggage might have included silken hangings brought from home that were unpacked for the duration of her confinement at Jesi, perhaps curtains like those strung on rods between the columns of the imperial palace in the mosaics of Ravenna.

The furniture of the time was less massive, less permanent than one might think, for given the multiple purposes of each room, it had to be easily moved. The tables were boards laid on trestles – the chronicler Richard of Devizes tells us that Johanna possessed, as part of the *donatio* made by her future husband at the time of their marriage, a gold table board with two tripods of gold to support it. But most people dined off wood. Beds were normally mattresses placed on a frame strung with cords, with carved wooden supports that could be dismantled. Poetic license describes

> a bed of which the hooks are of silver, the knobs are of red gold, and the frame pieces are all of ivory. All the cords are of red silk. There are two or four padded mattresses, and bolsters and sheets of velvet, and pillows, and a coverlet of marten's fur embroidered with birds, beasts, and flowers.[13]

The bed itself could have been curtained, with draperies that were not generally used except for periods of illness or labor. This information, specified in a contemporary source,[14] sheds light on a question that is of interest to us: the degree of privacy in which childbirth normally took place.

It is generally assumed that the notion of privacy is entirely modern (Italians still don't have their own word to express this concept and have to make do with ours) and that castle life in the Middle Ages was one great bawdy tumble of birth, death, and lovemaking in plain sight of all those present. The rigid division between the male and the female quarters was to protect the women's chastity rather than their modesty.

One scholar points out that in the preface to the longest of the three Madrid treatises, attributed to Trotula, 'the author states her or his reasons for writing . . . [and] adds that "shame-faced on account of their fragile condition and of the diseases which afflict them in such a private place, women do not dare reveal their distress to a male physician."'[15] Whether it is female empathy speaking here or merely a literary convention, such feelings of modesty were obviously not unknown to women of the Middle Ages. Any woman who has experienced childbirth would instinctively attribute to Constance the desire to seek a private, sheltered spot in which to undergo this dangerous ordeal. Yet privacy was the one luxury that Constance could not afford.

Royal adultery is a frequent theme in courtly literature.
In this case, Tristan and Iseult are the guilty couple.

~

'The function of marriage was to ensure that the manly virtue of valor was passed on in honor from one generation to the next.'[16] In this statement by Georges Duby, *valor* is a key word. Power and riches could be transmitted by a variety of means, but valor, probity, and courage – the whole seemingly genetic basket of kingly virtues – could be transmitted only, it was thought, through legitimate sex. In twelfth-century literature, the chastity of the queen, or the lack thereof, becomes almost an obsession that was fanned, according to Peggy McCracken, by the behavior of Eleanor of Aquitaine in her relationship with her uncle at Antioch.

But Eleanor was never formally accused of adultery, and the cases in which formal charges were laid against a queen were very few. The legitimacy of royal succession had such great import that it seems to have inhibited the sexual behavior of medieval queens, or at least the tongues of their courtiers.

In *The Romance of Adultery: Queenship and Transgression in Old French Literature*, McCracken analyzes the many adulterous queens who populate French romances of the twelfth and thirteenth centuries. The mother of them all was Guinevere, who betrays King Arthur for Lancelot. In almost all cases, McCracken points out, these queens are barren: it is not the royal succession that is at stake, but the situation of the court itself: 'In romance narratives accusations of adultery focus on the sexual rather than on the dynastic.' Furthermore, in these romances, 'the integrity of the queen's body symbolizes the integrity of the king's sovereignty.'[17]

When a medieval queen was charged with adultery, the one way she could clear her name was to submit to the *iudicium Dei*, the judgment of God. Her culpability was determined by means of a physical ordeal, such as placing her hand on a hot iron: a cleanly healed wound signified innocence, while an infection meant guilt. Although the use of the ordeal seems to have been very rare by the end of the twelfth century and was abolished altogether by the Church in 1215, the principle behind it would have taken longer to die: 'The ordeal provides a visible judgment inscribed on or by the body: the burned hand, the floating body. Like magic tests of chastity, the unilateral ordeal is a spectacle in which the body is displayed and scrutinized, and in which a truth about that body is revealed.'[18]

Not that anyone had ever, as far as we know, accused Constance of adultery. The crowned heads of Europe often employed such an accusation as a convenient excuse for getting rid of a barren wife, but Henry never resorted to this tactic: no matter how valid he felt his own claims to the Sicilian throne to be, he would have had nothing to gain by repudiating its legitimate heir. Constance's problem was specular, but it did not involve the issue of paternity: rather, she had to demonstrate that her body was *not* intact and that it had indeed conceived a child. She herself, moreover, wished to prove that the child whom she was about to deliver bore not

In this illustration from a French romance, a woman accused of
adultery attempts to prove her innocence by submitting to an ordeal;
physicians from Salerno are pouring hot lead onto her hand.

only the genes, the *probitas*, of the Hohenstaufen, but those of the Hautevilles of Sicily as well.

It may well never have come to Constance's ears, but a great scandal had arisen in England just at this time. A French historian tells us the story as related in a biography of the Bishop of Lincoln:

> Thomas, an elderly man, had a wife, Agnes, who was sterile. His very large estate would therefore revert to his brother on his death. But Agnes disliked her brother-in-law, and detested the prospect of becoming his ward. 'With the cunning of a viper' she conceived a plot. She pretended to be pregnant by hiding a cushion under her robes. Her brother-in-law suspected a ruse, but how could he prove it? Eventually, moaning as if in the throes of labor, Agnes took to her bed and feigned giving birth to a daughter, Grace. Agnes had obtained the baby girl from a poor woman in a nearby village, whom she now hired as a wet nurse.[19]

The story is a long one, with confessions, excommunications, and an evil neighbor who, in order to get his hands on the inheritance, defies canon law by marrying little Grace when she is but four years old. This fraud was documented, and there were doubtless other similar cases that went unrecorded because the inheritance was negligible or the local bishop had no biographer. That such suspicions should fall upon Constance and her child was almost inevitable.

~

News was trickling in from Sicily. Sometime before the first of November, Henry had crossed the Straits of Messina together with his army. The city of Messina had welcomed him with open arms, always glad for an opportunity to cross its archrival, Palermo, which supported the claims of the boy-king, William III. From Messina Henry marched west toward the capital, his troops traveling both by land and by sea.

On learning of his approach, Queen Sybilla sent her son and his crown south to the castle of Caltabellotta, perched high on an isolated mountaintop overlooking the southern shores of the island. At this point, the city of Palermo decided to offer its surrender to the Emperor and sent its envoys to Henry, who by that time was camping in the castle of Favara, just outside the city walls.

Little remains today of Favara, the summer palace built by an Arab emir and reconstructed by Roger II for his own pleasure and delight. The palace is a warren of apartments and stables, and the great reflecting pools in its park are drained and planted with neat rows of cabbages and onions. But we have a contemporary description of its former splendor written by Roger's secretary, the Arab poet Abd ar-Rahmaàn al-Itrabànishi:

Favara of the two lakes, you are the sum of all desires; pleasing sight, most marvelous spectacle.
Your waters divide into nine rivulets; O most beautiful and branching currents!
Where your two lakes meet, there love had made its camp, and beside your canal has passion pitched its tents.
O splendid lake of the two palms, O royal hostel which this embraces!
The limpid waters of your springs resemble lustrous pearls, and the surrounding meadows are the sea.[20]

The poet goes on to describe the garden, the orange and lemon trees, and the fish swimming in the shadow of palm trees. Henry had certainly never seen such exotic opulence before, and although we may reasonably doubt that it triggered his sensuality, it certainly whetted his avidity for the even greater riches that awaited him within the city walls.

The Emperor sent envoys to Queen Sybilla, promising that he would give Tancredi's former fiefs in Lecce and

Henry accepts the homage of the people of Palermo, as the weeping Queen
Sybilla loses her crown in the castle of Caltabellotta. The Emperor's triumphant
entry into Palermo is accompanied by a fanfare of trumpets.

Taranto to her and her son, in return for the surrender of the fortress of Caltabellotta, the crown, and the royal insignia. The Queen Regent accepted his offer in good faith, and on the twentieth of November Henry made his triumphal entry into the city of Palermo, as described by a German contemporary:

> Meanwhile the townspeople, deeply fearful of the Emperor's animosity, surrendered without hesitation and pleaded for his benevolence and for conditions of peace, offering themselves and all their belongings in return. After the city was delivered into his hands, the Emperor granted them his favor, and ordered that the imperial insignia should be flown from every tower.
>
> With great zeal and expenditure the townspeople prepared the triumphal procession: all the streets of the city were festooned with tapestries and different draperies, and inside and out the city was perfumed with incense, myrrh and other essences. . . .
>
> The Emperor, having himself disciplined the army with no lesser zeal, and having decreed that any soldier who demonstrated Teutonic arrogance or showed disrespect for the Palermitani would have his hands cut off, ordered that his men should display the splendor of their arms as they marched slowly through the city. And he followed upon them, dressed in the magnificence of his imperial vestments, while all shouted his praise. The townspeople who were gathered in the streets, seeing the might of the army and the splendor of its leader, shouted his praises and fell on their knees, bowing their faces to the earth.
>
> Once he reached the royal palace, he set about the business of peace. And the townspeople honored him with many gifts, with magnificent horses, golden saddles, bridles embossed with precious metals, and other objects of gold, of silver and of silk.[21]

Together with the news of his triumph, Henry no doubt sent word to his wife of his intention to receive the crown of the Kingdom of Sicily on Christmas Day, as had his father-in-law, Roger II, before him.

~

Preparations were under way in Jesi as well as Palermo, as the holy festivity approached. Polisena was surely readying her patient for the moment of birth, administering both tisanes and encouragements.

> Using great caution the patient should be induced to sneeze, holding her nostrils and mouth tightly closed so that the greater part of the energy and force be directed towards the uterus. . . . Above all she should be protected from chill, and suffumigations of aromatic substances should be placed far from her nostrils, but near the orifice of the vagina, since the uterus has a propension for sweet smells and shrinks from the fetid. . . . Musk, amber, aloe wood and similar substances are suitable for the rich; while aromatic herbs such as mint and oregano will do for the poor.[22]

As an empress, Constance probably rated suffumigations of incense and myrrh, and she might also have had to drink, poor dear, a solution recommended by Trotula (perhaps available only to the lucky few of noble blood who had easy access to falcons) that contained 'that famous white matter that is to be found in the excrements of the sparrowhawk.'

These were cures to accompany a normal delivery, but what if there were problems? In the face of a difficult delivery Trotula first instructed her contemporaries 'to apply for the help of God, and then, with regards to inferior aids,' she suggested a series of sneezings and baths and massages. 'Let the

This woman in labor is surrounded by a number
of midwives, but their assistance appears to be mainly
verbal encouragement.

woman be led about the house with slow steps; those who
assist her should not look her in the face, because women
usually feel shame during and after birth.' Turning a baby in
the uterus appears to have been a common practice: 'If the
baby does not present itself in the proper position, as in the
case where a leg or an arm issues first, then a midwife with a
small and delicate hand should assist, wetting [her hand first]
in a decoction of linseed and fenugreek, and bringing the child
around into the right position.'[23]

The rest of Trotula's remedies deal with more extreme circumstances. Little could be done to save the child, if anything

December

went wrong, and precious little could be done to save the
mother. We have no statistics as to the number of women who
died in childbirth in the twelfth century, but the number was
doubtless very high, and a first birth at an advanced age rendered survival even more problematic. Constance would have
had care to prepare her soul as well as her body for the coming
ordeal.

She would not have had, one hopes, a presentiment of
death, which is said to have been a common feature of
medieval dying; nor would she have taken those steps – the
disposition of her belongings and choice of her sepulchre, the
farewell to those around her, the commending to God of her
own soul and the care of those she loved – that constituted the
necessary attributes of a good death. Not yet.

But surely she sought absolution for her sins through confession, that her soul might be ready to enter the Kingdom of
Heaven if it were called, and surely on the morning of Christmas Day, supported by Nahid and Polisena and surrounded by
the members of her court, she heard the Christmas Mass and
lifted her voice with the others to give thanks for the birth of
the Son of God. Perhaps she was able to attend mass in the
Cathedral of Jesi; more likely a special celebration of the rites
was performed for her in a private chapel. As she prayed, her
thoughts must have wandered to the Cathedral of Palermo,
where her husband was that day receiving the crown of her
kingdom.

～

In the middle of the main piazza of Jesi stands an obelisk,
mounted on an imposing base and guarded by lions. It is said
to mark the spot where, in the last days of December of 1194
and in obedience to the orders of the Empress, a tent was
erected.

Tents were an important symbol of status at that time
(William had given one to Johanna along with the golden

231

table board), and Constance's tent would at the very least have been made of brocaded silk, perhaps like the one that, according to Chrétien de Troyes, had astonished Perceval, 'on one side of scarlet fabric, on the other green, with a border embroidered in gold. At the top of the tent pole, above the pennant, a gilded eagle gleamed in the clear rays of the sun.'[24]

The chronicles tell us that it was in this piazza, and in such a tent – some say in the presence of fifteen bishops, while others claim the entire populace of Jesi as witness – that on the twenty-sixth of December, the feast day of Saint Stephen, the Holy Roman Empress, Constance of Hauteville, gave birth to a male child. His given names were Frederick Roger; posterity remembers him as the Emperor Frederick II, *Stupor mundi*, the Wonder of the World.

PART THREE

THE FUTURE

CHAPTER NINE : JANUARY

This day has restored the joy –
therefore let us, the faithful, sing jubilantly –
to all mankind.
Let us rejoice in our earthly exile,
let us sing praises to God.
> – *Dies ista gaudium*
> Anonymous, twelfth century[1]

Constance had survived her ordeal. She had demonstrated to the world that she could become a mother and could guarantee the Hautevilles' legitimate succession to the throne of Sicily. An illuminated codex in the Vatican Library shows her tucked into bed in a tent, her newborn child in her arms, with the townswomen standing around her. Yet historians, and in particular male historians, seem to have a hard time digesting the story of the tent, dismissing it as far-fetched, a mere legend, or else as mundane – a simple transposition of what was always, given the structure of the medieval castle, a fairly public event. Ever ready to blame Constance for the fate of her father's kingdom, they seem loath to credit her with courage.

Other sources tell us that Constance demonstrated the veracity of her motherhood by nursing the baby in public. As a rule, babies of noble and royal families were turned over immediately to wet nurses, for it was believed that nursing impeded the mother from becoming pregnant and thus from producing as many heirs as possible from the valorous seed of her husband's family.

If Constance did breast-feed the young Frederick, one wonders if it was solely to prove to the world that her body had

The illuminator of this codex opted for the townswomen as witnesses,
and for a very elegant tent with a brocade lining.

indeed gone through the process of childbirth and that her
breasts were now capable of producing milk, or whether she
saw it as a further means of transmitting her own inheritance
to her son. All children were breast-fed in the Middle Ages, if
not necessarily by their mothers. In those times, unburdened
by the erotic imagery of the twentieth century, breasts were
seen as a source of health and life and strength.

Mother's milk – powerful, life-giving, and of female origin –
would not, of course, have been regarded without ambivalence by the thinkers of the period. The anatomists of the
Salerno school, working from Arab sources, identified maternal milk with menstrual blood and hypothesized a special vein
that connected the liver, where blood was manufactured, to
both the uterus and the breasts. During pregnancy, menstrual
blood was diverted to the uterus, where it fed the fetus, while
after birth it went – well cooked and refined from red to white
– to the breasts as milk.

Although Islamic scholars attached no particular stigma to
menstrual blood, those of the Judeo-Christian tradition, even

as they recognized that menstruation was a beneficial purgation, and that failure to menstruate was a sign of illness and malnutrition, saw menstrual blood as a dangerous pollutant. Indeed, the insufficient and corrupt nourishment that it provided during pregnancy rendered the newborn child, unlike the newborn beast, too weak to walk at birth.[2]

Despite such mixed messages from society, nursing her son might well have meant to Constance an ulterior sharing of her lineage, in the tangible bond that is still echoed today in the heartfelt cry of the Sicilian mother, both in joy and in desperation, as she embraces her child: '*Sangue mio!*' Blood of my blood!

In any case, the odds were against her: in the long run, she could not prevail against the violence of the sympathies and antipathies that her son, once grown, would suscitate, nor could she hope to set the record straight once and for all. A chronicle, written twenty-five years after her delivery, tells us that:

This is what is said to have happened. . . . Constance, in her sixties when she married the Emperor, was feared to be permanently sterile. Wherefore the Emperor turned to the counsels of doctors that this sterility be overcome and she be made fecund, lest the Kingdom of Sicily remain without an heir. The doctors lavished their services on her, and by means of medicines they made her uterus gradually swell, so that the Emperor believed that she was indeed pregnant.

In the meantime the doctors procured several pregnant women, so as to have an infant ready, and when it came time for Constance to be delivered, they secretly plotted to seize the infant and introduce him into the palace and to the bed in which Constance had been brought to birth. Thus the child of others was taken for the son of the Emperor and his wife just as if he had been born of Constance herself. They also say that there are doubts as to whether this child was the son of a physician, or of a miller, or of a falconer.[3]

Fortunately Constance never saw this chronicle, and as yet no shadow marred the perfect happiness with which she must have contemplated her baby son as she held him to her breast.

~

How was the newborn child cared for? Right after birth he would have been bathed and then wrapped in a swaddling cloth. Perhaps his head would be covered with a close-fitting cap, for 'the ears of the baby should immediately be compressed, over and over again many times. Care must be taken that no milk enter into the ears or the nostrils during nursing. The umbilical cord should be tied at the height of three fingers, measured from belly: the degree of contraction of the cord will determine if the virile member be greater or smaller.'[4]

> There was no sewn clothing for the newborn baby. A large square of soft fabric covered the umbilical binding and enveloped the baby completely, covering the head like a kind of hood. Later, the baby was swaddled in a woollen blanket. . . . The arms were generally strapped into this bundle and the whole kept in place by broad bands. . . . Rich infants wore very fine white linen, bound with red braid as recommended in medical treatises.[5]

The red of the braid was repeated in the tiny horn of coral that Nahid, if not his mother herself, hung around the baby's neck to ward off the evil spirits. The pendant of coral was important in the Islamic tradition, but Trotula too considered it to be a valid aid to women in childbirth. Renaissance paintings often show the Christ Child wearing a branch of coral, and even today the South of Italy is festooned with similar amulets.

The feast of Epiphany, the sixth of January, was always an occasion for great celebration, and although no document tells us what happened in 1195, it is easy to imagine that the

Even the infant Jesus gets a bath
directly after birth.

prelates, nobles, and all who wished to win the favor of the
Empress would have brought gifts to her son just as the
Magi had brought gifts to the Christ Child. The Epiphany,
or 'manifestation' of the divinity and majesty of Christ, had
long been a feast of great importance in the Eastern Church,
and as such it would have been celebrated in the Greek rite
churches of Constance's childhood. At this time it was also
gaining importance in the West, thanks in great measure to
Constance's father-in-law, Frederick Barbarossa, who in 1164
had ordered that the relics of the Magi be translated from a

church in Milan to the Cathedral of Cologne: 'Milan, in rebelling against her natural lord, who was the Holy Roman Emperor and King of Germany and Italy, had lost all rights of custodianship over the relics of the three perfect vassals of the King of Kings.'[6]

What would have been more logical than for Constance – to whom the symbolic significance of her child's birth, a mere day apart from the Nativity, had not only personal emotional valence but potential political utility as well – to exploit this coincidence to the utmost, presenting her own son and heir to the imperial and royal vassals on the feast day that commemorated the presentation of the baby Jesus to the homage of the Magi.

~

Aside from this hypothetical public appearance, the days that followed were private ones for Constance. She was still considered polluted from childbirth and would be for forty days, until it was time for her to be purified, or 'churched,' at the beginning of February. She remained closed in the women's chambers, resting from the fatigue of her delivery, nursing her child and watching over him as he slept, still not quite able to believe that she had really been able, after so long, to produce this tiny living and breathing creature, and that the festive attention that had always been directed elsewhere was this time centered on herself and her own baby. Far from being an imposition, these forty days of seclusion must have meant hours and hours of uninterrupted joy.

Let us pass these weeks of January with Constance in speculation about her thoughts and emotions as she contemplated her son. How did she feel about herself now that she had become a mother, had produced the heir that had been expected of her? When I speculate about this, I unavoidably turn to my own emotions of some thirty years ago, when I myself became a mother.

I grew up in the 1950s, in that generation and that part of American society where girls and women were ruled by the mixed messages of the so-called Cinderella complex. My father, consumed by a brilliant and absorbing career, was absent from most of my childhood and died while I was in my last year of high school. My mother made it clear to me that I was to fulfill all the intellectual promise that I was showing in school, but that my choices would be limited to what were considered 'good careers for women,' those that would allow me ample time for fulfilling the duties of wife and mother. Science, for example, was out.

Thus I had no paternal expectations to trigger my ambition, and my mother projected acute ambivalence: I was to have the career that she gave up in order to follow my father, but I was not to invalidate in any way her sacrifice by refusing the roles that she had chosen. Like so many women of my generation, I had to do it all.

I was lucky enough to marry a Sicilian who had no expectations of me other than that I be myself – a great refuge in my confusion. But in marrying him, I married into a society that had strong and traditional views about the role of women. During the three years that passed before I succeeded in becoming pregnant, his family watched with barely veiled impatience, and I knew that even my mother's disapproval of this Sicilian marriage was softening when, at the announcement of an impending grandchild, her first thought was to order me a complete set of Beatrix Potter. The lack of any career possibilities for me in Palermo lost importance for her once I was launched on the career of motherhood. Everyone's expectations were fulfilled.

It was 1968, but the ripples launched by Women's Lib had yet to reach Sicilian shores and complicate my reactions: motherhood was straightforward, exhilarating, and, ultimately, empowering. By producing a child (and eventually a second) I had justified my existence. I had a role to play, and I could march into battle to defend my children's rights in situations where I would have been much too timid to defend my own. For a time I even tried to buck the Italian bureaucracy by writing 'mother' instead of 'housewife' in the space given for one's profession on the myriad forms and documents required by life in this country. But while the Italians both celebrate and bewail what they call their *mammismo*, they consider mother-hood to be a destiny or a calling, never a career.

The knowledge that I could function successfully as a mother gave me the courage to expand in other directions. My involvement in Italian society and politics started with the schools; my first literary effort was a children's book.

For some of my friends, the discovery that they were competent mothers gave them the self-confidence to go on to other conquests, while others felt professionally diminished by the sacrifices necessary in caring for small children. Circumstances placed me in the first category, and I have unabashedly appropriated Constance to membership as well. At the moment in which Constance gave birth to a son, she entered the ranks of royal mothers and redeemed her ten years of sterility, her failure as a woman and as a queen. Her entire self-image changed. How could this transformation have been other than empowering?

~

But am I not here doing exactly what all contemporary medieval historians warn against? Am I not projecting across nearly a millennium the feelings and thought patterns of a twentieth-century woman onto those of a very different mentality? How can I dare to hypothesize what Constance felt about herself?

Indeed, did she know she had a self? If she didn't, how can I understand what that means, or even imagine how it feels to be a person without personality, an individual without individuality? Does the self, once discovered, impinge so totally on any attempt at empathy as to nullify it? These questions have accompanied me in my research, and I have wrestled with them, as suspicious of my intellectual temerity as a twelfth-century nun might be about her intellectual pride. As Constance watches over her newborn son during these dark winter days, I shall propose the fruits of this research for my readers' contemplation.

~

For much of the twentieth century, historians argued over the degree to which the growth of humanism – a development previously attributed to the fifteenth century – could be claimed for the period at which we are looking, and whether it was proper to speak of a 'twelfth-century renaissance.' The debate narrowed in scope in the 1970s, with the publication of a book by Colin Morris entitled *The Discovery of the Individual 1050–1200*. In the first paragraph of the concluding chapter, Morris claims:

> The discovery of the individual was one of the most important cultural developments in the years between 1050 and 1200. It was not confined to any one group of thinkers. Its central features may be found in many different circles: a concern with self-discovery; an interest in the relations between people, and in the role of the individual within society; an assessment of people by their inner intentions rather than by their external acts. These concerns were, moreover, conscious and deliberate. 'Know yourself' was one of the most frequently quoted injunctions. The phenomenon which we have been studying was found in some measure in every part of urbane and intelligent society.[7]

Morris's conclusions were greatly qualified, if not rebutted, by Caroline Walker Bynum, in an article published in expanded form in 1982, entitled 'Did the Twelfth Century Discover the Individual?'

The twelfth-century discovery of self or assertion of the individual is . . . not our twentieth-century awareness of personality or our stress on uniqueness; the twelfth-century emphasis is not the modern sense of lifestyle as expression of personality nor the modern assumption of a great gulf between role or model or exterior behaviour and an inner core of the individual. The twelfth-century person did not 'find himself' by casting off inhibiting patterns but by adopting appropriate ones.[8]

The Empress Gisela died in 1043 and was buried in the Cathedral of Speyer. On this burial crown, found inside her tomb, are inscribed the words *Gisle Imperatrix*.

Bynum goes on to say that 'the goal of development to a twelfth-century person is the application to the self of a model that is simultaneously, exactly because it is a model, a mechanism for affiliation with a group.'[9]

To understand, therefore, the implications of motherhood for Constance's image of herself as a queen, we must look at the models that were available to her. Just what did queenship mean at the end of the twelfth century? How did Constance see the role that she was called upon to play?

The early Middle Ages were rife with powerful women. In the ninth century the Lombard queen Angilberga was honored with the title of *consors regni*. In the tenth century

Theophano, a Byzantine princess married to Holy Roman Emperor Otto II, ruled the empire after her husband's death as regent for the young Otto III. The *consors imperii* Gisela, wife of the Salian emperor Conrad II, reigned with her husband in the eleventh century. These are but a few of the women who exercised power and authority in the Germanic tradition. At the beginning of the twelfth century, Constance's own grandmother Adelaide of Savona governed Sicily as regent until her son Roger II came of age.

All of these women reigned in a period that made no neat distinction between the private sphere and the public, between the king's household and his court. A queen was of no help on the battlefield – women were forbidden to bear arms and shed blood – but as manager of the royal household and, most often, as strategist for royal marital alliances, she exercised considerable authority, patronage, and political influence. She took part in the royal councils, expressed her opinions in public, and advised the king in the intimacy of the royal bed-chamber.

By the middle of the twelfth century, this arrangement was changing. The distinction between public and private spheres was growing sharper, and 'the rise of professional administrative bureaucracies, coupled with changes in inheritance patterns and marriage customs, were combining to erode women's freedom to act in the public sphere.'[10]

At the same time, the tendency to idealize and spiritualize womanhood, as seen in courtly literature and in the increasing importance of the cult of the Virgin Mary, might be regarded as a reflection of women's curtailed material power. Placing a woman on a pedestal has always been a good way of getting her out from underfoot.

Modern studies indicate that toward the end of the twelfth century, two major spheres of power remained for a queen. The first was the power she acquired through her son, whether it was institutionalized as a regency or was merely an addition (based on a special relationship between mother and son) to whatever power was conceded her by her husband. The second sphere was that of family diplomacy, in which she prepared her daughters for marriage and chose their husbands: 'despite their membership in patriarchal families that traded them in marriage, noblewomen's unique participation in matrimonial politics did afford them opportunities to claim power and to achieve some degree of self-realization.'[11]

All of the queens I named above, and almost all of those whom I have not listed, were either queens consort or queens regent; they were almost never queens regnant – ruling in their own name rather than deriving their authority from their husband or son. In the first half of the twelfth century, there were only four queens regnant in western Europe, two of whom, Petronila of Aragon and Urraca of León-Castile, lived in the Iberian Peninsula, where Visigothic law was traditionally tolerant of women's rights of inheritance. The other two were closer to the Norman world: Melisende, daughter of King Baldwin II of Jerusalem, and Matilda, daughter of the English king Henry I (and consequently the grandmother of Johanna). Both of these women had been designated by their fathers as legitimate heirs to their thrones. Except for Constance, there would be no more such queens until the very end of the thirteenth century.

No concrete contemporary evidence substantiates the story that at an assembly in Troina in 1185, William II designated his aunt as his heir and made his barons swear fealty to her before she went off to marry the German. Some scholars say that William, certain that he would in time have children, could never have intended to sanction in this manner a possible union of the two realms. Yet such were the uncertainties of the age that to leave the question of succession open when no heirs were on the horizon was surely a risky decision, and election by the barons was an important step in the Norman king-making process. Whether or not this assembly actually took place, however, does not alter the substance of what interests us here.

Constance was the last legitimate member of the Hauteville family. Nothing in Norman law or in the feudal regime forbade her, as a woman, to inherit her family's throne. Now that her husband had conquered Sicily and taken his place on the Norman throne, she was queen consort. Now that she had borne a son, she was potentially queen regent.

Henry's ideas were undoubtedly very clear in this regard: he was now king of Sicily by right of conquest and by right of imperial rule. The Holy Roman Empire's claim to Sicily had first been stated by Frederick Barbarossa, long before he made peace with the Norman king William II and betrothed his son to Constance, and it was echoed by his son. As early as 1191, in negotiating with Pisa and Genoa for the support of their fleets, Henry used the same words his father had used before him, making no reference to the rights he had gained by marriage.

Moreover, among the numerous privileges which the Emperor granted to subjects of the kingdom between 1191 and 1197, only one [from May of 1191] contains a reference to the Empress's right of inheritance, and even then it was coupled with and preceded by an unqualified statement of the imperial claim, since the document in question says that the Emperor was at Montecassino: *pro obtinendo regno Siciliie et Apulie, quod tum antiquo iure imperii tum ex hereditate illustris consortis nostre Constantie Romanorum imperatricis auguste ad imperium devenatur* [in order to obtain the kingdom of Sicily and Apulia, which belongs to the empire both by ancient imperial law and by the inheritance of our illustrious consort, Constance, august Empress of the Romans].[12]

David Abulafia reads the situation differently: he claims that while Henry 'possessed to the full his father's belief in the claim to universal authority of the Holy Roman Emperor,'[13] he considered that his claim to the Kingdom of Sicily came to him through his wife, and that he intended to maintain his two

During the years in which Matilda of England struggled to assert her claim to her father's throne, she coined silver pennies with her image on them. The inscriptions read *Imperatrix* (she had been married to the Emperor Henry V) or *Comitissa* – on her coins she never dared to designate herself queen.

realms separately. Sicily was not to be annexed to the empire but was to remain 'the private possession of the Hohenstaufen dynasty, a power base over which the German nobles had no claim whatsoever.'[14]

No notes indicate on what Abulafia bases this reading of Henry's intentions, but in actual practice it makes little difference to Constance's situation. As far as Henry was concerned, the power in Sicily was his, and he was going to be the one to wield it.

Public opinion about the eventuality of being ruled by a woman is harder to pinpoint, but on the whole the people of the Middle Ages seemed more comfortable with a woman who, they thought, derived her authority from her family context, as wife or mother, regardless of the other realities of her claim to power. Lois Huneycutt has done an interesting study of what churchmen, normally the most forceful castigators of the weaker sex, had to say about Melisende and Matilda, the two candidate queens of the first half of the twelfth century. 'In both cases, the diplomatic evidence shows that the women in question saw themselves as true heirs and rulers in their own right, but the narrative evidence from chronicles, letters and other expository prose shows that the idea of a female wielding power in her own right was literally inconceivable to many twelfth-century commentators.'[15]

Sex is never referred to in discussing the rights of these women to inherit their thrones, and Huneycutt claims that 'contemporaries overlooked the sex of the lawful candidate in order not to sacrifice the larger principles of hereditary right.'[16] Her conclusions are relevant, I believe, to the atmosphere in which Constance was to find herself.

Medieval thinkers did not need to reject explicitly the misogyny they inherited from antiquity in order to construct a legal framework centered on the family. With few exceptions, these commentators never viewed Melisende and Matilda as 'female claimants' or as women exercising power in their own right. Rather, they were portrayed as representatives of their families, agents for their fathers, husbands, and sons. As long as women in positions of public

A queen regent could wield power through her influence
on her son's education. Here Blanche of Castile lectures
her son, the young Louis IX.

authority could be seen as acting for another, they posed no threat to the feudal order.[17]

The behavior of Berenguela of Castile is a case in point. In 1217 she was placed 'by right of inheritance' on her father's throne, but she abdicated soon afterward in favor of her son. She thus ensured the exercise of her considerable power and authority, first as queen regent and then as queen mother, until her death in 1246.[18]

At this point we must return to the debate over the development of the individual. How ironclad were the models of queenship that society proposed to Constance, and what exceptions to the general lack of self-awareness might we postulate? What factors might have induced Constance to look beyond the ambivalence of her contemporaries and see herself as queen in her own right?

The Russian historian Aron Ja. Gurevich believes that Christianity itself posed a major barrier to introspection in its modern form, in that 'this religion, which condemns the sin of pride, thereby renders impossible the spontaneous expression of self awareness.'[19] But he also claims the possibility of exception 'in those places where ethical control, as expressed in the demands for self-restraint and humility . . . had been undermined as a result of an individual's own psychological idiosyncrasies.'[20]

To talk about psychological idiosyncrasies with regard to Constance may be stretching a point, but several aspects of her life need to be examined in this light. First is the fact that she belonged to the category of royal brides: women who, according to the historian John Carmi Parsons, gained both a sense of group belonging and a heightened sense of self-awareness through their participation in matrimonial and succession politics. Constance was a latecomer to this game, for she had no daughters to marry off and not even much in the way of relatives for whom to matchmake, while questions of succession had long been hypothetical. Yet how not to recognize her in Parsons's description of this category?

> [A] man's place in the medieval world was defined by his membership in a single patrilinear family, a woman's place by multiple family allegiances – a point fundamental to medieval women's understanding of themselves. Women's passages from one family to another – daughter, wife, mother, widow – distinguished their lives from men's. Royal women experienced these passages in exaggerated form as they crossed cultural, geographical, and linguistic boundaries as well as familial – transitions that, with attendant choices and decisions, might well give them a strong sense of self.[21]

Here we have come back to the idea of passage, of voyage as the expression and resolution of alienation. Whether it was a pilgrimage undertaken in penitence, a chivalric quest such as that of the Knight of the Lion, or the nuptial voyage of a royal princess, the act of travel presented the individual traveler with conflicting values and cultural norms that could not help but stimulate a greater self-awareness.

Scholars are just becoming interested in the exogamous voyages of these medieval noblewomen. In his chapter 'The Spermatic Journey,' Eric Leed notes, 'The dialectics of gendering may go unnoticed in travel literature, dominated as it is by male activities, while the journeys of women are secret, necessitated, or accomplished through the agency of men.'[22] He gives an example from Icelandic literature, the story of Olaf the Peacock.

> Olaf's travels from Iceland through Norway to Ireland and back are prescribed to him by his mother, Melkorka, the daughter of an Irish king taken as a concubine by Vikings and sold to Hoskuld of Iceland for three marks of silver. Melkorka, in her transportation, is deprived of her native tongue and pretends dumbness until she is overheard speaking Irish to her newborn child, through whom her lost identity and status are made known and recovered. When

Olaf comes of age, Melkorka supplies her son with trade goods . . . [and] with tokens . . . with which to stimulate the recognition of his Irish relatives. . . . On his return home, he is recognized not as a son of Melkorka the concubine but as a great man and the son of a princess.[23]

Olaf's journey, Leed goes on to say, is 'one that makes visible a prior female journey in which a self was stripped away, to be restored by the son.'[24] But the female self was restored, one might add, to the greater glory of the son, and only in second place to the mother. The great travelers are not women but men: Olaf, Gilgamesh, Odysseus, Yvain. 'Within the traditions of Western civilization, and of heroic journeys in particular, travel is clearly an assertion of the power of male narcissism. . . . The connectivities of civility established in travels are a compensation for a rooted absence of connection to the species.'[25]

Man is biologically alienated from the species that he engenders in the instant of ejaculation, and according to Leed, patriarchy is a fiction that serves to hide this fact. 'All of the classical myths instituting civilization represent male sexuality as the generative, world-creating sexuality. The heroic journey is essentially a spermatic journey in which the male seed is broadcast, rooted in localized wombs, generating lineages and connectivities.'[26]

How can we measure a myth? What sort of tool can calibrate the hazy shape of prehistory? Here too it appears that the new science of genetics is giving us an answer: the male heroic journey is indeed a myth. An Italian newspaper recently interviewed Luigi Luca Cavalli-Sforza, an Italian geneticist who teaches at Stanford University. He and his team have been working on the mutations of the male, or Y, chromosome, research that 'has made possible a reconstruction of the geneological tree of humanity: a tree which superimposes and completes that obtained thanks to the mitochondrions. Work

252

on the Y chromosome furnishes us with authoritative confirmation, also because, despite appearances, the male is more stable, and travels less than the female. Genetics demonstrates that the woman, in primitive societies, moves more than the man, probably because of exogamy.'[27] So the real – as opposed to the mythic – heroic journey becomes the ovular journey, the cross-cultural bridal journey.

This discussion seemingly has taken us a long way from Constance, and we cannot possibly claim for her, as she moved from Sicily to Germany and then south again, any sense of being an archetypal traveler or even of being heroic. For ten years travel had been a part of her daily life, too natural to elicit any self-examination. And yet I am convinced that in the year 1194 the coincidence of passage is very relevant; that the physical suspension between two worlds resonated upon how she passed from barren to fruitful, from queen consort to queen regent, from failure to completion, enabling her to stand back from the world around her. I am convinced that this coincidence of journey and pregnancy was doubly empowering to her, influencing the way in which she was to act in the future. At the end of her travels, she had gained a greater sense of herself, as a woman and as an individual. Perhaps she could even imagine herself as a queen regnant.

CHAPTER TEN : FEBRUARY

> Then they laid the child in a little cradle,
> wrapped in a white linen cloth;
> beneath his head
> they placed a fine pillow
> and over him a coverlet,
> hemmed all around with marten fur. . . .
> As they traveled from town to town
> they stopped to rest seven times a day;
> they had the child nursed,
> changed and bathed.
>
>   – *The Lai of Milun*
>   Marie de France, twelfth century[1]

With the onset of February, Constance's period of seclusion came to an end. The second day of the month was the feast of the Candelora, or Candlemas, commemorating the presentation of the infant Jesus at the temple, and the purification of the Virgin Mary. No day could be more suitable for the churching of the Empress.

In truth, Constance was pushing things a bit, as her forty days were not quite up. But the Middle Ages attached much greater importance to the symbolism of dates than to their accuracy. We know the precise birth date of very few medieval people, and if Frederick's has been recorded so carefully, it is probably because of its proximity to Christmas and his father's coronation in Palermo.

The Empress was in fact lucky: had she borne a daughter, she would have been excluded from entering a church for eighty days, one more example of medieval misogyny. Yet this

manic attention to detail leads at times to touching conclusions, as in Jacobus de Voragine's thirteenth-century
description of the original purification ceremony:

> [T]he Blessed Virgin offered to the Lord a pair of turtle
> doves, which was the offering of the poor, a yearling lamb
> being the offering of the rich. It might be asked, in this
> regard, whether the Virgin Mary, who had received a large
> sum of gold from the Magi, could not have bought a lamb.
> But we may think, as St. Bernard says, that instead of
> keeping this gold for herself, the Blessed Virgin had at once
> given it to the poor, or perhaps saved it for the seven years of
> her sojourn in Egypt.[2]

The purification of Candlemas, a Christian feast of Judaic
origin, is embedded in an earlier, Celtic commemoration, that
of Imbo, the feast of the purifying fires of winter, sacred to the
goddess Brigite of the luminous crown. On February 2nd the
Cathedral of Jesi would have been filled with candles, relics of
the pagan bonfires that burned away the evils of winter and
announced the coming of spring. I have been unable to find a
description of the medieval rite, but the Book of Common
Prayer gives as the Gospel reading for that day a passage from
St. Luke. It begins: 'And when the days of her purification
according to the law of Moses were accomplished, they
brought him to Jerusalem to present him to the Lord.' The
closing words also would have held special meaning for Constance: 'And the child grew, and waxed strong in spirit, filled
with wisdom: and the grace of God was upon him.'[3]

The Christian religion eventually replaced this presentation
with the rite of baptism, but the reports of Frederick's baptism
are contradictory and incomplete. The confusion may be due to
a change in names: some chroniclers say that Constance gave
him the names of Constantine and Roger to emphasize his
southern heritage, Byzantine and Latin, while Henry at a later
date imposed the names of both grandfathers, Frederick and

The presentation of the infant Jesus in the temple, as depicted in the mosaics of the Palatine Chapel, a scene that Constance had known since childhood.

Roger, thus stressing his Hohenstaufen blood as well as that of the Hautevilles.

Most modern historians believe that the child was not baptized until 1197 or after, a postponement due to Henry's desire to see his son baptized by the pope and at the same time crowned emperor. But three major contemporary chronicles all refer to the birth and the baptism in the same sentence, and if the Chronicle of Stade speaks of fifteen bishops and cardinals, it may imply a recycling of the same prelates who had been summoned as witnesses to the birth, rather than a later and elaborate ceremony.

However ambitious Henry's plans might have been, I find it very hard to believe that Constance would have tolerated her one and only child being left unbaptized for long. Infant mortality was very high, and although by the twelfth century the hellfire that Saint Augustine had believed to be the fate of the unbaptized infant had been replaced with a less cruel limbo, baptism was thought to ensure not only eternal salvation but a better chance for survival on earth. The sacrament was seen as a sort of antibody that rendered the child less susceptible to disease and death.

The actual baptism, which normally took place one week after birth, was presided over by the child's godparents rather than the blood parents, since the mother, not yet churched, could not be present at the ceremony.

[T]he baby was still presented virtually naked to this washing and oiling with sacred oils, before being wrapped in its swaddling clothes again. The fine linen cloth then wound around the baby to envelop it completely symbolised the spotless purity of the new Christian, cleansed of original sin.[4]

Baptism was an important ceremony and an occasion for celebration. 'In prosperous circles it was customary for the godparents and relatives to send the mother presents: cakes and sweetmeats, candles and torches for the celebration, rich fabrics and lavishly ornamented trays known as the "birth tray."'[5]

Would this ceremony have taken place at Epiphany or later, at Candlemas? In any case, most likely only with herself churched and the child baptized would Constance have dared to undertake the dangers of the road once more.

≈

Where did she go next? At this point I must offer an hypothesis: sometime during the month of February, a messenger arrived in Jesi, bringing with him orders from the Emperor in Palermo. The messenger was to escort the Empress and her child to Foligno, where the young Frederick was to be left in the care of the Duchess of Spoleto, and then Constance was to proceed to Bari, where on Easter Day she would be crowned queen of Sicily.

This messenger was probably the Duke of Spoleto himself,

Conrad of Urslingen. Conrad was one of the most faithful of the *ministeriales*, the men who formed the backbone of the imperial bureaucracy. In 1183 he had been named duke of Spoleto, at the same time as his more famous colleague, Markward of Annweiler, was named duke of Molise; by this move the Germans ensured their control of the eastern half of central Italy, guaranteeing themselves a safe corridor for the control of the South.

Most *ministeriales*, Markward among them, were not free men. They were given a fief in payment for their services, but it was not hereditary, and they were bound by law to the service of the emperor. Conrad, an exception to this rule, was an *Edelfreier*, a descendant of a family of what might in later ages be called landed gentry, who owned their own land in freehold but did not belong to the nobility.

Other than this, we know little about Conrad. Judging from the documents from the imperial chancery in which his name appears as witness, he seems to have spent most of the ten years following his appointment in his new duchy keeping order there and coming to the Emperor's assistance when needed. He was present at the coronation in Rome in 1191 and then at the siege of Naples, and he had rejoined Henry and his army in 1194 during the rapid march on Sicily. He remained at the Emperor's side for the Palermo coronation, and on the second of February he was part of the Candlemas court held in Messina. But he was not witness to the documents drawn up on the fifteenth of February, still at Messina, or those of February 25th at Catanzaro, on the mainland. Why not suppose that he had been sent ahead to meet the Empress at Jesi or Foligno?

Nothing at all is known about Conrad's wife, but since it is on record that the young Frederick spent the first years of his life in the Umbrian town of Foligno, which lies about eighteen miles north of Spoleto, and that he was in the care of the Duchess of Spoleto, it is thought that Conrad had married into the local nobility. Most probably his wife was a daughter of the Antignano family of Foligno, to whom Henry VI awarded a large fief in 1197, possibly in gratitude for the care they bestowed upon his son.

Constance would surely have wanted to accompany the baby as far as Foligno herself. She had more than a month before her appointment in Bari, and she would have wanted to see the child safely installed and ensure a smooth transition from her own breast to that of a wet nurse, for the child would not be weaned from human milk until he was about two years old.

It is remotely possible that the Duchess herself was to serve as wet nurse: 'The children of royalty were sometimes nursed by women of the minor nobility, who (apparently), in contrast to other wetnurses, brought their own infants to the royal residence and suckled both their own and the royal children together.'[6] Great care would have been taken, in any case, to select the best possible candidate, ideally a woman about twenty-five years of age, who had been delivered of her own child about two months before the birth of the child to be suckled, and who was fair of complexion and amiable in character, possibly similar in temperament to the child's mother. Had Henry been present, he would have been active in the process of selecting the wet nurse, to which great importance was attached; as it was, he had probably delegated the responsibility to Conrad.

∾

It was time for Marcella and me to return to the road. We walked back into the center of Jesi, hoping to find that, siesta over, some new door had been opened into the twelfth century, but the town was still closed up and sleepy. A last stroll around the piazza, a last glance at the very phallic and most unevocative monument, surrounded by rather dismal lions, that marks the spot of Frederick's birth – a tribute to the son's virility rather than the mother's courage, I would say – and we were off toward Foligno.

The twelfth century was waiting for us in Móie, a little village just up the road from Jesi, where we stopped to look at a small and sweet Romanesque church with a very simple façade. A young girl on a bike was riding in circles outside the front door, waiting while her friend inside the church made her confession. Her whisperings echoed unintelligibly against the brick walls and up into the little dome, the intricate patterns of the brickwork unspoiled by any superfluous decoration.

The landscape around Móie was a joy to our eyes, as it must have been to those of Constance: once more we saw olive trees, their shaggy silver-green shapes fitting into our vision like the missing piece in a jigsaw puzzle, and cypresses too, solitary in a garden, marching down a road or clustering in a cemetery. But this landscape didn't last, and it soon became clear why Constance had stopped at Jesi. The valley of the Esino River narrows here, and the road begins to climb through wooded hills: we threaded our way on and off an autostrada that was gradually eating up the old road, passing through tunnels where the valley floor is too narrow to accommodate a widening of the roadbed. Another little detour took us to San Vittore delle Chiuse, advertised in the guidebook as 'one of the most significant Romanesque monuments in the Marches.' The church and its adjacent abbey sit in a meadow in a small opening in the mountains, where a stream from the northwest feeds into the Esino; a path leads under an arched tower and across a footbridge to a handful of houses on the stream's farther bank.

The abbey had a tall fortified tower to guard the confluence of the waters, and the church, dating from the eleventh century and showing its Byzantine roots, was in the form of a Greek cross. The interior was similar to that of Móie, but here the patterning of the walls was designed in stone, the same gray stone of all the buildings in the valley. It was a pleasure to come back to gray after so much pink marble and brick.

Clouds were drifting through the passes, and the air was

The Abbey of San Vittore delle Chiuse,
guarding our passage through the mountains.

chilly even if it was June. In February there might well be snow here, if not down on the valley floor, at least on the Apennine peaks that rose sharply in the near distance, some more than three thousand feet. In the twelfth century these roads would not admit a litter: Constance would have returned to her saddle, her fur-lined great-cloak wrapped around herself and the baby in her arms. Or would the baby, wrapped in linens and woolen blankets faced with miniver and marten, be riding in a basket entrusted to Nahid and her sure-footed mule?

The landscape opened up a little more as we approached Fabriano, a town that even in the time of Constance was famous for its papermaking – by the second half of the 1300s its annual production was over a million sheets. We had hoped to spend the night there and visit the paper museum the next morning – and were even more eager to do so once we discovered that the center of town was all decked out for the first evening of its traditional festival, the Palio di San Giovanni. Brightly colored banners hung from the windows of medieval

and Renaissance houses, and some of the streets were garlanded with greenery; here and there young people were
strolling about in medieval costume, waiting for some sort of
parade to begin.

We wanted so to stay and participate, but the hotels were
few, hard to find, and sold out, and the sun was about to set.
With great regret we drove on, following along a wider valley
to Gualdo Tadino. Here too there were banners everywhere,
all of them red and white, and our spirits lifted – until we
learned that, although the town is divided into neighborhoods
known as *ponti* and has its own *palio* in September, these
banners were celebrating the local soccer team, which was to
play the next day in a match that could (and did) win it promo-
tion into the B League.

Early the next morning a drive through more wooded hills
brought us to Foligno, a good-sized town in the center of
Valle Umbra, Roman in origin and medieval in aspect. On
Sunday mornings much of the old center is closed except to
foot traffic, and we drove in several circles before we found a
place to leave the car, on a side street that runs under the walls
of the Monastery of Santa Lucia, a huge complex in pale pink
stone. The walls were high enough that only the roofs of the
buildings were visible, but it looked well cared for and quite
wonderful.

We spent the morning walking around Foligno, looking for
the few remains of the twelfth century. The small church of
Santa Maria Intraporta was the only well-preserved building
from that period. The cathedral had been altered so many
times that nothing was left of the original to see, and even its
façade, lovely as it was, with three rose windows and the sun,
moon, stars, and signs of the zodiac moving in concentric
arches over the main portal, belonged to the 1300s.

The later Middle Ages were kind to Foligno. Although it
had belonged to the Duchy of Spoleto when Constance came
through, not many years passed before it became an independent commune and a prosperous commercial center. Merchant

families built handsome palazzi along the narrow cobbled streets, which wind at odd angles around the cathedral square and the crenellated tower, the Torre Civico, symbol of the town's civic pride.

We were lucky to see it when we did. Not much more than a year later, in September of 1997, the world watched as this tower crumbled and fell, a rain of bricks caught by the television cameras that had been rushed into the area after the earthquake that shook all of Umbria and did such terrible damage to the Basilica of St. Francis in nearby Assisi. This very day, as I am writing, a solemn ceremony is under way to celebrate the reopening of the basilica; its frescoes have been restored, its priceless beauty is saved. The Italian government is justly proud to demonstrate to the world the excellence of its restorers and the remarkable commitment and speed with which they have worked, but many Italians are asking themselves when their country will show the world equal speed and efficiency in civil reconstruction. The old centers of Foligno and Gualdo and Nocera are still roped off, and the families who lived there are facing their third winter housed in containers.

Map in hand, we took a different route back to the car, passing through the Piazza Garibaldi. Inside the Church of St. Augustine, a wedding was taking place, and outside, dwarfed by the solemn façade of dark stone columns and marble statues, an ancient and tiny black Fiat 500 was parked. The car was decked with white ribbons tied in bows, and the luggage rack on the roof held a large glass demijohn encased in straw like a Chianti bottle, a red-and-white rope-edged lifesaver, a large umbrella of striped cotton, an old-fashioned black suitcase with brown leather edgings, and a canary singing in a birdcage. The friends who had organized this enchanting spectacle were waiting outside, hardly able to contain their pride and their impatience for the ceremony to be over, so that the bride and groom would come out and discover their handiwork.

We lingered for a while, wanting to see the scene, but the

ceremony showed no sign of ending, and as usual we were in a hurry, so we packed ourselves and the sandwiches we had bought at a bar into the car and set off to look for the road – hardly more than a country lane – that would lead us to San Giovanni Profiamma, which was on the map, and the Rocca Agnano, which wasn't.

There had once been an imperial palace in Foligno, perhaps built in the thirteenth century by Frederick II as a monument to the city of his infancy. But its few remaining stones were cloistered, incorporated into the Franciscan monastery, and so we had to settle for the Rocca Agnano, which, according to a friend of my daughter who lived in Foligno and had done some research for me, is thought to be the remains of the Antignano family castle. A *rocca*, or 'rock,' is a small fortress, often simply a tower built on a stony outcropping. Central and southern Italy are full of them, vestiges of the early feudal age, constructed when the economy destroyed by the barbarian invasions began to pick up the pieces and rebuild itself, and destined to be the strongholds of local lords. In some places a village would grow up around the *rocca*, which would then be transformed into a proper castle; elsewhere the settlement died out, and the *rocca* dwindled into a solitary ruin on the horizon.

We found the road and San Giovanni Profiamma, but hunger overtook us before we were able to find the *rocca*, so we parked on the roadside and ate our sandwiches overlooking a valley with cherry trees full of fruit and a cuckoo calling in the distance – not the view we had wanted, but very pretty. Reluctant to give up, I insisted that we go a little farther up the valley, and presently we saw some ruins sticking up in the woods on the hillside opposite the road. The trees hid all but the upper rim of what seemed to be a square tower, a dark reddish brown in color; at a distance it was impossible to distinguish whether the building material was brick or stone.

The tower was completely surrounded by trees, and there was no sign of human habitation elsewhere in the little valley that lay between us and the ruin. In its dark solitude it bore a striking resemblance to Trifels, even though the Agnano tower was built halfway up the hill and not, like Trifels, on the summit. I couldn't help but wonder if Constance too had been struck by this similarity when she arrived, and how she had felt, knowing that she would have to leave her baby there.

~

In 1960 the French demographic historian Philippe Ariès published a book known in its English translation as *Centuries of Childhood*. It made an enormous splash when it came out, and when I read it some years later, it almost induced me to abandon the idea of writing a book about Constance. According to Ariès, the people of the Middle Ages had no particular idea of childhood as a special stage of development. The high rate of infant mortality provoked a defensive reaction of indifference toward small children, who might so easily die: 'People could not allow themselves to become attached to something that was a probable loss.'[7] The ones that survived until the age of seven became part of an undiscriminating adult world. 'The age groups of Neolithic times, the Hellenistic *paideia*, presupposed a difference and a transition between the world of children and that of adults, a transition made by means of an initiation or an education. Medieval civilization failed to perceive this difference and therefore lacked this concept of education.'[8]

What bothered me above all was the idea of maternal indifference. I could imagine it in a mother whose child was the fruit of rape, or who in her own childhood had had no experience of affection or bonding. But that the mothers of the Middle Ages would uniformly and deliberately steel themselves to remain unattached to their babies, given the poor probability that they would survive, was more than I could accept. Mine was a gut reaction, instinctive and unscholarly; if this were true, I had understood nothing of Constance, and the empathy on which this whole project was constructed was merely an anachronistic illusion, a projection of my own experience of motherhood onto someone of a different era who had felt nothing of the sort. The more scholars I consulted, the more it was made clear to me that my idea and experience of motherhood – far from being universal – was entirely determined by the particular historical moment and the particular society into which my own mother had borne me.

Fortunately I was not alone in my reaction. A host of medieval historians, most of them women, bridled and rose to the challenge. Ariès's analysis was weighted heavily in favor of iconography: his challengers marshaled innumerable citations from educational and childcare manuals, from saints' lives and miracle stories, from courtly poems and Cistercian sermons, that evidenced the delight and affection with which the people of the Middle Ages observed and cared for their children.

The ideal of motherhood was the Madonna, the universal mother, loving and nurturing, feeding her child with what was essentially her own blood. Caroline Walker Bynum shows (in a book that lies outside the Ariès controversy) how the mother-child relationship became a favorite analogue for the relationship between God and the soul, and between the abbot and his monks. 'Medieval images of the maternal also stressed mother-love as instinctive and fundamental: the mother is tender and loving, sometimes dying to give the child life; she tempts or disciplines only with the welfare of the child in mind.'[9]

Bynum is quick to point out that this idealized vision of motherhood does not in any sense correspond to an 'increased respect for actual women.' The clerics who used the maternal imagery had renounced the world and the flesh; and 'there was in the general society no mystique of motherhood; both medical texts and exhortations to asceticism dwell on the horrors of pregnancy and the inconveniences of marriage.'[10]

Other studies have further pointed out that the growing cult of nurturing motherhood reflected not only a masculine idealization of a female role but also an appropriation of

This miniature of the Madonna and Child, painted in Sicily in
the years following Constance's death, bears the same tragic
expression as the statues of the Madonna Addolorata that are
still paraded through the Sicilian streets on Good Friday.

female power. '[T]he male powerholder, unable to participate in the reproduction of the species as intimately or visibly as the female, is consequently envious and fearful of women's reproductive power. Therefore, women's biological role is decentered in favor of the nurturing role, which can be shared by men and women alike.'[11]

But outside monastery walls, and despite clerical exhortations, strictures, and fantasies, men and women were procreating, and many texts evince parental concern and love for the children of all that lust, and interest in the way in which they develop. Trotula herself has suggestions that are not strictly medical: indeed, she and other writers urge conditions of childbirth that sound quite modern, insisting on the necessity of avoiding a violent contrast of light and temperature between the conditions of birth and those of the womb.

> As soon as he is born the eyes should be covered; and great care should be taken to keep him from too much light. Different paintings, materials of different colors and pearls should be hung before him. In his presence one should use rhymes and simple words, and not sing in a strident or hoarse voice. . . . One should speak frequently to him and pronounce easy words.[12]

As one might expect, a greater supply of affection was available to male children. Females were generally weaned earlier – one text cautions mothers to feed their daughters only the minimum necessary to keep them alive[13] – and their childhood, such as it was, ended earlier. Marriage and motherhood came at a very early age, although among the nobility at least, childhood marriages such as that of eleven-year-old Johanna were usually not consummated until the bride reached an age when bearing children would not put her life at risk.

It was the male child that received the most enthusiastic welcome, as we can see from the description of the birth of Parzival, the Knight of the Grail:

When the queen recovered consciousness and took her baby into her arms, then she and the other ladies intently observed the tiny pizzle between his legs. He could not be other than fondled and cherished, for he was possessed of the organ of a man. Later on, he was to be a very smith for the swords with which he struck fire from helmets, and his heart had manly courage. It was the queen's delight to kiss him over and over again, and always she kept calling him '*Bon fils, cher fils, beau fils.*'[14]

Medieval writers observed and appreciated other attributes as well – the way babies react to music and sounds, their halting attempts at speech, their smiles and their laughter – and they expressed curiosity about how they learn. The baby Frederick himself is said, as a grown man, to have undertaken an experiment: he had children from different backgrounds raised by wet nurses, who were ordered to care for them lovingly but never to speak to them. The object was to discover in what language a child would naturally begin to talk, but all the children died before any conclusions could be drawn.

Queen and peasant alike must surely have delighted in their child's first word, but parenting was haphazard at best, and for the great majority of babies born in the Middle Ages, life was as brief and grim as it is for many third world children today. Taking as her source the accounts of the many miracles involving children that were attributed to the Virgin Mary, Clarissa Atkinson sums up the situation:

The numerous children and infants in the stories present a poignant and complicated glimpse of medieval childhood. Children faced mutilation and death by fire and water, disease and accident; they were promised to the Devil by wicked or careless parents; they were neglected and abused as well as loved and cherished by parents and parental surrogates. Their presence in such numbers, with the assumption that they and their circumstances are touching and pitiful, argues against the 'indifference' to children sometimes attributed to medieval adults. On the other hand, the stories do not supply evidence of careful and empathetic parenting – far from it: Mary is a much more satisfactory parent than any of the adults.[15]

The controversy stirred up by Philippe Ariès's book dies hard. In his introduction to a collection of essays entitled *Medieval Man*, Jacques Le Goff dissents from the conclusions of one of his contributors: 'I continue to think that Philippe Ariès was correct in affirming that in medieval Europe the child was not a highly valued object – which did not prevent parents from loving their children, but loving them particularly in view of the adults that they would become.'[16]

Considering the pressure to perform under which so many young children labor today, and the growing request for genetically engineered and even cloned babies, I can only remark that we of the twentieth century are still quite close to the Middle Ages.

∾

The news that Conrad of Urslingen brought with him to Foligno was not good. Sicily had been pacified, but at a price. In January Henry had ransacked the royal palace and its treasury: the treasure of the Norman kings, the gold coins and jewels and precious silks, were on their way to Germany. Traveling with them as captives went the nobles and prelates who had been the most fervent partisans of Tancredi and his family, arrested on what were probably trumped-up charges of conspiracy against the Emperor, together with the former royal family: Sybilla, her young son William III, her three daughters, and her young daughter-in-law, Irene of Byzantium.

It was Irene who fared the best. The widow of Tancredi and Sybilla's eldest son, Roger of Apulia, who had died shortly before his father, the beautiful young princess, who had the added advantage of being the daughter of Isaac Angelus, Emperor of the Eastern Roman Empire, caught the eye of Henry's brother, Philip of Swabia. The two were betrothed in Palermo and returned to Germany together to be married in Augsburg. Irene, described by the poet Walther von der Vogelweide as a 'rose without a thorn, a dove without gall,' became the star of the German court, shining with a light that Constance had never been able to achieve.

The deposed boy-king, William, was taken to the fortress of Hohenems, near Lake Constance, imprisoned, and not surprisingly died shortly thereafter. Sybilla and her daughters were enclosed in the Alsatian convent of Hohenberg and were eventually released. The daughters Elvira and Constance married well, while the third, Medania, who reportedly 'had no man,' perhaps became a nun.

We know absolutely nothing of Conrad of Urslingen's

Tancredi's supporters are accused of conspiracy against the Emperor and are brought as captives before him for sentencing.

personality and can only hope against all expectations that he was a gentle man, sensitive enough to understand Constance's divided loyalties, and to tell her of these tragedies with tact. One wishes at least that he might have spared her the cruder details, which if she learned them at all might have come via Nahid from the boasting of the soldiers in the escort: how the Germans, when they entered Palermo, had slaughtered or carried off the animals in the palace menagerie; how Henry had ordered that the tombs of the usurpers, Tancredi and his son Roger, be opened and despoiled of the royal insignia; and how the five-year-old William was to be blinded and emasculated before being left in a cell to perish.

~

With no authority, no stand from which to countermand the orders of the Emperor, Constance had little choice but to leave her child in Foligno. A tiny baby was in any case ill suited to mountain travel in the early spring, when snow still lay in the passes to be crossed, and the streams to be forded were gorged with spring floodwaters. The loyalty of the Apulians and the Calabrians to the son of Henry VI was yet untested, and her own experience as captive and hostage must have loomed large in her memory.

Does that mean that Constance was indifferent to this parting or that it was painless for her? For an answer, we might turn to one of the earliest medieval texts to be written by a woman, a manual from around 841 by a Frankish noblewoman named Dhuoda. In the summer of 841, Dhuoda's husband, Berhard of Septimania, ordered that their fifteen-year-old son be sent as a hostage to the court of Charles the Bald; their second son, just a few months old, was also taken away from his mother. Some historians see these actions as proof of Berhard's unusual cruelty and the powerlessness of medieval women in general, although others suggest that the illness of which Dhuoda speaks in her writing was leprosy, which would certainly explain the hasty removal of the as-yet-unbaptized infant.

Dhuoda was an extraordinary woman, endowed with sensitivity and a strong personality, and she was very learned in a period when few laymen, and even fewer women, were literate. The manual that she wrote for her son's edification opens for scholars a window onto the Carolingian world. It predates our period by over three centuries, but nonetheless I think its opening words are significant:

> Having noticed that most women in this world are able to live with and enjoy their children, but seeing myself, Dhuoda, living far away from you, my dear son William, filled with anxiety because of this, and with the desire to be of aid to you, I am sending you this little manual, written by me, for your scrutiny and education, rejoicing in the fact that, though I am absent in body, this little book will recall to your mind, as you read it, the things you are required to do for my sake.[17]

The Pietro of Eboli codex contains a picture of Constance, riding sidesaddle on a dappled steed. Armed knights are leading the horse to the right, but the Empress turns backward, across the horse's rump, holding in her hands a baby wrapped in swaddling clothes and wearing a tiny crown. A woman standing behind the horse holds a blanket in her outstretched arms, ready to receive the royal child.

Constance's brows are knit, and the corners of her mouth turn down in a distinctly troubled expression. The artist has made a special effort toward realism here, in contrast to the rather complacent countenances in the dramatic scenes of death and triumph depicted in the manuscript. It is not indifference that he has portrayed, but grief.

CHAPTER ELEVEN : MARCH

I nurtured a falcon   for more than a year.
When I had him tamed   exactly as I wished
and had gracefully decked   his feathers with gold,
he raised himself so high   and flew to other lands.

Since then I've seen that falcon   flying freely;
he was wearing silken   jesses on his feet
and the whole of his plumage   was all red gold.
May God bring those together   who want each other's love.
                                    – Der von Kürenburch, twelfth century[1]

The last embraces were over, and the painful parting accomplished. If – as one hopes – Constance was consoled by the thought that her fledgling was in good hands, then it would feel good to be in the saddle once more, to start out again with new purpose and urgency. This was no longer the slow and dawdling journey of the previous year, in which the rhythm of her gestation set the pace and haste was of no avail, nor February's short ride, worrisome and vulnerable, with its frequent stops to nurse and change the baby.

Marcella and I, too, intended to set a steady pace once we finished our Sunday picnic at the Rocca Agnano. We had promised Marcella's parents to spend that night and the next at their home in Stroncone, just south of Terni, and I needed to be back in Palermo by Friday night. It was as if we, too, had been cradled in an inner time, inflated far beyond the five days that it had actually taken us to travel from Milan to Foligno. Now, with the baby safely born and lodged at Foligno, priorities shifted, and the outer world impinged. Like Constance, we had appointments to meet, family commitments to honor. Henceforth it would be even harder to choose between pressing on and stopping to look.

~

We were driving south, following once more the Via Flaminia up the Valle Umbra past Spoleto and Terni, where it turns west toward Rome. Stop we did, of course, and almost immediately, at Trevi, a small town tightly gathered on top of a hill that looks down over the olive groves and vineyards of the valley floor.

It was family impinging again, for what I really wanted to see here was a show at the Trevi *Flash Art* Museum of Contemporary Art, a small museum founded by the editor of *Flash Art* magazine, which my son had mentioned to me. But we were much more pleased with the art we found in the making. Trevi was celebrating the feast of Corpus Domini on Sunday, and preparations similar to those we had seen in Chiaravalle della Colomba were under way: the townswomen of Trevi were down on their hands and knees, laying out the *infiorata* for the afternoon's procession in the middle of the street.

Whether it was because the dampening austerity of the Cistercian heritage was lacking, or because spring was further along this far south, or simply because of tradition, the somber evergreens of Chiaravalle had given way to riotous color. The sides of the street were piled with sacks and cartons filled with flower petals – yellow broom, white and pink roses, pale orange carnations, and bright red poppies. There were crates and crates of brilliant green fennel weed chopped in small bits, and a sack of coffee grounds with which to draw dark outlines around the patterns.

The project was much more ambitious than that of Chiaravalle, for it was executed outdoors, on the asphalt and then on the patterned cobblestones of the street that led through the main gate of the city. The route passed under the arch and then curved uphill to the main square, ending at the doors of the cathedral. It appeared to have been divided up among groups of women, each doing the designs of its choice. Some were quite simple, while others were more complicated: a yellow sun in a green field, a star, a crescent moon, a geometric pattern of pink and white stripes boxed in a yellow square. The single motifs, each a few feet apart from its neighbors, were almost completed, but the outlines chalked on the cobbles indicated that each one would be joined to the next by greenery.

The bustle and excitement were contagious. Young children, hardly able to contain themselves, were dancing around the edges and leaping over the petals heaped in piles of dazzling color. They had been armed with plastic spray bottles filled with water to squirt on the flowers, keeping them fresh and heavy enough that the slight breeze that stirred the larger flakes of poppy and rose would not ruin the designs. It looked like a borderline situation to me, with water battles or worse threatening to take over at any minute, but as long as it held, the scene was enchanting.

The pièce de résistance was being laid out just in front of the gate: a very ambitious still life with a huge urn made of pinecones and filled with fruit – oranges, peaches, cherries, bananas, a large slice of watermelon, and even a pineapple. We wondered if here we weren't seeing the influence of the *Flash Art* Museum. The architects were two young women, dressed in gray knit jogging clothes and black baseball caps worn backward, intense and serious and rather smug as they crept about their creation – an act of faith and of one-upsmanship.

The Trevi cathedral, twelfth century reworked, was pleasant outside, uninteresting in. A distracted young priest full of tics and fidgets offered to show us the Church of San Francesco, and we accepted. It was deconsecrated and not terribly distinguished. It had bits and pieces of frescoes and a large plate for offerings next to the guest book. The ownership of the building was about to pass from the diocese to the town, and the priest wanted to make hay while the sun shone. Once the hay was in the plate, he left us.

We were half-tempted to stay long enough to watch the procession, although it would have been heartrending to see all that bright flowering trodden underfoot. But it would have been worse still to see all those petals being washed down the streets by the thunderstorm that seemed imminent. As we drove out of Trevi, dark rain clouds were gathering to the south, and the air was very hot and still.

$\sim$

Trevi was our detour for the day. From there on in, we steeled our hearts and kept our eyes straight forward, unyielding to the siren call of the fountains and temple of Clitunno (not our period), nor to the many attractions of Spoleto, where surely Constance had stopped, a guest in the palace of the Duke.

Shortly below Spoleto, the wide valley came to a narrow end, and the road ran through deep woods of chestnuts and oaks, much lusher now than they would have been in March as Constance rode through, and brightened by big clusters of robinia trees in bloom, splotches of yellow gorse, and the white flowers of the elderberry bushes. In what seemed to be the middle of nowhere, an elderly peasant woman hailed us from a stool where she sat alone at the edge of the road, dark woods stretching in all directions around her. She wore long skirts to protect her from the chill of late afternoon, and a bright blue-and-red kerchief was tied under her chin. She was surrounded by crates of cherries, pails of wild asparagus shoots, and baskets of eggs. Deep under scarves in one of the baskets was a still smaller basket, where she had hidden a handful of pungent black truffles wrapped in silver foil. She complained about her abscessed tooth and her corns and her rheumatism and called us 'darlings, my treasures, my loves' –

and sold us two of her truffles at what we later discovered was an exorbitant price.

'*Contadino, piede grosso e mente fino,*' said Marcella. The peasant has large feet and a sharp mind. It was dark by the time we reached Stroncone.

~

We took the next day off, rising late and making good use of Mrs. Serangeli's washing machine, admiring the progress of the garden and digging up a plant of sweet marjoram to be potted and borne off to Sicily. Marcella's mother brought her up to date on the gossip of the town. I was intrigued as always by the intricacies of life in a small town like Stroncone, its outward aspect and inner relationships unchanged since the Middle Ages.

The Serangeli house and its garden were tucked into a curve in the road that leads up to the gates of the town, which is still contained within its tenth- and eleventh-century walls. When Marcella took me on a tour that afternoon, we had to leave the car in one of the surprisingly large and pleasantly landscaped parking lots at the base of the walls. Most of the town streets are too narrow to admit four-wheeled vehicles, and as they weave up and down the ridge of the little hill on which the town is perched, they break frequently into flights of stairs.

Stroncone is rapidly becoming a ghost town. Few of its families have the money or desire to renovate their awkward little medieval houses so as to make them comfortable for family life, and most have preferred to move into the all-mod-con apartment buildings on the outskirts of Terni. Only a few small grocery shops remain to serve those still living within the walls; the streets are almost empty as we walk through, and silent but for our footsteps echoing on the paving stones.

It's a very pretty town, not spectacular like Spoleto or Todi, yet charming in its completeness. But unless some wealthy foreigners discover it and buy up the houses, which can be had for very little now, it will slowly empty and fall, one more among the growing number of medieval ghost towns that are scattered throughout the Apennines.

~

Once more we had to make arbitrary choices, as there are no indications as to the route that Constance followed in her journey from Spoleto to her appointment with Henry in Bari. In southern Italy as well, the network of Roman roads had fallen into disrepair. The medieval roads were precarious, light and elastic, rarely allowing more than passage by foot or on horseback. Unlike the Roman roads, which had traced straight lines across the lowlands and river valleys in order to accommodate the long-distance traffic of imperial armies and merchant caravans, the medieval roads connected the hill-towns, climbing up to one *rocca*, then winding down again until the next. Cut into the hillsides by constant use, they disappeared once settlements and commerce shifted, and they have left few traces.

The main road from Spoleto and Terni ran southwest toward Rome: there was no major route east until much farther south, where the old Via Appia cut across from Naples via Benevento and Venosa to the Bari coast. But for Constance to reach that road would have meant going south along the spine of the Apennines, through high mountain passes, where in March bitter winds would still have been blowing and treacherous snowdrifts were yet unmelted.

Constance would also have had to skirt the territories of the pope, whose relations with the empire were notoriously antagonistic. Earlier in the century Frederick Barbarossa had reestablished his authority over the duchy of Spoleto, which had been an imperial fief since the time of Charlemagne, and in 1183 had placed it in the hands of Conrad of Urslingen. And the mountainous region of the Abruzzi, to the southeast of Spoleto, had been part of the Norman Kingdom of Sicily since 1154. But between them and to the west lay the Papal States and the territory of Benevento, the old Lombard princi-pate that Charlemagne had given to the papacy and that, after a Norman interlude, had reestablished its loyalty to the Church in the preceding century. The Papal States and Ben-evento were not outright enemies of the empire at that moment, but neither were they friends, and Constance was all too well aware of her potential value as a hostage.

Although Pope Lucius III had consented to and, according to some sources, even encouraged the betrothal between the heir to the Norman throne and the heir to the Holy Roman Empire, the papacy had been resisting imperial claims to sover-eignty over southern Italy for many years. Despite the Peace of Venice in 1177 and the new treaty signed in Constance six years later, which had appeared to issue in a period of unprece-dented peace between papacy, empire, and the Sicilian Kingdom, Lucius's successors did not share his enthusiasm for the union.

If the Church's problems with the empire were notorious, its relations with Norman Sicily had not been much better. The seed of discord was sown in 1098 by Urban II, the preacher of the First Crusade, when he bestowed upon the Great Count Roger, Constance's grandfather, the status of apostolic legate in Sicily, enabling the Count to act in his stead upon the island. The gesture was unprecedented and has been much debated by historians, although according to Abulafia, 'the explanation is simple: Urban II could see that Sicily, lacking any firm ecclesiastical institutions after centuries of Muslim rule, needed to be assigned diocesan boundaries, needed to be brought out of Greek obedience into the Latin, needed too a vigorous programme of missionary work among the Muslims.'[2]

The Pope thought he was merely making an emergency concession to a military conqueror who was his vassal in Sicily and was in an excellent position to achieve the objectives of the Church there. But Roger's successors were quick to claim the apostolic legacy as their hereditary right. The tangled story of this disagreement, punctuated in each generation by a grudging truce, is irrelevant for us, except to say that in 1156 Pope Hadrian IV confirmed the rights and privileges of the Norman rulers in Sicily in return for an oath of fealty sworn to him by William I; in 1188 William II had repeated this oath.

When William II died childless, Pope Clement III was horrified to think of his territories clamped in a vise created by the union of German and Sicilian rule. He had immediately supported Tancredi, and now Henry's refusal to swear fealty for a kingdom which he claimed by ancient imperial right was exacerbating the situation. For the Church, Henry ruling Sicily as Constance's husband was preferable to his ruling there as emperor, which would have much graver implications for the future, so the Pope chose to champion Constance's claim over that of her husband. Even so, the general hostility of the current pope, Celestine III, to her husband's conquest of Sicily must have weighed on Constance; she could not travel near the papal borders in peace of mind.

~

The first stage of our resumed journey was obligatory, and lovely: the Via Salaria carried Marcella and me past the Marmore waterfalls, through woods and past lakes and nature reserves that cried out for a visit. We were headed toward Rieti, the town where Constance had been handed over to the Germans as Henry's bride-to-be. It was here that she had parted from the world of her youth, said good-bye to the barons and the bishops that had accompanied her from Sicily and made her first acquaintance with the German knights in whose company she would spend the next decade. Very likely, the same Conrad of Urslingen with whom she was riding now, in 1194, had commanded the escort in which I have given a starring role to Frederick von Hausen.

Constance had come full circle: she was returning to her

kingdom in triumph. Yet I imagine that if she passed through Rieti in 1194, her visit was colored by a certain sadness, a weariness. After ten years she was still traveling, and in the meantime so many people were gone. William was dead; Johanna had gone to Jerusalem and then sailed back to the south of France as the wife of Count Raymond of Toulouse (to whom the following year she would give one son and later die during the birth of a second). Even Tancredi was gone and Sybilla prisoner in Germany; German friends too, her father-in-law, the poet with him, and then the many knights and clerics who had died outside the walls of Naples in 1191.

As they moved east from Rieti, along the gorges of Antrodoco, following the Via Sabina toward L'Aquila, the landscape distracted her from these sad thoughts. To the north rose the magnificent peaks of the Gran Sasso, snow-covered still in March, and through the dramatic gorges carved into the rock, the mountain waters rushed toward the Velino River. The gorges marked the border of the Abruzzi: although Constance had never been here before, this region was part of her kingdom. She had come home.

We drove past L'Aquila and southeast toward Popoli, skirting small towns and following the Via Claudia 'nova' down a long straight valley gaudy with late spring color. Great swatches of brilliant red poppies and blotches of bright yellow mustard flowers followed the contour of the land and spilled over low stone walls from field to field. Near Popoli we had to choose between the mountain route, leading down through Sulmona, Isernia, and Campobasso, all places where we would have had no time to stop, and the road east to the sea along the Via Claudia Valeria and the valley of the Pescara River.

We went east. We were, once again, drawing straws, but perhaps this time we picked the right one. I later discovered that these Roman roads – the Via Claudia 'nova' and the Via Claudia Valeria – were still in use in the thirteenth century, and that Frederick II, grown to manhood, had traveled over them frequently. The Via Claudia Valeria follows the base of the

San Clemente a Casàuria as we saw it, looking very sunny and southern.

foothills, slightly above the level of the valley floor, and was crowded with lines of heavy trucks bringing out stone and timber from the mountains to the shore. We were in fact driving between two of Italy's loveliest mountain parks, the Gran Sasso to the north and the Maiella to the south, but the foothills above us and the large trucks before us blocked out any scenic vistas.

Italy never lets you down, however. On the road map, in tiny letters, we discovered a place-name underlined in green: San Clemente a Casàuria. The green meant 'go,' so we went, lured by the guidebook's promise of an important Benedictine abbey with a church dating from the twelfth century. It turned out to be easier to find on the map than in timber and stone, but once we saw a German tourist bus parked off a small street, we knew we were close.

The Abbey of San Clemente a Casàuria was founded in 871 by the Emperor of the West, Louis II, Charlemagne's great-grandson, in obedience to a vow he had made while prisoner in Benevento. The following year, he obtained the pope's permission to have the bones of Saint Clement translated there. Despite severe damage at the hands of the Saracens in the tenth century, the abbey and its church, the latter rebuilt in the twelfth century, remained wealthy and influential throughout the Middle Ages.

The abbey was an imperial foundation, therefore; surely if she passed this way, Constance would have found hospitality there, and surely she would have rejoiced as she rode up the path leading to the front door of the church, over a paving of cobbled squares outlined in narrow slabs of stone, the same design that can be seen all over Sicily, even in the courtyard of my farmhouse. On either side of the path – now, at least – are oleander bushes, and a palm tree; the very vegetation spoke of home. The golden sunlight of late afternoon, glowing on the pale rosy-yellow stone so foreign to the north but so typical of the South, lit up the triple arches of the portico, which cast warm shadows over the carvings of the portal.

In the tympanum the Queen of Heaven sits upon her throne, and to her left the Emperor offers her the church, just as William II offers the Abbey of Monreale to the Madonna on a capital of that abbey's cloister. Across the bottom of the tympanum, a strip of carved figures tells stories that I was unable to read. In one scene some people, among them the Emperor Louis and a knight identified as Count Heribad, are gathered about a table. Lying on the table is what looked to me like an artichoke, complete with stem and leaves.

I confess to a minor obsession about the history of artichokes. I collect iconographical evidence in the hope of discovering whether it was the Saracens who first cultivated edible artichokes from cardoon plants and introduced them into Europe through Sicily, or whether the Romans were already eating them. (I belong to the latter school of thought and have a photograph of an artichoke in a fourth-century Roman mosaic in Tunisia that proves my point.) I couldn't

The portal at San Clemente, complete with artichoke.

imagine, however, what an artichoke was doing on the façade of San Clemente. Artichokes would have been ripe in March, but it was a little far-fetched to think that Constance may have noticed it and felt her mouth water. Someday I will have to go back with binoculars – just about the only thing we didn't have in the car – and a better guidebook.

As I retraced our journey afterward, I read about the places we discovered and wished that we had had more information with us on the spot. The texts say that the columned pulpit and the tall paschal candlestick carved of marble that fill up the narrow central nave of San Clemente show Cistercian, proto-Gothic influences and are perhaps the work of some itinerant stonecarver, working his way home from a pilgrimage to the Holy Land. When I was at San Clemente, I didn't know enough to pick out these nuances by myself, and yet I felt at home in that church, as I do in the Norman churches of Palermo, as I did last year when I entered the Cathedral of Salerno. San Clemente is a church of the South.

Thinking back on it, the abbey church was amazingly small in scale for such an important institution, which is probably why we had such a hard time finding it. The easy, well-paved roads that had whisked us through the Apennines had numbed us to the sense of scale that we had felt on the Spluga Pass, and the cumbersome trailer trucks had blotted out the tiny, antlike groups of riders toiling up a mountainside that we might have imagined there.

In the Middle Ages, vast tracts of southern Italy were covered by almost-empty forests, alternating with untilled pastures populated only by shepherds and their flocks. Nearer the villages, the traveler rode past small fields that had been wrested from the trees, where fava beans rotated with spelt and barley, and nearer still, vegetable patches and grapevines clustered close to the village walls. The walls themselves were little more than a palisade of saplings, and the houses mere huts of mud and thatch. Ephemeral settlements with few inhabitants, many of them would return to dust, emptied by the plagues and famines of the following centuries, unless pinned to the map by a castle or a monastery. In such a wilderness, San Clement would have acquired greater stature, an imposing fortress of faith and a hope of refuge.

We visited a last lonely Cistercian abbey, San Giovanni in Venere, that stood on a hilltop overlooking the Adriatic, then turned south down the coast, out of the Abruzzi and into the Molise, a mountainous region of the Italian interior that here reaches briefly to the sea; its only port is the town of Tèrmoli. As we drove in, the sun was about to set, and we walked out onto the spit of land where the old city stands, to look at a little castle founded by our baby, Frederick. The church next door had medallions of inlaid stone, like those of Salerno and Palermo, between the brick arches of its apse, and the sun's red wake was in the wrong place, just as in Ancona. Here we spent the night – and finally found a restaurant that would give us the *zuppa di pesce* that Marcella had been looking for ever since Ravenna.

∼

Just south of Tèrmoli, the Molise ends, and we were in Apulia. This was truly Norman country, where the Norman conquest of the South began.

The northern part of Apulia is known as the Capitanata, although the guidebooks usually neglect to explain that this word comes via medieval Latin from *catapano*, the Byzantine term for a provincial governor. A rich plain of flat and dusty farmlands, some truck gardens, but mostly wheat fields already bleached by the early summer sun, the Capitanata has as its hub the agricultural town of San Severo. Here we turned east, following the signs for San Marco in Lamis.

A long line of trucks passed us going west, each carrying a precarious three-storied wooden cage filled with live sheep. It was a modern mechanized version of the *transumanza*, the ancient seasonal migration of the shepherds and their flocks as they abandoned the arid fields of the South. Frederick II would make an attempt to regulate this practice in the code of laws known as the Constitutions of Melfi, which he promulgated in 1231. The sheep we met were coming from the Gargano peninsula and had but a short ride to endure; others would be crossing the Tyrrhenian Sea on the ferryboats from Sardinia. All were headed for the rich grasses of the Apennines that would tide them through the summer months, until the autumn rains turned their home pastures green once more.

We were looking for a minor road, a shortcut that would take us to Siponto, but we missed it somehow and found ourselves climbing up into the foothills of the Gargano, the mountainous, tree-covered spur that juts out into the Adriatic from the boot of Italy. I have long wanted to visit the shrine of Monte Sant'Angelo, the grotto that passed from pagan shrine to Christian in the fifth century, when the Archangel Michael appeared to the bishop of Siponto in a dream. I yearn to see the procession of pilgrims who push their bicycles up the mountainside to the grotto and then, after paying their respects to the saint, decorate their bikes with multicolored feathers and descend triumphantly, clothes and feathers fluttering as they coast down the curving road to the bottom. This happens in May and again in September, but we were there in June, slim consolation for not having time to visit Monte Sant'Angelo.

Constance may well have taken the time to do so. Michael was a warrior saint, very dear to the Normans both past and present, and Monte Sant'Angelo is the southern equivalent of the shrine of Mont-Saint-Michel on the coast of Normandy. Legend tells us that on this mountain the Lombard prince of Bari, Meles, first met with some Norman knights who had come on pilgrimage on their way home from the Holy Land, and he asked for their assistance in driving the Byzantines from Apulia. The moral of that legend is, never ask a Norman for help. They assisted the Lombards right off the map.

The hills we were driving through were quite barren, but just beyond we could see the green of the Gargano, true *macchia mediterranea*, a scrubby cover of low-growing oaks and olives mixed in with resinous perfumes of terebinth and rosemary and rockrose. We hadn't wanted to be up where we were, but we soon changed our minds. The road that we chose at random took us around the town of Rignano and then down the side of a cliff in breath-catching switchbacks; below us the whole Tavoliere, or tableland, of Puglia spread southward, its endless wheat fields glistening gold in the morning sun, its high skies and distant horizons.

~

I love Puglia. If I weren't so happy in Sicily, I think I would go there to live. It has been a long romance. In 1961 my mother was living in Florence in a splendid fourteenth-century villa on the hill of Bellosguardo, with cypresses in the garden and umbrella pines placed strategically to embellish the view over the valley of the Arno. I spent the summer there, and each day I would go down into Florence to the National Library, where I was reading for my undergraduate thesis on Frederick II. (At twenty, my thoughts were all for the amazing son; it took me longer to appreciate the mother.)

When the library closed for lunch, I would go to a bar to eat a ham roll and a *granita di caffè con panna*. (I had a round of five bars, one for each weekday, so that I wouldn't have to go to any one too often, a neat schedule that went in tilt when the married, middle-aged waiter at one bar asked me out for dinner.) I lingered over my lunch as long as I dared, then spent the remaining hour until the library reopened walking through the hot and empty streets of Florence. Fast-food dispensers and big-name designers had not yet overtaken the city, and although plenty of tourists were about, at that hour Florence, in all its sober elegance, was mine. I thought I was in the most beautiful place on earth.

And then I went south. My mother proposed that we spend a week in Puglia, touring the castles and churches that were related to Frederick. It was August, but Puglia had not yet been 'discovered.' Very few tourists were about, and we never saw another woman at the wheel. Each time we stopped for gas, the whole village would turn out to stare, while the man at the service station insisted on checking the oil and the water, measuring the air in the tires, and washing all the windows, so as to make the spectacle last as long as possible. If we protested, they were kind but firm: '*Signora*, we must! What if you were to have a *disgrazia* on the road!' – a phrase that became part of our family lexicon.

I never recovered from that trip, from the warmth of the people, the beauty of the churches, the intensity of the light and colors, the bunches of tiny red tomatoes hanging against freshly whitewashed walls, the brilliant blue of sea and sky behind the pale gold stone of the Trani cathedral, the old woman in black sitting outside her door near San Nicola in Bari and greeting us as we walked by – so much so that I have spent the rest of my life in southern Italy, albeit in a different region.

So I felt I could share with Constance something of her

gladness of heart as she began to feel that she was really in the South again. At the end of March, the wheat would have been green still, and much of the land a pasture where the spring flowers were starting to bloom, but even in the depths of winter, the southern sun is strong and limpid, and the colors vibrate in its light.

I have perhaps dwelt overmuch on color in this book, but the more I read about the Middle Ages, the more I saw color as a tool with which to interpret Constance's moods. Today we picture medieval life as in an illuminated manuscript, rich and glowing and variegated in its hues, but in truth most of the color was isolated on these pages of painted parchment. Color was an urban phenomenon, concentrated in the stained-glass windows and polychromed carving of the churches, in the clothes and ornaments of the rich in their castles.

Color was the symbol of status, hard to come by and reserved to God and the aristocracy, for pigments and dyes were extremely expensive. The rest of the population lived in a world made of monochrome materials: brick and stone, wood and unglazed clay, natural fibers badly dyed at best.

Think also of Trifels in winter, its dark stone, leafless forests, and snow-covered fields; and then consider Sicily, where the winter wheat greens the fields as soon as the rains begin; where the dark emerald citrus trees are luminous with golden fruit; where the omnipresent wildflowers, timid only in the coldest months, become bawdy and aggressive as spring arrives. I do believe that in all the years in which she lived in the north, Constance wore her Sicilian gowns like a banner blowing in a winter wind.

≈

We finally found our way to San Leonardo di Siponto, a small church with a few adjacent walls that is all that remains of the abbey which in the early twelfth century was entrusted to the

The Teutonic Knights (here, the thirteenth-century German poet Tannhäuser)
wear austere white cloaks, decorated only by a black cross.

Order of the Teutonic Knights, that they might offer hospitality to pilgrims on their way to and from the Holy Land. The southern leg of the Via Francigena passed here, in fact, for those who planned to embark directly at the port of Siponto (long since silted up), as well as for those who were continuing south by land to the more trafficked ports of Bari and Brindisi.

The church is an unusual box-shaped building with two small octagonal Byzantine domes on the roof. Two magnificent lions flank the entrance on the northern wall. The lion on the right is devouring some beast unidentifiable because its head was already well into the lion's gullet, and the other is roaring – with rage, perhaps, since the prey that he once held in his paws has been stolen from him. They were by far the fiercest lions we had seen: the Teutonic Knights were a stern bunch, and maybe they wanted to warn arriving guests of the dangers inherent in their pilgrimage.

Once we passed a beautifully carved portal, there was just enough light from a small window of filigreed stone to illuminate massive columns within a small, dark, and strongly circumscribed space. Many of the abbeys that Marcella and I had visited, engulfed as they were by urban development, have lost the sense of haven that still imbues San Leonardo, where no other construction rises from the waves of golden wheat that stretch to the horizon, and nothing but our car, parked in the shade of a crumbling wall, intruded upon our medieval fantasies.

It was only a short drive from San Leonardo to the sea. The road, a heavily trafficked alternative to the autostrada, skirts the famous salt flats of Puglia, the *saline* of Margherita di Savoia. According to the map, they were enclosed in a nature reserve, but from the road all we could see were large industrial machines and a gray coat of salty brine that covered everything like a blight. They were nothing, I thought, compared with the salt flats of western Sicily, a checkerboard of salt pans that stretch south of Trapani to the lagoon of Mozia, shifting from blue to gray to white according to their salinity

The lion of San Leonardo di Siponto bewails his stolen prey.

and to the changing color of the sky reflected in their still sur-
faces. The pans are divided by walkways on which the brilliant
white crystals are piled in neat heaps and covered with weathered terra-cotta roof tiles that keep them from dissolving in the
rain. Here and there windmills, once used to mill the salt,
break the flatness, and in the distance the sea spreads its restless
colors – one of the most beautiful sights in Sicily.

Maybe it's a question of age. Once I asked the owner of
some Sicilian salt flats, which date from the time of Phoenician
colonization, about the *saline* of Puglia. With a truly Sicilian
sense of time, he told me that the Pugliese salt flats were *much*
more recent – they were Roman! Or perhaps we just took the
wrong road. In any case they would have looked less industrial
when Constance went by, and she was sure to have noticed
them, since they belonged to her.

Salt was a natural product, in the sense that it could not be
made to 'grow' like wheat; it could not be harvested in the
same way as the product of Man's toil. It was, as a natural
good bestowed by divine blessing, the prerogative of God's

representative on earth, the king, who was the custodian of the public good. The idea of minerals, sea-produce, treasure trove, as public good, for which the ruler was custodian, was derived straight from the Roman law-codes; it was also highly convenient to a monarchy that believed in making money.[3]

Salt was very valuable in the ancient and the medieval world – a good soldier was said to be 'worth his salt,' which made up part of his monthly wages. One should not underestimate the economic motives here, but how ecologically correct it sounds, and how contemporary, this concept of the king as the steward of the earth.

It was past noon by the time we reached Trani, and I was feeling quite desperate at the thought that our long, unintended detour into the foothills of the Gargano, however beautiful it had been, might mean finding the cathedral closed for lunch. That would have been a real loss to me, for the cathedral at Trani is one of my favorite churches. Built on the very edge of the sea, its apses point east across the Adriatic in the direction of Jerusalem, so that as we approached it from the city, we saw the medieval building against the blue, quite alone thanks to the work of restoration done in the 1950s that removed the cathedral's later accretions.

Unlike the rather squat churches to which we had become accustomed, this cathedral is taller than it is wide, with a façade that rises to a high peak at the roof beam. The effect of height is accentuated by the doors of the façade, which open out onto a porch well above the level of the piazza. A double staircase leads the eye up to the porch, and the tall, spired bell tower that pierces the sky on the right is built over a high archway. Beneath these arches one can see through to where the waves are breaking, so that even the bell tower seems to be on stilts.

The color of the stone is absolutely marvelous, a warm creamy gold that glows against the blue background, and inside the church the windows, paper-thin panes of alabaster,

The façade of the cathedral at Trani is lit up against
the sky and sea behind it.

The light filtering through the alabaster windowpanes
floods the cathedral interior with pale gold.

filter a golden light that, even in the relentless sun of noonday, lies gently upon the arches and columns of the lofty interior. We were lucky, closing time had been delayed because a wedding was in progress, so we tiptoed in. Only the glow of the candles and the bouquets of white flowers tied to the ends of the pews leavened the austerity of walls stripped to bare stone.

What decoration has survived the rigor of the restorers is on the outside façade: high up a rose window; below that another window within a portico supported by elephants and surmounted by lions; more lions at the portal, odd ones wrestling with men. (The men are losing.) Around the arch of the doorway, a design of vines weaves together monkeys and griffins and other mythical beasts. Yet all the carving is on a scale small and delicate enough that, as we looked back at the church, the effect was one of great simplicity and of indescribable beauty. It was hard to leave.

~

After her coronation in Bari, Constance doubled back to Trani together with her husband, stopping long enough to preside over a high court, her first as Queen of Sicily, her last outside the confines of her native island. But now, on her way south, she was in a hurry: she had to press on to Bari. There Henry was waiting for her, crown in hand.

CHAPTER TWELVE : APRIL

> She stands by the king, clothed
> in the splendour of a golden robe,
> as do royal daughters.
> Behold, from the South comes the Queen,
> whom the divine wisdom
> of Solomon ennobles.
> She is dark but comely,
> around her myrrh and incense
> and aromatic plants burn.
> Thus it is that a day of grace
> has revealed to us what was
> hidden by obscure figures and symbols.
>   – 'Quam dilecta tabernacula'
>   *Liber Sancti Jacobi*, twelfth century[1]

Constance was crowned queen of Sicily in Bari on the second of April, 1195. It was Easter Sunday, a feast that was considered as propitious as Christmas for such a ceremony: the imperial coronation in Rome in 1191 had also been held at Easter.

It is a temptation to think that the crown placed on Constance's head that day in Bari looked like – or actually was – the one that was discovered in a wooden casket in the sarcophagus of her daughter-in-law, Constance of Aragon, now on display in the treasury of the Palermo cathedral. A stunning cap of crimson silk embroidered with a cross of seed pearls and golden threads and studded with cabochon gemstones, it has long golden pendants on either side – intricate structures of chains, diamond-shaped plaques, and crossbars that look like enormous and elaborate earrings.

But this is a Byzantine *camelaucum*, reserved for the emperor and his son, and we have no iconographical evidence that a woman ever wore such a crown. Abulafia suggests that it was Frederick II's own, placed there by his own hands in 1222, in a torment of grief at the death of his first wife, a Spanish princess ten years older than he, to whom he had been married at the age of fifteen.[2] If the disparity in age echoed that of his parents, the marriage differed: Constance of Aragon had been friend and counselor to Frederick as well as wife and mother of his firstborn son.

Queens and empresses, instead, wore an open coronet with round or ogival peaks pointing upward. Such is the crown barely distinguishable in the only official portrait of Constance, enthroned on the wax seals of her documents. Her actual crown has not survived, although it might have been one of the two Sicilian women's crowns that, like so many other royal treasures, were carried off to the north, to Bamberg in Germany, where their presence was recorded as late as the seventeenth century.

Not even queens and empresses, however, were ever permitted to outshine their husbands in sartorial splendor. It is easier for us, and more accurate perhaps, to imagine Henry at Bari, his gaunt, dark figure almost lost in the folds of the magnificent mantle that had been made in the royal *tiraz*, the silk workshops of Palermo, for his father-in-law. Had none of the glittering churches and mosaicked halls of the Norman period survived, this frail silken cloak, now to be seen in the Imperial Treasury in Vienna, would still suffice to tell us of the majesty and the splendor of that court.

The mantle is a perfect half-circle of scarlet samite – a heavy silk woven with a minute tracery of vine branches, probably imported from Byzantium – divided in two by a palm tree, the sacred seven-branched tree of life that unites heaven and earth. On either side, symmetrically displayed, a lion poses victorious on the back of a crouching camel. The beasts are embroidered in golden thread, each part outlined by stitching of dark blue silk and a double row of seed pearls. The mantle is bordered at the front by a design of quadrifoils beaded with tiny pearls alternating with diamond-shaped gold plaquelets, while around its bottom hem runs an inscription in Kufic calligraphy stitched in gold:

> [This mantle] belongs to the articles worked in the royal workshop, in which fortune and honor, prosperity and perfection, merit and distinction have their home. May the king rejoice in good acceptance, thriving magnificently, in great generosity and high splendor, renown and magnificence and the fulfillment of wishes and hopes; may his days and nights be spent in enjoyment, without end or change; in the feeling of honor, dependency and active participation in happiness and in the maintenance of well-being, support and suitable activity; in the capital of Sicily in the year 528.[3]

The year 528 of the Hegira corresponds to 1133–34 in the Christian calendar, so this cloak was made not for Roger's 1130 coronation but afterward, for use on state occasions. It has often been suggested that the lions triumphing over the camels symbolize the Norman conquest of the Arabs, but according to Rotraud Bauer, the mantle has a greater, more cosmic significance: the rosettes embroidered on the face and joints of each lion correspond to the stars in a medieval Egyptian engraving of the constellation Leo. 'Together with the symbolism of the Zodiac, the West took over a further Oriental tradition, that of clothing the sovereign with a celestial mantle.'[4]

The cloak appears in an inventory of the imperial treasure at Trifels that was drawn up in 1246 at the order of Frederick II's son Conrad. For a long time scholars believed that it made the journey north to Germany only after Frederick II wore it at his imperial coronation in Rome in 1220. But an Austrian researcher has now shown that Frederick wore a different cape, one decorated with the eagles of Swabia, produced in

Palermo around 1200 and now preserved at Metz.[5] Why not think then that Henry wore Roger's robe as his coronation mantle on Christmas Day in Palermo, then brought it with him as he traveled north and wore it again at Bari on Easter?

Constance would have known that cloak, would have seen her uncle and then her nephew wear it, and having grown up in the palace, she would have understood the symbolism. The lions settled upon the shoulders of her husband reflected the weight of cosmic responsibilities, the same responsibilities that she herself assumed, standing at his side and clothed in similar if lesser splendor, in the moment that she felt the weight of the crown placed on her head.

She was no Leo, proud and aggressive, but a Pisces swimming at once both north and south, torn between two families and two worlds. From the point of view of karmic astrology, her north node was in Capricorn.

> Many individuals with these nodes are strongly wrapped up in the business of their country. They personalize government for to them it is still part, in a larger sense, of their own family. . . .
>
> The major karmic lesson in the Capricorn North Node is to identify with an ideal bigger than the personal life. The individual must ultimately come to stand for something. . . . He must understand true responsibility.[6]

Yet even as she felt the burden of divine anointment, Constance must have looked uneasily upon Henry wrapped in her father's robe. Not that she would have envied him the wearing of it: that was a male prerogative that it would never have occurred to her to question. Yet she cannot have greeted with equanimity the discovery that her husband had taken Roger's splendid mantle away from the gilded palace in which it had been created, away from the throne whose majesty it expressed, and that this quintessential emblem of Norman regality was soon to be imprisoned in the cold, dark recesses of Trifels.

Under Byzantine dominion, the city of Bari had been the capital of southern Italy. In 1071, after three years of siege, it was captured by Robert Guiscard, one of the first Hautevilles to settle in the Italian South, and it henceforth grew in importance, especially after a group of Bari sailors raided the city of Myra, in Asia Minor, and brought back to their native city the relics of Saint Nicholas, Bishop of Myra, who was greatly venerated in the Orthodox world.

The Benedictine abbot Elias set out to build a basilica to receive the saint, using as the foundation the remains of the palace of the Byzantine *catapano*, which were incorporated in the crypt. Pope Urban II came in person to inter the holy relics, which became an important center for pilgrimage, and less than a decade later Bari became the launching spot for the First Crusade.

In 1156 the people of Bari revolted against William I and were punished: only the Basilica of San Nicola was left standing. The Spanish rabbi Benjamin of Tudela reported that when he passed through Bari in about 1165, neither Jew nor Gentile lived there, in consequence of the destruction.

In the intervening years, much of the city was reconstructed, including the cathedral, which unlike the basilica had not been spared. The new church, built under the guidance of Archbishop Rainald, was modeled on the basilica, and by 1195 the work of reconstruction must have been well along.

I have no memory of visiting the cathedral on my first visits to Bari, although in many ways it is so similar to the basilica that perhaps the two have blended in my mind. Their interiors have the same structure, and both have been restored to their pristine Romanesque simplicity, with Corinthian columns dividing the naves and holding up the triple arches of the clerestory. Both have the same octagonal marble canopy over the main altar, and behind it a *cattedra*, the bishop's throne that is the mark of a cathedral. Especially lovely is that of

The Basilica of San Nicola in Bari, the only church that William I
left standing when he razed the city in 1156.

It was most probably here, in San Nicola, that Constance
received the crown of her kingdom.

Abbot Elias in San Nicola: his throne is held up by men, the
footrest borne by lions.

My memories of San Nicola are very clear. Built almost on
the shore, it is tall and fortresslike, designed to withstand
attack, and it is surrounded by walled courtyards that could be
defended if necessary, all in a grayish-white stone that is brilliant in the southern sun. An enamel plaque in the basilica
treasury shows Roger II being crowned by the saint, a reference to his conquest of Bari and the basis for a legend about
his actually having been crowned here, one that pleases the
Baresi but has no historical grounds.

Well before the Bari sailors brought his relics from Myra,
Nicholas had been the center of an active cult among Normans
both in the South and in Normandy, so most probably it was in
his church, older and sanctified by the presence of the saint's

relics, that Constance's coronation took place, followed by a great imperial diet held immediately afterward.

On the preceding Good Friday, Henry had secretly taken the cross of the Crusader from the hands of the Bishop of Sutri. At the imperial diet, he made his crusading intentions public and announced his arrangements for the government of the kingdom during his imminent return to Germany. There is no clear agreement among the sources as to whether Henry vowed that he would actually participate in the coming Crusade or merely intended to promote and support it: he was no soldier, and his health had never completely recovered from the severe bout of dysentery that he had contracted during the siege of Naples four years earlier. His piety and religious ardor were beyond question, but it was no secret that he was campaigning for the goodwill of the pope, without which he would not be able to carry out his plans for his heir. Henry was also in negotiation with the German princes, offering them substantial concessions: in return they were to recognize the hereditary character of the imperial crown, which the pope would then confer on the infant Frederick as soon as the baby was big enough to hold his head up under such a weight.

I suspect that Constance was not in the least upset by the thought of packing Henry off to the Holy Land. She knew full well that better men than he had never returned, and at the very least it would mean a year or so of freedom to rule her kingdom as she wished. But any notions that she would rule alone in his absence were soon dismissed: Constance was to be coregent, but Markward of Annweiler, to whom Henry awarded his freedom, was made duke of Ravenna and Romagna and markgraf of Ancona, while Conrad of Urslingen, the Duke of Spoleto with whose wife Constance had left her son, was nominated *regni Sicilie, ducatus Apulie et principatus Capue vicarius*, the viceroy of the realm.

From Bari the royal couple moved north again, to Trani and then to Barletta, where they held court on April 13th. From there Henry headed north, stopping here and there on imperial business. By the beginning of June he was once more in Milan, and on the eighth of July he held court in Frankfurt.

After Barletta the newly crowned Constance turned south once more, traveling fast, heading for Sicily. She would not feel that she was truly in her kingdom until she reached Palermo, and until her people – that undisciplined and difficult admixture of Normans, Greeks, Arabs, and Jews – had welcomed her as their queen. She would not be home until she had entered the royal palace, no longer as an awkward if beloved aunt, no longer as a hostage, but as its mistress. A letter she wrote to the pope some months later makes clear her priorities. Sicily was hers by reason of *paterna successione et imperiali adquisitione*: her husband the Emperor might have acquired the kingdom, but her paternal succession, her hereditary rights, came first.

~

Marcella and I had visited Bari together in 1980, when we spent three weeks camping in Puglia with our respective families. At that time we had resolved the problem of where to leave cars laden with suitcases by parking in front of a local branch of the Italian Communist Party. Marcella's husband, who worked for a trade union, had gone in and asked the *compagni* to keep an eye on our things. But this time we were afraid that such precautions would not be sufficient. In the intervening years, Bari had acquired a very ugly reputation for petty street crime, and the closer we got, the more uneasy we felt about our baggage, our purses, and my daughter's computer. It was very hot, we had seen it before, we were pressed for time: we copped out. Or so we thought.

The big highway coming down to Bari from the north circles inland around the city before it continues south along the coast to Brindisi. We were looking for the exit that would take us southwest, not along the sea but inland, straight down to the instep of Italy's boot. The traffic was heavy, the signs were confusing, and the turnoff we chose proved almost immediately to be the wrong one: a badly paved road that petered out into nothing in the middle of a half-built residential district. There were no other cars, no one of whom to ask directions. We decided to retrace our route back to the highway and try again, so I circled the car over the bumpy, unfinished road and started back.

Suddenly from nowhere two boys on a motorbike appeared, passed us, and then stopped without warning, just in front of us, fiddling with their controls as if the bike had stalled. I braked hard and slid over the gravelly surface, stopping just inches from their taillight as a loud bang sounded from the back of the car. Two more boys on another bike had bumped into us from behind, and one of them was striding toward my window, protesting loudly about my driving.

Whether it was because of Bari's reputation, or because something similar had recently happened to friends in Sicily, I do not know. Perhaps it was simply Constance, keeping an eye on us, a hawk circling too high above for us to notice. Somehow my usual combination of gullibility and easy guilt gave way to clear thinking: the sound at the back had been the whack of a hand hitting the lid of the trunk, and the boy walking toward me was taking an excessive interest in the contents of the backseat.

'Lock, lock, lock, lock, lock!' I was unable to be any more articulate as I shouted at Marcella, but she took my point. Fortunately the back doors were already locked and our purses were out of sight, and even more fortunately our motor was still running. I jammed the stick into first gear, hit the accelerator, and swerved barely enough to miss the boys in front of us, who had in the meantime dismounted and were gathering in menacing fashion. We departed in a spray of gravel, leaving four very surprised young men behind us.

I stopped as soon as it seemed safe. I was shaking so that I could barely keep the car straight, and at the same time I felt exultant, empowered by my own quick reactions. And although it came to me considerably later, in some strange way I was also grateful for this unpleasant experience: it was as though having faced ambush and having triumphed had brought me closer emotionally to Constance's mode of travel, to her vulnerability and her anxiety, than all the hairpin turns and gaping chasms of the Alpine passes, or all the marble lions that had guarded our route.

Despite this misadventure, I still wanted to see Bari again, and so three years after my trip with Marcella, I went back with my husband. We came by ferry to Naples, then drove through the medieval towns of Benevento, Melfi, and Venosa, where the huge Benedictine abbey church of the Santissima Trinità, left unfinished in the twelfth century, raises its columns and arches to the open sky.

In Bari we stayed at the house of friends, and our hosts accompanied us into the old medieval city, where I rediscovered the cathedral and found the basilica as beautiful as ever. We brought no purses with us, I kept my camera hidden deep in a pocket. The visit was well worth whatever moments of apprehension it had cost us.

~

Marcella and I pulled ourselves together, returned to the highway, and found the right exit. We were relieved to get away from Bari's unfinished suburbs and enter the rich farmlands of Puglia, traveling through miles and miles of vineyards, table grapes growing on trellises, many of them covered with sheet plastic to hasten the ripening. The road south took us past Gioia del Colle, and here we made our only stop, to look at the castle.

This was a detour in time if not in place. Originally a Byzantine fortress, the castle at Gioia was amplified during the Norman period and then given its present form by Frederick II in 1230. It is an imposing building, a massive square of heavy stone walls, with a square tower rising at both corners of the

The much-restored throne room at Gioia del Colle.

principal façade. It would be much more impressive had the town not so encroached upon it that it is now difficult to see it from anywhere but right under the walls themselves.

I had fond memories of this castle from 1961, when I came here with my mother. Certainly it is far less beautiful than Frederick's masterpiece, the octagonal Castel del Monte that stands on a hilltop to the northwest of Bari, but I had liked the courtyard, where a handsome staircase leads up to the *piano nobile*. The balustrade is carved with a frieze that suggests the royal hunt: a grimacing lion chases a boar and a deer, and a man on horseback gallops to the top carrying a falcon at his wrist. Upstairs my fantasy had been aroused by the great hall with its decorated dais, and by the great stone chair carved with falcons that proclaimed itself the throne of Frederick II.

On my first visit, this castle had seemed the perfect setting for the man with whom I had been infatuated ever since my history tutor at Harvard had assigned me the Ernst Kantorow-icz biography to read. I was dazzled, stupefied by the *Stupor mundi*, the Baptized Sultan, the primordial Renaissance prince, patron of the arts and sciences, builder of castles, author of the Western world's first scientific treatise, Holy Roman Emperor, and Antichrist.

During Frederick's reign the major knots of the previous century – the often deferred but never ultimately resolved relationships between papacy and empire, between empire and southern kingdom, between southern kingdom and papacy – came to the fore once again, exacerbated by the force of the personalities involved. Pope Gregory IX and his successor, Innocent IV, asserted the absolute supremacy of the papacy, while Frederick maintained his ancestors' claim to divinely appointed rule. The cities of northern Italy, united once more in a reborn Lombard League, played off Emperor against Pope to their own purposes. In the end the Pope declared a crusade against the Emperor, and the rhetoric and invective spun off in the course of these struggles became gossip, then legend, then history.

I blush now to think how much of this I accepted unquestioningly when I wrote my undergraduate thesis. Drawn by Frederick's exotic aspects, and not terribly discerning in my use of sources (habits over which I hope I have since gained better control), I saw a brilliant, tolerant, skeptical man of the future seated on that throne.

I knew better now. The art nouveau falcons on the throne at Gioia were a dead giveaway: much that had struck me in 1961 about that building was the fruit of very imaginative if unreliable restoration at the beginning of the twentieth century. As for the throne itself, 'there can surely be no doubt by this time that the Emperor would never have deigned to take his seat on such an ignoble object and that the artist responsible for its clumsy design would have been left to starve.'[7] So much for my fantasies.

If we are to accept the thesis of Frederick's latest biographer, so much for the fantasies of many medieval historians as well. As its subtitle, *A Medieval Emperor*, indicates, David Abulafia's book gives a much-reduced reading of this multifaceted man, portraying him as sincere in his dedication to the Church, conservative in his political thought, patron of a court far inferior in magnificence and in cultural production to that of his Norman grandfather, and less effective and charismatic as a military leader than his German grandfather. The only claim to glory that survives undiminished is his authorship of *The Art of Hunting with Birds*. Frederick inherited from both sides of his family a consuming passion for falconry, and his treatise is 'a thoroughly remarkable piece of science, describing in exact and unadorned detail the nesting habits of falcons and their prey, dismissing contemporary hocus-pocus, the product of experiment and long thought.'[8]

Hence the falcons that decorate his spurious throne at Gioia. On the one hand, it is somehow comforting to see the man in place of the superman, yet Abulafia seems almost too systematic in his work of demolishing Frederick's exceptional attributes. (His work naturally enjoys only limited popularity in Frederick's own kingdom today.) The debate will continue, I expect, for a long time to come. I still take great pleasure in tracing how a simple reading assignment changed the course of my life and brought me eventually to live on a farm in what is known as Bosco Falconeria, 'The Falconry Woods,' where I like to think that the young *Stupor mundi* himself might have hunted. But now I find the figure of Constance to be more approachable and more interesting.

The concluding words of Abulafia's biography describe Frederick as

a victim of his dual dynastic inheritance. Yet among his great ideals was the preservation of that inheritance, not solely to achieve power for himself, but to pass on to his heirs, intact, the lands, titles and rights that he believed God had called him to possess. He was not a Sicilian, nor a Roman, nor a German, nor a *mélange* of Teuton and Latin, still less a semi-Muslim: he was a Hohenstaufen and a Hauteville.[9]

The mother's concern was to preserve the Hauteville inheritance; the son, in choosing both, ultimately squandered both. Neither empire nor kingdom would ever recover.

~

From Gioia, Marcella and I cut straight down to the Ionian Sea and circled the instep west, across the bit of coast that belongs to the Basilicata and then into Calabria, driving through a long string of dismal beach resorts still battened down from the winter, in search of a bed for the night. This is one of the less beautiful stretches of the Calabrian coast, a narrow plain invaded by tacky summer houses and cheap hotels, saved only by its proximity to the mountainous forests of the Pollino National Park that rise behind it. We finally found a hotel and a seafood restaurant, neither of them memorable, in the town of Trebisacce.

The next morning we continued down the coast, following in the footsteps of Robert Guiscard as he went south to add Calabria to the growing list of Norman conquests in southern Italy. At Sibari, site of the ancient Greek city that invented the sybaritic lifestyle, we had to decide, once again with no clues to guide us, how Constance might have crossed the Calabrian peninsula.

Sibari lies at the mouth of the Crati River. The most usual route across Calabria runs upstream along this river, first west to the point where the valley meets the big north-south Autostrada del Sole, and then south following the bend in the river. In April it was probably too early to worry about the malaria that then plagued the Calabrian lowlands, but the spring thaw would have made the floor of the river valley marshy and dangerous. Nonetheless it is possible, even probable, that Constance followed this route, traveling high enough in the hills to avoid the flooded lowlands.

But I had another plan. I wanted to go via San Giovanni in Fiore, a small town up in the mountains of the Sila, to see the

312

abbey of Joachim of Fiore, the visionary monk whose prophecies were capturing the imagination of learned men throughout twelfth-century Europe. An exchange of letters took place between the Abbot and Constance herself, and we can imagine how eagerly she must have sought any prediction about the future of her child and her kingdom. Might she not have visited him in person on her way south across Calabria?

So we continued along the Ionian shore past Sibari, following the coastal railroad. There were in fact few towns on this stretch of coast, which had been subjected to centuries of attack and piracy, but it was dotted with train stations that served the towns perched up on the more defendable hilltops. At the station of Mandatoriccio, we turned inland and started a steady, twisting climb up through mountains covered with scrub oak and, as we climbed higher, chestnut forests. The clearings blazed with yellow clumps of flowering gorse, and the roadside mixture of scarlet poppies, orange calendulas, and purple mallow made a vivid border for the dark forests behind. Pass after pass, valley after valley, we finally reached San Giovanni, on the very edge of the mountainous area known as the Sila. It was in this ancient Greek town, built on an impervious peak at an altitude of almost 3,500 feet with a glorious view in all directions, that Joachim sought refuge from the world.

Having passed through San Giovanni some twenty years before, Marcella had memories of a pretty medieval village, but in the overflow of recent construction, we had a very hard time finding it. A littering of five- and six-story apartment buildings slithered down the hillside in what was perhaps the worst example of unrestrained real estate speculation that we had ever seen. We circled at length in search of the abbey. Not only were there no street signs, often there wasn't any street, and no sign of urban infrastructure, much less planning, to tie the buildings into a coherent design. If here and there tar had been poured onto the open spaces, often nothing connected one bit of tar with the next, and even if B was visible from A, it took a devious imagination to find a paved route connecting the two.

313

The abbey, when we finally found it, was not on the crest of the hill as we had expected but quite far below. It was built in 1189 after Joachim, dissatisfied with the growing worldliness of the Cistercian order, broke off to found his own monastery in the lonely wilderness of Fiore. My strongest impression, as I think back to our visit, is one of darkness, an effect heightened by the clouds that covered the sun as we arrived. The stark, single-naved church, illuminated only by what light could penetrate the small windows of the flat apsidal wall, had all the austerity of a Cistercian church, combined with an uneasy obscurity that spoke of its builder's preoccupation with the Apocalypse.

Joachim, who lived in the second half of the twelfth century and died in 1202, had wandered as an itinerant ascetic through the mountains of his native Calabria before joining the Cistercian order, and although his intellectual training reflected the Latin order, his writings were heavily influenced by the ideas of the Greek monastic tradition that had dominated the region before the arrival of the Normans. He saw the unity and trinity of the Christian God paralleled in human history, which he divided into three ages: the Age of the Father, an age of obedience to an angry god that corresponded to the period of the Old Testament; the Age of the Son, that of the New Testament, in which man is guided by the teachings of Christ and lives in faith and acceptance; and the Age of the Spirit, yet to come, in which man would live in everlasting joy and contemplation of God. According to Joachim's calculations, the Age of the Spirit would be ushered in by the sword, accompanied by the rise and fall of the Antichrist. More precisely, this was to happen in the year 1260.

Joachim was in fact prophesying a specifically Christian, very medieval New Age, a vision based on his interpretations of the Book of Revelation. Born of a rejection of the increased temporality and worldliness of the Church, and a yearning for greater simplicity and charity, Joachim's writings were imbued with a sense of expectation not at all foreign to our own era, one

The Great Red Dragon – *Draco Magnus et Rufus* – of the Apocalypse,
as shown in Joachim of Fiore's *The Book of Figures*, has many heads,
representing the six kings, from Herod to Saladin, who persecuted the
Christian Church. The seventh head is reserved for the Antichrist, whose
arrival Joachim thought imminent and whom some contemporaries
identified as Frederick II.

that found great resonance in the years after his death, in particular with the new order of itinerant monks founded by Saint
Francis of Assisi.

Given the imminence of the Age of the Spirit, and of all the
untoward events leading up to it, on which Joachim dwelled
with gloomy satisfaction, it is not surprising that the rulers of
the world were interested in having a firsthand account. In
1191 Richard I of England, waiting at Messina to sail to the
Holy Land on the Third Crusade, paid a visit to Joachim and
plied him with questions. Both Henry and Constance were his
patrons, making grants of land and gold to the monastery and
confirming its privileges.

Fortunately Joachim was a prophet and not a fortune-teller.
His concerns were eschatological and cosmic, without regard

for the individual and personal. Whatever he might have said to Constance, he could not tell her what awaited her in Sicily. He could not tell her that it would be her very own son, Frederick II, whose death in 1260 would be interpreted by many as the fall of the Antichrist; he could not foresee that she herself had only four more years to live.

~

The story of Constance's last years is not a happy one, and San Giovanni in Fiore, with its aura of ancient doom and modern decay, is as good a place as any to tell it.

Constance arrived in Palermo in June of 1195 to find the treasury ransacked and the coffers empty. Though she set about with energy and intelligence to restore order in her kingdom, all that she had hoped to achieve in her husband's absence was cut short by Henry's return at the end of 1196. The Emperor installed Germans in the positions of power, taxed the Sicilians relentlessly, and brooked no opposition: it was a reign of terror 'unrivalled in its intensity.'

The oppression was too great, and in June of 1197 the people of Sicily rebelled. According to many sources, it was with the knowledge and consent of Constance that the conspirators planned to do away with the Emperor and to elect their own leader, William Monaco, as king. But with the help of Markward of Annweiler and the German troops, Henry ruthlessly quelled the revolt and punished its perpetrators. Whether or not Constance actually participated in the conspiracy, her husband certainly thought she had, for he required her to be present at the public ceremony in which the conspirators were burned or crucified, and a crown of red-hot iron was nailed to the head of the man who had dared to call himself king.

Even in an age in which the public display of physical punishment was the norm, the insistence with which the chronicles remark on her forced attendance suggest that this was indeed a ruthless yet subtle reward for treachery.

Release came unexpectedly: just a few months later, Henry caught a chill while hunting in the forests near Messina, which brought on a return of his old dysentery. A brief recovery was followed by a relapse, and the Emperor was brought to Messina, where on the twenty-eighth day of September, 1197, he died, leaving his infant son Frederick as heir to both the Holy Roman Empire and the Kingdom of Sicily.

Constance spent the following months in the role of the sorrowing widow, traveling between Palermo and Messina to arrange a suitably prestigious burial for the father of her son and to prepare for the arrival of Frederick himself, whom she had ordered to be brought south from Foligno to Palermo. In a magnificent ceremony on the feast of Pentecost, the seventeenth of May, 1198, the three-year-old boy was crowned King of Sicily and coregent with his mother. Once he wore the Sicilian crown, no further reference was made to any other title. Supported by the local nobility, Constance expelled Markward of Annweiler from the kingdom and prepared to oppose all German interference in her realm.

Yet she too felt her health failing. This time the presentiment of death was pressing, and the need to put her spiritual and temporal affairs in order was urgent. Faced with the need to protect her child and her realm, she turned her back on his German heritage, and in a letter to the newly elected Pope Innocent III, she named the Pope regent of her kingdom and guardian of the young king. In return she was required to forswear her predecessors' claim to the apostolic legacy.

For centuries, Sicilian historians have claimed that Constance, in turning to the Pope, sold out her birthright and betrayed her kingdom. Others now tend to acquit her of this charge: 'against the claims of imperial overlordship, she preferred those of the papacy itself. The formal submission of the king to the pope had been insisted on from her father's time; since 1156, friendship between the kingship and the papacy had become not only traditional, but a guarantee that imperial power in Italy could be checked.'[10]

And again: 'She was a determined, able woman, but she needed to make her kingdom inviolable. . . . Innocent, as overlord of a minor, Frederick, hardly needed to be appointed his guardian; it was his feudal duty as suzerain of the king of Sicily, to protect his ward once Frederick's parents were both dead. By actually appointing him as Frederick's guardian in her will, Constance reminded the world of the inviolability of her son's inheritance. Sicily was ruled by a minor, but protected by a pope. It was a policy that made considerable sense, given the emergency.'[11]

In any case, she did not capitulate easily to the terms imposed by the Pope: negotiations with the curia were still under way when the end came. Constance died on the twenty-seventh of November, 1198, at the age of forty-four. At the order of her son, her body was later placed in a porphyry sarcophagus, one of the four that now stand under marble canopies in a side chapel of the Cathedral of Palermo. Next to her lie her husband Henry, her father Roger, whom she never knew, and her beloved son Frederick, whom she had known but little.

~

The sun came out again as Marcella and I drove west across the plateau of the Sila. The road took us along the shores of the Lago del Ampollino, a large artificial lake surrounded by gentle mountains covered with beech, oak, chestnuts, and larch pines, the remains of a magnificent forest that once covered much of the region. Ducks were swimming in the lake, and a couple of swans enjoyed the peace and quiet of early summer before the arrival of the vacationers with their motorboats and water skis. We stopped briefly to count the wildflowers blooming exuberantly by the edge of the road; in my notes there is a list. 'Flowers we saw in Sila: violets, strawberries, orchids, cornflowers, broom, gorse, vetch, sweet peas, bugloss, chestnuts in flower, lots of oak and ilex.'

This is the other face of Calabria, perhaps the most dramatic region of Italy: it is spectacular in the natural beauty of its unspoiled beaches and highlands, and tragic in its poverty. Slashed by rugged and impervious mountain ranges and bordered by narrow and swampy, fever-ridden lowlands, it was part of the South 'destined to the role of prey,' yet it was isolated throughout history. Even today much of the traffic between Sicily and the north prefers to skip it altogether by taking the sea route from Palermo to Naples.

Originally a western province of the Byzantine Empire, for two centuries preceding the Norman conquest it had been the locus for a fierce power struggle between the Greeks and the Saracens of Sicily, with an occasional invasion by the Lombard prince of Salerno. The contending armies had marched back and forth across the mountains, the fleets had battled and raided up and down the coasts.

Under the Normans the area made a minimal recovery as the local barons flourished in newfound security, but the Angevins imposed a strict feudal regime, while the Aragonese and then the Bourbons gave fairly free rein to the rough and quarrelsome local nobility. Violent earthquakes added to the region's collapse.

Even today, despite the postwar land reform, a good part of the region's impoverished interior is still divided into large landholdings, and in many areas the rule of the barons has been supplanted by that of the bosses of the *'ndrangheta*, a word of Greek origin denoting the Calabrian version of the Mafia. Given all of this, it was not difficult to understand the degradation we had seen in San Giovanni in Fiore, and of which we were to see more when we reached the western coast.

Yet here, at least, sitting by the lakeside and counting the wildflowers, it was easy to admire Calabria's other face and to imagine how it must have presented itself to its queen as she passed through on her first visit to this part of her kingdom. Speaking of how Calabria 'offered a unique environment in western Christendom for such an awkward, uncompromising figure as Joachim,' Donald Matthew goes on to write about the Italian South in words that move me each time I return to them:

> Potentially the Christian kingdom could draw upon spiritual, as well as material, resources of exceptional quality. Foreign visitors of the period were impressed by what they saw and not, like those of later times, depressed by evidence of poverty, superstition or degradation. The South did not at this time pose a problem: it presented itself as a promised land.[12]

We followed a lovely winding road down from the Sila and onto the Autostrada del Sole for a stretch of viaducts and tunnels that offer no alternative roads. As soon as we could, we left it to follow the old road south through Mileto and on to Bagnara Calabra. We knew here that we were on Constance's route: this was the main road south, the overland route taken by all the messengers and armies and crowned heads passing this way. It is described by the chronicler Roger of Hoveden in his account of Richard I's passage here on his way to Messina, where he spent the winter of 1190–91 in uneasy rivalry with Philip Augustus as they waited for the onset of good weather to embark for the Holy Land. Jealous of his aristocratic prerogatives regarding falconry, Richard got himself into a rather undignified squabble along the way:

> [T]he king of England, departing from Melida [now Mileto] with a single knight, passed through a certain small town, and, after he had passed through, turned to a certain house in which he heard a hawk, and, entering the house, took hold of it. On his refusing to give it up, numbers of peasants came running from every quarter, and made an attack on him with sticks and stones. One of them then drew his knife against the king, upon which the latter giving

him a blow with the flat of his sword, it snapped asunder, whereupon he pelted the others with stones, and with difficulty making his escape out of their hands, came to a priory called Le Baniare; but, making no stay there, he crossed the great river.[13]

The battle of the hawk continues to this day: courageous members of wildlife protection associations keep vigil over the nests to protect them from falconry enthusiasts who attempt to steal the fledglings and smuggle them north into Germany and, on the Sicilian side of the straits, to guard the migratory flight of the peregrine falcons from the assault of local men, for whom the slaying of such a trophy is, still today, a rite of passage into manhood.

In Constance's time, the harbor of Bagnara Calabra was the principal port from which to navigate the dangerous currents of the Straits of Messina, the 'great river of the Faro,' as English chroniclers called them, in order to land in Sicily. Its strategic importance was not lost on the Lionheart, who later in his stay turned the priory into a garrison and shut his sister Johanna up there while negotiating with Tancredi for the return of her dowry.

We had thought, as we zigzagged down the steep hillside to the narrow strip of coast on which the town was built, that it would be fitting for us to spend our last night on the road in Bagnara, but the little town was too dismal, too shabby and forlorn. Not one fresh coat of whitewash was to be seen on any of the rows of turn-of-the-century houses, the stores seemed bereft of customers, and the local youth milled idly in the streets in an unrelieved distillation of the unemployment and general hopelessness that infect so many small towns in southern Italy. So we moved on, to a rather squalid hotel just north of where we would put the car on the ferry for Messina.

≈

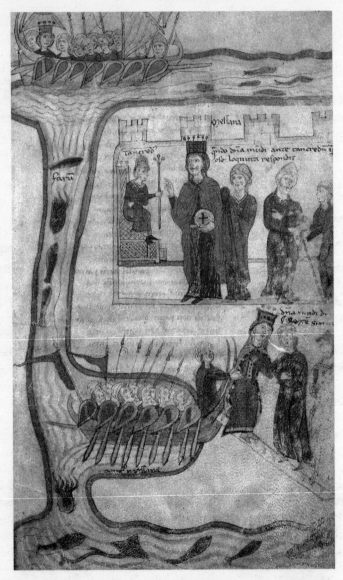

Journey's end: Constance, 'in golden robes, / In gowns adorned with precious gems,' steps off the ship that has brought her home to Sicily.

April

It is at Bagnara, however, that our story ends. I have chosen to part company with Constance here, for she deserves to live on in our minds in the moment of her triumphant return, as she first catches sight of her promised land and sees the spit of land embracing the port of Messina, the green heights of the Caronia mountains, and to the south the great hulking volcanic cone of Etna, its eternal plume of smoke rising above the glistening remnants of the winter snows.

I do not believe that Constance was unaware of what awaited her, that she thought that her husband could bring anything but evil to her kingdom, or that the task in store for her would be anything but daunting. I have chosen not to dwell further on the the tragic events of the last three years of her life, on her desperation in the face of death, and on the drastic choices that she had to make, as she lay dying, for the sake of her son. I leave her at the doorstep of her kingdom, a different woman from the sad and passive Constance who set out from Trifels twelve months earlier. Transformed by the miracle of a late motherhood, she had shrugged off the resignation induced by her failure to conceive; now she was eager to fulfill the role bequeathed to her by the father she had never known.

Pietro of Eboli describes Constance as she looked when she landed in Messina four years earlier, the hostage of her usurper Tancredi. She was dressed, according to Pietro, as befitted a queen and an empress, putting on a good show, keeping a stiff upper lip in her humiliation. At the end of April in the year 1195, Constance once more took ship for Messina, once more dressed in full regalia. But this time the splendor reflected in Pietro's words was no longer the pretense of wounded pride; this time she came to reclaim her birthright, the earthly paradise invoked upon the walls of the palaces where she spent her childhood, the Garden of Eden from which she had long been exiled.

Already a safe ship, manned by a hundred rowers,
    Moves swiftly as soft Zephyrus ruffles the waves.

323

O new counsel! O great prudence!
  Like a new bride she dresses, in golden robes,
In gowns adorned with precious gems,
  Her tresses dressed with art and ornament.
Roses adorn her tunic, nor does she lack for perfumes,
  The golden orbs of Phoebus dangle at her ears.
On her breast the horns of her moon-shaped necklace meet,
  And she is robed in the gleam of jewels.[14]

A CHRONOLOGY OF THE HISTORICAL EVENTS
DISCUSSED IN THIS BOOK

1060 Norman knights of the Hauteville family under the leadership of the Great Count Roger undertake the conquest of Sicily from the Arabs.

1130 The Great Count's son, Roger II, is crowned king of Sicily in Palermo on Christmas Day.

1154 Roger II dies in Palermo shortly before his third wife, Beatrix of Réthel, gives birth to a daughter, Constance of Hauteville.

   William I, Roger's son by his first wife, is crowned.

1161 The barons under Matthew Bonello revolt; the palace in Palermo is sacked.

   William I's son Roger is killed.

1166 William I dies.

   William II, the twelve-year-old son of William I, is crowned, with the Queen Mother, Margaret of Navarre, as regent.

1171 William II takes over full powers as king.

1176 William II's ambassadors visit London for his betrothal to Johanna Plantagenet, daughter of the English king Henry II and Eleanor of Aquitaine.

1177 Johanna arrives in Palermo.

   Under the Treaty of Venice, the Holy Roman Emperor, Frederick Barbarossa, makes peace with the papacy, with Sicily, and with the Lombard League.

1183 The Treaty of Constance is concluded between Frederick Barbarossa and the Lombard League.

1184 In May, Barbarossa's son Henry of Hohenstaufen (the

future Emperor Henry VI) is knighted at Mainz.

In October, Constance's betrothal to Henry of Hohenstaufen is announced at Augsburg.

1185   In August, Constance sails to Salerno and is handed over to the Germans in Rieti.

1186   On January 27th, Constance marries Henry at Milan.

For the next two years, Constance and Henry travel through northern Italy.

In October, they hold court in Ravenna.

1187   Jerusalem falls to the infidel. The Pope calls for a Crusade.

1188   In January, Constance and Henry go north to Germany.

In December, Frederick Barbarossa and the poet Frederick von Hausen take the cross at Mainz.

1189   On November 18th, William II dies childless in Palermo.

1190   In January, Tancredi of Lecce, illegitimate grandson of Roger II, seizes power and is crowned king of Sicily.

Frederick Barbarossa and his followers depart for the East.

On May 6th, Frederick von Hausen dies on crusade.

On June 10th, Frederick Barbarossa drowns in Asia Minor.

In September, Philip Augustus of France and Richard the Lionheart arrive in Messina on their way to the Holy Land.

1191   In January, Henry and Constance cross the Alps on their first expedition to conquer the South.

In April, Henry is crowned Holy Roman Emperor in Rome.

Eleanor of Aquitaine arrives in Messina. Her children, Richard the Lionheart and the widowed Johanna, sail to the Holy Land.

In May, Henry besieges Naples. Constance is invited to Salerno.

On August 24th, Henry raises the siege of Naples and retreats north. Constance is betrayed by the people of Salerno and taken as a prisoner to Palermo.

In November, Archbishop Albert of Louvain is murdered.

1192   In February, Constance is rescued by German knights at Ceprano and returns to Germany.

In December, Richard the Lionheart, returning from the Crusade, is taken prisoner by Duke Leopold of Austria, who hands him over to Henry VI.

1193   Richard the Lionheart is held prisoner at Trifels, then at Haguenau.

In May, Tancredi's son Roger marries Irene of Byzantium.

In December, Eleanor of Aquitaine arrives at Speyer.

1194   In February, Henry holds court at Mainz, and Richard the Lionheart is released.

Tancredi's son Roger and then Tancredi himself die. His second son is crowned as King William III of Sicily, with Queen Sybilla as regent.

On Pentecost, May 9th, Henry holds court at Trifels. On May 15th, Constance and Henry set out once more to conquer southern Italy.

On May 29th, the imperial couple reach Milan. Constance, who is pregnant, remains at Meda.

On July 1st, Henry holds court at Pisa. On August 23rd, the imperial fleet under Markward of Annweiler enters the Bay of Naples, and in mid-September Henry razes the city of Salerno.

Henry reaches Messina at the end of October and enters Palermo in triumph on November 20th.

On Christmas Day, Henry is crowned king of Sicily.

On December 26th, Constance gives birth to Frederick Roger (the future Emperor Frederick II) in Jesi, near Ancona.

1195   In February, the alleged conspirators of Palermo are arrested, and Tancredi's family is sent to Germany.

Constance meets Henry at Bari, where Henry takes the cross, and on April 2nd she is crowned queen of Sicily.

Henry returns to Germany, and Constance proceeds to Sicily. By June, she is in Palermo.

1196   In December, the infant Frederick II is elected king of the Romans.

1197   In May, there is a second conspiracy against Henry VI. The conspirators are tortured to death in Constance's presence.

On September 28th, Henry dies in Messina.

1198   On Pentecost, May 17th, Frederick is crowned king of Sicily in Palermo.

On November 27th, Constance dies.

SUGGESTIONS FOR FURTHER READING

Since this is not an academic study, I am not including a complete bibliography of the works I have consulted in researching this book. Listed below are a few works in English, intended for the general reader, that I recommend to those whose curiosity has been whetted. More specialized publications referring to specific topics can be found in the Notes. My deep gratitude goes to all the authors, mentioned here or not, upon whose shoulders I have leaned.

Abulafia, David. *Frederick II, A Medieval Emperor.* London: Allen Lane, 1988.

Chrétien de Troyes. *Yvain, The Knight of the Lion*, trans. Burton Raffel. New Haven: Yale University Press, 1987.

Duby, Georges. *William Marshal, The Flower of Chivalry*, trans. Richard Howard. New York: Pantheon, 1985.

—*Women of the Twelfth Century*, 3 vols., trans. Jean Birrell. Chicago: University of Chicago Press, 1997.

The History of the Tyrants of Sicily by 'Hugo Falcandus' 1154–69, trans. Graham A. Loud and Thomas Wiedemann. Manchester and New York: Manchester University Press, 1998.

Fumagalli, Vito. *Landscapes of Fear: Perceptions of Nature and the City in the Middle Ages*, trans. Shayne Mitchell. Cambridge: Polity Press, 1994.

Gillingham, John. *Richard the Lionheart.* London: Weidenfeld & Nicolson, 1978.

Hartley, Dorothy. *Lost Country Life.* New York: Pantheon, 1979.

Holmes, Urban Tigner, Jr. *Daily Living in the Twelfth Century. Based on the Observations of Alexander Neckam in London and Paris.* Madison: University of Wisconsin Press, 1952.

Kantorowicz, Ernst. *Frederick the Second, 1194–1250*, trans. E. O.

Lorimer. New York: Frederick Ungar, 1957.

Labarge, Margaret Wade. *A Small Sound of Trumpet: Women in Medieval Life*. Boston: Beacon Press, 1986.

Leed, Eric J. *The Mind of the Traveler*. New York: Basic Books, 1991.

Le Goff, Jacques, ed.. *Medieval Callings*, trans. Lydia G. Cochrane. Chicago: University of Chicago Press, 1990.

Matthew, Donald. *The Norman Kingdom of Sicily*. Cambridge: Cambridge University Press, 1992.

Norwich, John Julius. *The Kingdom in the Sun*. London: Longmans, 1970.

Owen, D.D.R. *Eleanor of Aquitaine, Queen and Legend*. Oxford: Blackwell, 1996.

Petzold, Andreas. *Romanesque Art*. New York: Harry N. Abrams, 1995.

Piponnier, Françoise, and Perrine Mane, *Dress in the Middle Ages*, trans. Caroline Beamish. New Haven: Yale University Press, 1997.

Wilson, Katharina M., ed. *Medieval Women Writers*. Athens: University of Georgia Press, 1984.

NOTES

Note: If not otherwise specified, the English translations are my own. Abbreviations are used for the following collections of primary sources:

Monumenta Germaniae Historica Scriptores (M.G.H.SS.)
Del Re, Cronisti e Scrittori Sincroni della Dominazione Normanna nel Regno di Puglia e Sicilia (R.C.S.S.)

Prologue

1. Georges Duby, *The Knight, the Lady and the Priest: The Making of Modern Marriage in Medieval France*, trans. Barbara Bray (New York: Pantheon, 1983), p. 21.

PART ONE : THE DUBBING AT PENTECOST

Chapter One : May

1. This and all subsequent quotations from *Yvain, The Knight of the Lion* are taken from Burton Raffel's translation (New Haven: Yale University Press, 1987).
2. Karl Hampe, *Germany under the Salian and Hohenstaufen Emperors*, trans. Ralph Bennett (Totowa, N.J.: Rowman & Littlefield, 1973), p. 228.
3. *The Chronicle of Salimbene da Adamo*, trans. J. L. Baird, et al. (Binghamton, N.Y., 1986)p. 361.
4. Horst Fuhrmann, *Germany in the High Middle Ages, c. 1050–1200*, trans. Timothy Reuter (Cambridge: Cambridge University Press, 1986), pp. 32–33.
5. Quoted in Edith Ennen, *The Medieval Woman*, trans. Edmund Jephcott (Oxford: Blackwell, 1989), p. 145.
6. Georges Duby, *The Three Orders: Feudal Society Imagined*, trans. Arthur Goldhammer (Chicago: University of Chicago Press, 1982), pp. 306–307.
7. Frederick von Hausen, trans. Frederick Goldin, in Ingrid Walsøe-Engel, ed., *German Poetry from the Beginnings to 1750* (New York: Continuum, 1992), p. 33.

Notes

8. Quoted in J. E. Tyler, *The Alpine Passes in the Middle Ages* (Oxford: Blackwell, 1930), p. 30.

Chapter Two : June

1. Dante Alighieri, *The Divine Comedy*, book 3: *Paradise*, ll. 109–20, trans. Dorothy L. Sayers (Baltimore: Penguin, 1962), p. 76.
2. *The History of the Tyrants of Sicily by 'Hugo Falcandus' 1154–69*, trans. Graham A. Loud and Thomas Wiedemann (Manchester and New York: Manchester University Press, 1998), p. 255.
3. Ibid., pp. 258–59.
4. Ibid.
5. Ibid.
6. Ibid., pp. 259–60. The translation is misleading here, since the only carvings are on the painted wooden ceiling; I have taken the liberty of correcting it.
7. Rosario La Duca, *Il Palazzo dei Normanni* (Palermo, 1997), pp. 53–56.
8. John Julius Norwich, *The Kingdom in the Sun* (London: Longmans, 1970), p. 24.
9. *History of the Tyrants of Sicily*, p. 138.
10. John Carmi Parsons, *Medieval Queenship* (New York: St. Martin's Press, 1998), p. 69.
11. Norwich, *Kingdom in the Sun*, p. 301.
12. Benedict of Peterborough, *Gesta regis Henrici Secundi* (London, 1867), p. 115.
13. Roger of Hoveden, *The Annals*, trans. H. T. Riley (London, 1853), II, p. 413.

Chapter Three : July

1. Michel Pastoreau, 'L'Uomo e il colore,' supp. no. 5 to *Storia e Dossier* (March 1987), pp. 19ff.
2. Ibn Jubayr, 'Viaggio in Sicilia,' in Leonardo Sciascia, ed., *Delle cose di Sicilia: Testi inediti o rari* (Palermo, 1980), I, pp. 108–9.
3. Pietro Colli, *Meda: Mille anni di storia all'ombra di un monastero* (Meda, 1988), pp. 7–10.
4. Peter Munz, *Frederick Barbarossa: A Study in Medieval Politics* (Ithaca, N.Y.: Cornell University Press, 1969), pp. 359–60.
5. *Annales Austriae Continuatio Zwetlensis Altera*, M.G.H.SS. IX, p. 242.
6. Frederick Goldin, 'The Array of Perspectives in the Early Courtly Love Lyric,' in J. M. Ferrante and G. D. Economou, eds., *In Pursuit of Perfection: Courtly Love in Medieval Literature* (Port Washington, N.Y.: Kennikat Press, 1975), p. 54.
7. W.T.H. Jackson, *The Challenge of the Medieval Text* (New York: Columbia University Press, 1985), p. 37.

Notes

8. Anonymous, 'The Weingarten Travel Blessing,' trans. Carroll Hightower, in Ingrid Walsøe-Engel, ed., *German Poetry from the Beginnings to 1750* (New York: Continuum, 1992), p. 11.

9. Frederick von Hausen, my adaptation of Hugo Bekker's translation in his *Friederich von Hausen: Inquiries into his Poetry* (Chapel Hill: University of North Carolina Press, 1977), pp. 89–92.

10. Chrétien de Troyes, *Yvain, The Knight of the Lion*, trans. Burton Raffel (New Haven: Yale University Press, 1987).

11. Jackson, *Challenge of the Medieval Text*, p. 181.

12. Robert W. Hanning, *The Individual in Twelfth-Century Romance* (New Haven: Yale University Press, 1977), p. 4.

13. Quoted in Richard Barber, *The Devil's Crown: Henry II, Richard I, John* (London: BBC, 1978), p. 114.

14. Hildegard of Bingen, trans. Christopher Page, *A Feather on the Breath of God*, Hyperion CD no. 66039.

15. Jacobus de Voragine, *The Golden Legend*, trans. Granger Ryan and Helmut Ripperger (London: Longmans, Green & Co., 1941), pp. 522–23.

PART TWO : THE FOREST

Chapter Four : August

1. Frederick B. Artz, *The Mind of the Middle Ages, An Historical Survey A.D. 200–1500* (New York: Alfred A. Knopf, 1958), p. 242.

2. Peter Munz, *Frederick Barbarossa: A Study in Medieval Politics* (Ithaca, N.Y.: Cornell University Press, 1969), pp. 368–69.

3. *Annales Marbacenses*, M.G.H.SS. XVII, p. 163.

4. Ibid.

5. David Abulafia, *Frederick II, A Medieval Emperor* (London: Allen Lane, 1988), p. 67.

6. Vito Fumagalli, *Paesaggi della paura. Vita e natura nel Medioevo* (Bologna, 1994), p. 190. This interesting book has been published in English as *Landscapes of Fear: Perceptions of Nature and the City in the Middle Ages*, trans. Shayne Mitchell (Cambridge: Polity Press, 1994), but I have preferred to translate this quotation myself.

Chapter Five : September

1. Michel Pastoureau, 'L'Uomo e il colore,' supp. no. 5 to *Storia e Dossier* (March 1987), p. 60.

2. Eric J. Leed, *The Mind of the Traveler* (New York: Basic Books, 1991), p. 26.

3. Ibid., p. 44.

4. Ibid., pp. 56–58.

Notes

5. Carlo M. Cipolla, *Storia economica dell'Europa pre-industriale* (Bologna, 1975), pp. 209–10.

6. Dorothy Hartley, *Lost Country Life* (New York: Pantheon, 1979), p. 4.

7. Pier Paolo Mendogni, *Il Battistero di Parma. Arte, storia, iconagrafia* (Parma, 1996), p. 7.

8. Jacques Le Goff, 'Il Tempo del lavoro. Agricultura e segni dello zodiaco nei calendari medievali,' Supp. no. 22 to *Storia e Dossier* (October 1988), p. 35.

9. Kitty Hatcher, personal correspondence, quoted by permission.

10. Le Goff, 'Il Tempo del lavoro,' p. 29.

11. Chiara Frugoni, 'I Misteri dello scultore,' *Storia e Dossier* 3, no. 18 (May 1988), pp. 43–47.

12. Chiara Frugoni, 'La Mappa delle meraviglie,' *Storia e Dossier* 2, no. 3 (January 1987), pp. 26–30.

13. Francesco Gandolfi, 'La Cattedra "Gregoriana" di Salerno,' *Bollettino storico di Salerno e Principato Citra* II, no. 1 (1984), pp. 5–29.

Chapter Six : October

1. Translated by Meg Bogin in *The Women Troubadours* (New York: W. W. Norton & Co., 1980), p. 119.

2. Vito Fumagalli, *Paesaggi della paura. Vita e natura nel Medioevo* (Bologna, 1994), plate following p. 159.

3. Emilio Sereni, *Storia del paesaggio agrario italiano* (Bari, 1982), pp. 75–77. This book has been translated into English as *History of the Italian Agricultural Landscape* (Princeton, N.J.: Princeton University Press, 1997).

4. Ernst Kantorowicz, *Frederick the Second, 1194–1250,* trans. E. O. Lorimer (New York: Frederick Ungar, 1957), p. 7.

5. Nicetas Acominatus, *Istoria degli imperatori Bizantini*, Italian trans. M. Ludovico Dolce (Milan, 1854), II, p. 146.

6. My translation was done with the help of Regine Hundemer.

7. Austin Lane Poole, 'The Emperor Henry VI,' in *Cambridge Medieval History* (Cambridge: Cambridge University Press, 1957), V, p. 458.

8. John Julius Norwich, *The Kingdom in the Sun* (London: Longmans, 1970), p. 348.

9. Acominatus, *Istoria*, pp. 140–41.

10. Eve Borsook, *Messages in Mosaic: The Royal Programmes of Norman Sicily, 1130–1187* (Oxford: Blackwell, 1998), p. 63.

11. Ibid., pp. 72–73.

12. David Abulafia, *Frederick II, A Medieval Emperor* (London: Allen Lane, 1988), p. 89.

Chapter Seven : November

1. Franco Cardini, *I giorni del sacro. Il libro delle feste* (Milan, 1983), p. 109.

Notes

2. Georges Duby, *Women of the Twelfth Century*, vol. 2: *Remembering the Dead*, trans. Jean Birrell (Chicago: University of Chicago Press, 1997), p. 9.
3. Romualdo Guarna, Archbishop of Salerno, *Cronica*, in R.C.S.S., p. 19.
4. John Julius Norwich, *The Kingdom in the Sun* (London: Longmans, 1970), pp. 98–99.
5. Paulette L'Hermite-Leclerq, 'The Feudal Order,' in Christiane Klapisch-Zuber, ed., *A History of Women in the West* (Cambridge, Mass.: Harvard University Press, 1992), II, p. 204.
6. Raymond H. Schmandt, 'The Election and Assassination of Albert of Louvain, Bishop of Liège, 1191–92,' *Speculum* 42 (1967), p. 649.
7. Ibid., p. 659.
8. Benedicta Ward, *Miracles and the Medieval Mind: Theory, Record and Event, 1000–1215* (Aldershot: Wildwood House, 1987), p. 129.
9. Ibid., p. 98.
10. Alexander Neckam, quoted by Urban Tigner Holmes, Jr., in *Daily Living in the Twelfth Century. Based on the Observations of Alexander Neckam in London and Paris* (Madison: University of Wisconsin Press, 1952), p. 88.
11. Michel Pastoureau, 'L'Uomo e il colore,' supp. no. 5 to *Storia e Dossier* (March 1987), p. 46.
12. Roger of Hoveden, *The Annals*, trans. H. T. Riley (London, 1853), II, p. 197.
13. Gislebert of Hainaut, *Chronicon Hanoniense*, M.G.H.SS. XXI, p. 574.
14. Norwich, *Kingdom in the Sun*, p. 384.
15. Bruno Figliuolo, 'Salerno,' in *Itinerari e centri urbani nel Mezzogiorno normanno-svevo* (Bari, 1993), pp. 195–224.
16. Georges Duby, *William Marshal, The Flower of Chivalry*, trans. Richard Howard (New York: Pantheon, 1985), p. 95.

Chapter Eight : December

1. Robert Hanning and Joan Ferrante, trans. and eds., *The Lais of Marie de France* (Durham, N.C.: Labyrinth Press, 1982), pp. 128–29.
2. Trotula de Ruggiero, *Sulle malattie delle donne*, ed. Pina Boggi Cavallo, Italian trans. Piero Cantalupo (Palermo, 1994).
3. John F. Benton, 'Trotula, Women's Problems, and the Professionalization of Medicine in the Middle Ages,' *Bulletin of the History of Medicine* 59, no. 1 (1985), pp. 30–53.
4. Monica Green, 'Women's Medical Practise and Care in Medieval Europe,' in Judith M. Bennett, et al., eds., *Sisters and Workers in the Middle Ages* (Chicago: University of Chicago Press, 1989), p. 44.
5. Margaret Wade Labarge, *A Small Sound of Trumpet: Women in Medieval Life* (Boston: Beacon Press, 1986), pp. 20–21.
6. Trotula, *Sulle malattie*, p. 73.
7. Ibid., p. 75.

8. Ibid., p. 77.

9. Ibid., p. 81.

10. Franco Cardini, *I giorni del sacro. Il libro delle feste* (Milan, 1983), pp. 137–38.

11. Eve Borsook, *Messages in Mosaic: The Royal Programmes of Norman Sicily, 1130–1187* (Oxford: Blackwell, 1998), p. 37.

12. Georges Duby, *Women of the Twelfth Century*, vol. 2: *Remembering the Dead*, trans. Jean Birrell (Chicago: University of Chicago Press, 1997), p. 106.

13. From the *La Mort Aymeri*, quoted in Urban Tigner Holmes, Jr., *Daily Living in the Twelfth Century. Based on the Observations of Alexander Neckam in London and Paris* (Madison: University of Wisconsin Press, 1952), p. 85.

14. Holmes, *Daily Living*, p. 283, n. 38.

15. Green, 'Women's Medical Practise,' p. 66.

16. Georges Duby, *The Knight, the Lady and the Priest: The Making of Modern Marriage in Medieval France*, trans. Barbara Bray (New York: Pantheon, 1983), p. 37.

17. Peggy McCracken, *The Romance of Adultery: Queenship and Transgression in Old French Literature* (Philadelphia: University of Pennsylvania Press, 1998), p. 33.

18. Ibid., p. 72.

19. Paulette L'Hermite-Leclerq, 'The Feudal Order,' in Christiane Klapisch-Zuber, ed., *A History of Women in the West* (Cambridge, Mass.: Harvard University Press, 1992), II, p. 204.

20. Abd ar-Rahmaàn al-Itrabànishi, in Leonardo Sciascia, ed., *Delle cose di Sicilia: Testi inediti o rari* (Palermo, 1980), I, p. 26.

21. Otto of St. Blaise, *Chronici ab Ottone Frisingensi – Continuatio Sanblasiana*, M.G.H.SS. XX, pp. 325–26.

22. Trotula, *Sulle malattie,* p. 83.

23. Ibid., p. 85.

24. Chrétien de Troyes, *Perceval* (Milan, 1989), p. 12.

PART THREE : THE FUTURE

Chapter Nine : January

1. Philip Weller, trans., for the Discantus Ensemble recording *Campus stellae* (Paris, 1994), Opus III, CD no. OPS 30-102.

2. William F. MacLehose, 'Nurturing Danger: High Medieval Medicine and the Problem(s) of the Child,' in John Carmi Parsons and Bonnie Wheeler, eds., *Medieval Mothering* (New York: Garland, 1999), p. 6.

3. *Annales Stadenses II*, M.G.H.SS. XVI, p. 357.

4. Trotula de Ruggiero, *Sulle malattie delle donne*, ed. Pina Boggi Cavallo, Italian trans. Piero Cantalupo (Palermo, 1994), p. 87.

Notes

5. Françoise Piponnier and Perrine Mane, *Dress in the Middle Ages*, trans. Caroline Beamish (New Haven: Yale University Press, 1997), p. 103.

6. Franco Cardini, *I giorni del sacro. Il libro delle feste* (Milan, 1983), p. 129.

7. Colin Morris, *The Discovery of the Individual 1050–1200* (Toronto: University of Toronto Press, 1987), p. 158.

8. Caroline Walker Bynum, *Jesus as Mother: Studies in the Spirituality of the High Middle Ages* (Berkeley: University of California Press, 1982), p. 90.

9. Ibid., p. 108.

10. Lois L. Huneycutt, 'Female Succession and the Language of Power in the Writings of Twelfth-Century Churchmen,' in Parsons and Wheeler, *Medieval Mothering*, p. 190.

11. John Carmi Parsons, 'Mothers, Daughters, Marriage, Power: Some Plantagenet Evidence 1150–1500,' in Parsons and Wheeler, *Medieval Mothering*, p. 65.

12. Dione R. Clementi, 'Some Unnoticed Aspects of the Emperor Henry VI's Conquest of the Norman Kingdom of Sicily,' *Bulletin of the John Rylands Library* 36 (1954), p. 329.

13. David Abulafia, *Frederick II, A Medieval Emperor* (London: Allen Lane, 1988), p. 79.

14. Ibid., p. 80.

15. Huneycutt, 'Female Succession,' p. 192.

16. Ibid., p. 194.

17. Ibid., p. 196.

18. See Miriam Shadis, 'Berenguela of Castile's Political Motherhood: The Management of Sexuality, Marriage and Succession,' in Parsons and Wheeler, *Medieval Mothering*, pp. 335–58.

19. Aron Ja. Gurevich, *The Origins of European Individualism* (Oxford: Oxford University Press, 1995), p. 242.

20. Ibid., pp. 244–45.

21. Parsons, 'Mothers, Daughters,' pp. 77–78.

22. Eric J. Leed, *The Mind of the Traveler* (New York: Basic Books, 1991), p. 221.

23. Ibid., pp. 221–22.

24. Ibid., p. 222.

25. Ibid., p. 223.

26. Ibid., p. 224.

27. Luigi Luca Cavalli-Sforza, interview by Franco Prattico, *La Repubblica*, November 4, 1999, p. 35.

Chapter Ten : February

1. Robert Hanning and Joan Ferrante, trans. and eds., *The Lais of Marie de France* (Durham, N.C.: Labyrinth Press, 1982), pp. 164–65.

2. Jacobus de Voragine, *The Golden Legend*, trans. Granger Ryan and Helmut Ripperger (London: Longmans, Green & Co., 1941), pp. 150–51.

Notes

3. Luke 2:22; 2:40.
4. Françoise Piponnier and Perrine Mane, *Dress in the Middle Ages*, trans. Caroline Beamish (New Haven: Yale University Press, 1997), p. 109.
5. Shulamith Shahar, *Childhood in the Middle Ages* (New York: Routledge, 1990), p. 47.
6. Ibid., p. 61.
7. Philippe Ariès, *Centuries of Childhood: A Social History of Family Life*, trans. Robert Baldrick (New York: Vintage Books, 1962), p. 38.
8. Ibid., pp. 411–12.
9. Caroline Walker Bynum, *Jesus as Mother: Studies in the Spirituality of the High Middle Ages* (Berkeley: University of California Press, 1982), p. 133.
10. Ibid., p. 143.
11. John Carmi Parsons and Bonnie Wheeler, introduction to John Carmi Parsons and Bonnie Wheeler, eds., *Medieval Mothering* (New York: Garland, 1999), p. xii.
12. Trotula de Ruggiero, *Sulle malattie delle donne*, ed. Pina Boggi Cavallo, Italian trans. Piero Cantalupo (Palermo, 1994), p. 89.
13. Angela Gillonga, *Il bambino medievale* (Bari, 1990), p. 28.
14. Wolfram von Eschenbach, *Parzival*, trans. H. M. Mustard and C. E. Passage (New York: Vintage, 1961), p. 63.
15. Clarissa Atkinson, *The Oldest Vocation: Christian Motherhood in the Middle Ages* (Ithaca, N.Y.: Cornell University Press, 1991), p. 136.
16. Jacques Le Goff, introduction to Jacques Le Goff, *Medieval Callings*, trans. Lydia G. Cochrane (Chicago: University of Chicago Press, 1990), pp. 16–17.
17. Dhuoda, *Manual*, trans. James Marchand, in 'The Frankish Mother: Dhuoda,' in Katharina M. Wilson, ed., *Medieval Women Writers* (Athens: University of Georgia Press, 1984), p. 12.

Chapter Eleven : March

1. Quoted in John Cummins, *The Hound and the Hawk* (London: Weidenfeld & Nicolson, 1988), p. 232.
2. David Abulafia, *Frederick II, A Medieval Emperor* (London: Allen Lane, 1988), p. 25.
3. Ibid., p. 45.

Chapter Twelve : April

1. Philip Weller, trans., for the Discantus Ensemble recording *Campus Stellae* (Paris, 1994), Opus 111, CD no. OPS 30-102.
2. David Abulafia, *Frederick II, A Medieval Emperor* (London: Allen Lane, 1988), p. 106.
3. Hermann Fillitz, *Catalogue of the Crown Jewels and the Ecclesiastical Treasure*

Notes

Chamber (Vienna: Kunsthistorisches Museum, 1963), p. 39.

4. Rotraud Bauer, 'Il Manto di Ruggero II,' in *I Normanni popolo d'Europa 1030–1200,* catalog of an exhibition held at Palazzo Venezia (Rome, 1994), p. 280.

5. The work of the Austrian scholar Bettina Pferschy-Maleczek is cited in Reinhard Elze, 'Le insegne del potere,' in *Strumenti, tempi e luoghi di communicazione nel Mezzogiorno normanno-svevo,* Atti delle undecime giornate normanno-sveve, 1993 (Bari, 1995), p. 121.

6. Quoted by Kitty Hatcher, personal communication.

7. C. A. Willemsen and D. Odenthal, *Apulia: Imperial Splendor in Southern Italy* (New York: Praeger, 1959), p. 38.

8. Abulafia, *Frederick II,* p. 269.

9. Ibid., p. 439.

10. Donald Matthew, *The Norman Kingdom of Sicily* (Cambridge: Cambridge University Press, 1992), p. 296.

11. Abulafia, *Frederick II,* p. 93.

12. Matthew, *Norman Kingdom,* p. 111.

13. Roger of Hoveden, *The Annals,* trans. H. T. Riley (London, 1853), II, p. 157.

14. From the Italian translation of Pietro di Eboli, *Liber ad honorem Augusti,* in R.C.S.S., p. 419.

ACKNOWLEDGMENTS

A great many people have stood by the roadside and cheered us on as Constance and I have made our stately and very slow progress toward publication. My thanks go first of all to Marcella Serangeli, who accompanied me from Germany to Sicily with tireless good humor and growing passion for the quest; to Jonathan Galassi, my editor, and to Robert Cornfield, my agent, for excellent advice and endless patience; to the Yaddo Foundation, for the weeks of peace and quiet in which I found the courage to start writing; to Caroline Walker Bynum, old friend and quintessential medieval scholar, for first encouraging me in my amateur endeavors; to Regine Hundemer and her sister Wiltrud Ziegler, to Kitty Hatcher, Giovanna Mazzei, Bruna Passarelli, and Sabrina Ricci for their enthusiastic help in research and translating; and to the many other friends and relatives, too numerous to be listed here, who offered advice and encouragement. A special thanks to my husband, Tonino, for putting up with me during a long and difficult gestation.

INDEX

Index

Index

Index

Index

ILLUSTRATION CREDITS

Illustration Credits

COLOR INSERT